My Life
Before I Decided To Commit Suicide
A Love Story

James Robert Murphy

BLBM

PUBLISHING

My Life
Before I Decided To Commit Suicide
A Love Story

2nd Edition, 2015
2920 Stone Edge Rd.
El Paso, TX 79904
(915) 526-0719
www.jamesrobertmurphy.com

On the cover: Jimmy Murphy in the den at
5208 S. Salina Street, Syracuse, NY around 1962.

Dedication

To my wife Margarita Viola Zavala-Murphy, my son Ian James Francis Murphy, and all of those interesting friends and cohorts I have had the pleasure of meeting and continue to meet along the way.

Message

This was a difficult writing project. The more I began to write about the incidents in my life that led to my breakdown, the more pieces of the puzzle I remembered, and thus, the angrier I became. This makes itself evident as my language becomes a bit more more aggressive when I enter my teenage and young adult years. I am apologizing for the cursing up front, but this is the way life presents itself sometimes. I hope a little sorted language doesn't deter you from absorbing my intended message; that beyond life's bumpy, thrashing roller coaster ride, it is every bit worth living.

Most importantly, while writing *My Life*, I learned that lying beneath all of the rigamarole was a rather humorous, quirky and beautiful side to nearly every challenge I faced. It is this descriptive verse that I think you will enjoy most.

With Special Thanks to Walter and Helen Mott

When I first arrived in El Paso, TX in February of 2004 and assumed my new position as managing director for El Paso Opera, I had the distinct pleasure to meet many of El Paso's most caring and most generous individuals. Caring because they loved the perfect musical genre; opera. Generous because they gave of their time and financial support to ensure that opera would succeed in this far western tip of the great state of Texas. Such dedication was very meaningful to me. Walter and Helen Mott were among this fascinating group of opera lovers. They were very knowledgeable, easy to talk to for a rookie like me, fun loving and down to earth. Everyone I've ever met through the ranks of El Paso Opera are gentle, unassuming souls.

As Helen, the self-proclaimed *Diva of Dale Road* states, "This area [El Paso] is unique in so many ways - accepting of the "outsider" and making him feel almost at once - that they are home again." The Mott's, "found the Promised Land and never contemplated leaving ever after." Helen and Walt were married for 50 years and four months until Walt's untimely death in October, 2014. Like so many others before them, they came to the Border Area through Walt's engagement in the U.S. Army. Together they gave untold hours in donated time and made annual contributions to benefit El Paso Opera. They were always bringing refreshments, snacks and more to rehearsals. Dear Helen is a long standing Opera Guild member and volunteer. Walter appeared in several operas as a supernumerary (a silent actor). Regarding Walt, Stephen Jackson, Director of Music at St. Mark's UMC remembered, "When I think of people in my life who truly reflect their faith on a daily basis, Walt is the first person who comes to mind." Walter and Helen Mott were honored as recipients of the Maestro Award for Excellence from El Paso Opera in 2015.

It has been my pleasure to know them both and I thank them from the bottom of my heart for their support. We, as individuals, cannot accomplish what is in our hearts that we seemingly must seek out. We can only succeed through the kindness of those who believe in us and are willing to carry us toward our dreams. Never think that you are alone. Someone will be there for you. Be patient.

Contents

Chapters

Auburn, NY

Move #2

Acknowledgements

Many friends have helped with my quest to sooth the egotistical being that resides inside me. I can't begin to tell you how thankful I am about that. Thanks to those who read my many varied versions of *My Life*. I appreciate all of you who took the time to assist me. I have to thank my mom and dad who were perfect parents and such normal, everyday Americans. And my siblings for unknowingly becoming my emotional scapegoats. I also wish to thank all of the innocent characters who played a role in this book. I love you all. I also want to thank the teachers and students of the Onondaga Central School District. You made life fun.

A personal debt of gratitude goes out to Richard and Cristina Palmer, Tom Riddell, and Bonnie Haines Church for their sincere reviews. I need to mention the kind heart of Jeanie Glenn. She is the proprietor of Book Publishers of El Paso. Jeanie is one of the sweetest people I have ever met. And my dear friends Ian Edwards and Kimberly Kyles who allow me to intrude on their privacy whenever I come home to Nedrow. Encouragement came from Patti Phelps Sunday, Kurt Moberg, Debbie Fredenburg, Valerie MacAllister, Sandra Lynch, Claire Lavin, Teresa Vanetti, Christine Busswell, Marie Hyland-Shields, Jack Parvese, Barbara Murphy, Rodolfo Sigala, Tina Giufre, Barnie Hill, Christopher Weiler, Katherine Kerlin-Owen, Leo Crandall, Bill Phelps, Matt Kerlin, Dave and Tom Watson, Bill and Betty Ott, Anne Cummings, Bob Alexander, Betty Lou Boyd-Beck, Steve Auborn, Donna Whedon, Deborah Abbott, and Linda Russell. Lastly, I sent my first tiny rough draft and initial rewrite to The Editorial Department in Tucson, AZ. Without their thorough reviews and rejections I never would have made it this far. I also want to say that Auburn, NY, the Valley, Nedrow and South Onondaga were such great places for a young kid to grow up. I enjoyed every moment.

Introduction

My Life Before I Decided to Commit Suicide is a collection of slightly embellished personal experiences from my youth, adolescent and young adult years. It begins as almost any young boy's life begins, with a mischievous exploration of one's surroundings. I truly believe that I'm born with superpowers and a unique understanding of life that few people, if any, possess. However, in the long run, my gifts cannot protect me from life's greatest challenges: finding love and friendship.

The purpose behind *My Life* is two-fold. To provide a glimmer of resolve for all those insecure souls contemplating suicide as I once did, and to provide a unique look at how silly life's foibles really are. "Hang in there," is my advice. All of the crappy stuff will soon pass. Everything thereafter is pretty darn good.

I was born in Auburn, NY. A sleepy little village surrounded by farm land, gigantic trees, flowing creeks, streams and rivers nestled against the northern tip of Owasco Lake. A 'finger' among New York's Finger Lakes. Members of the Onondaga Nation tell the story of the lakes origin this way, "…the Creator looked down upon this land with special favor and upon reaching out to bless it, left his hand prints." Apparently we're not quite in the image of our Creator because there are eleven Finger Lakes.

On the day of my birth, September 11, 1954, the headline of the Auburn Citizen Advisor read, "New York Drenched as Hurricane [Edna] Passes." Perhaps this was a telling sign of the future of those born on this cold and soggy day. I don't care what anybody says, a constant barrage of dark, rain-filled clouds is burdensome. These clouds are the reason so many New Yorkers have poor posture - everyone slogs along hunched over with their head pitched down against the wind, rain and snow.

Prologue

I hung myself on September 11, 1978. The same day I was brought into this world twenty-four years earlier. This specific date had nothing to do with anything. I didn't wake up knowing I was going to be dangling from an attic rafter of a house I had never been in before. It wasn't a planned hanging. And the hanging wasn't any different from any other self-imposed hanging that had taken place over millennia except I was working on a construction site with my dad building a dormer on the back of a house in Eastwood, NY. I used 12 gauge electrical wiring shielded in a rubber casing as a noose.

Hanging myself fucking hurt I can tell you that. But once you kick the ladder out from under you there isn't much you can do. I regretted it immediately. I fought to find something to stand on, kicking my feet like the near-lifeless idiot I'd now become. I couldn't really see anything because my neck was jammed backward and I was choking to death. I tried to grab onto the wiring and pull myself up to relieve the tension of my weight from the noose, but 12 gauge wiring doesn't bend like a nice rope would have, and it was slippery besides. Rubber coated wire and sweaty, trembling hands don't make for a happy ending. This was my life's final choice? God dammit!

After a half minute or so I realized I was done. There was no sense running in midair anymore or trying to cry for help. It was exhausting for one, and two, there were no sounds escaping from my collapsing throat. When you're in this state of proposed happiness and you do finally give up, you begin to think back on what the hell it was that led you here in the first place. What *was* it that was so fricking bad you killed *yourself* rather than killing someone else? Why would I take my *own* life? Son of a bitch! This is stupid. God dammit!

And just so you know, you don't die instantly when you hang yourself. It's extremely uncomfortable. No one hangs there thinking how great it is to be hanging. To comfort you in this time of desperation while the blood is slowly being cut off from your brain, your brain works feverishly trying to figure out how to save itself. It relaxes your body and hustles back to its time of conception in your squishy little head and reviews everything that might have caused you to end up doing such a dumb thing. After the review, in my case, my brain might come to the conclusion that I were right with my decision and continue with the hanging. I *was* a useless, skinny little messed up piece of shit kid and deserved to die, end of story ..... choke, cough, gasp, done. But my brain was also wishing that my body could die by myself and leave *it* the hell alone because my brain was having a great time sorting through all of my daily bullshit and now it wouldn't have anything to do......

Let's see now ...

Chapter 1
Auburn, NY
In the Beginning: Chocolate Quicksand and the King of the Dragonflies

We lived in a new housing development on Lakehurst Ave. There were no homes across the street or next to us where the strawberries grew in wild, unattended rows. We would eat them at will when they ripened. Up and down the rows we waddled searching for that perfect red diamond shape. We would sit there and eat four or five dripping morsels, waddle down the row a bit, sit back down, eat a few more and repeat that regiment over and over until we too resembled large over-ripened strawberries lying on our backs baking in the Auburn sun; rosy cheeks, white strawberry hair and little farmer jeans all rolled into one laying among our strawberry-bodied cousins. The next day there were even more cousins ready and willing to be devoured. There is nothing like fresh fruit. Wild berries, bananas, cantaloupe, cherries, apples, grapes, pears, watermelon, even grapefruit with a little sugar on top. Oh I love them all. I am them all.

Our house was a big white house with no grass, a dirt driveway and a rickety wooden sidewalk leading from the street to the glorious front door. My father built the entire house by himself. He laid the blocks for the foundation, studded up the walls, ran the wiring and the plumbing, hung and finished the sheetrock, put the windows in, put the clapboard siding on and the entire roof. He did it all. I'm sure he had a little help, but I am also sure he did 90% of it by himself. He told me so. That's the way he was. Want something done, just do it for Christ's sake. What are you waiting for and why are you waiting? Waiting is being lazy. Waiting is one of the biggest excuses lazy people have. "I'm waiting for them to call me." "I'm waiting for a ride." "I'm waiting for you so you can help me better myself." My father held a pretty good grudge against people who were waiting. As for me, I was born on a Saturday. I knew that waiting would not be a part of my life's equation. Saturday's child would work hard for a living.

Upon entering our glass-laced front door you were greeted by beautiful oak floors and an oak staircase with wide bottom steps that grew narrower toward the top as they swept gently to the left. A matching handrail joined spindled banisters that followed the outside of the stairs with a matching handrail bending along the curved wall. They were met at the top by an open hallway heading back toward the front of the house crafted in those same spindles and handrail. My dad was a master stair builder. Something even with all my powers I never quite figured out how to do. It was disappointing to say the least. I never really had the chance. He was the stair builder. The walls of our home were white and colorless so far, but it sure was a good beginning. Our Lakehurst home was a work in progress.

One damp day I wandered into the open field across the street. Nothing unusual. It was our job as kids to discover the world in any way we deemed fit. At the very far end of the field there was a chocolate muck hole filled with child-eating quicksand. I'm not kidding. Quicksand in Auburn, NY. It was amazing to see such a thing. Alive and gurgling, bubbling, popping the stench of death into the air .... blub, blub, blub, POP! .... stench ..... blub, blub ….. BURP-FART ..... stench ..... just nasty! The first time I ventured near that quicksand hundreds of gooey, skeletal arms with even gooier, skinnier fingers LEAPT UP and snatched onto my brand new rubber boot I had just received as a present from my parents and began shoving it into its fat, sucking mouth with my foot and my leg still in it! It started pulling me relentlessly into the center of earth's churning, chocolate chasm. I cried and I cried, screaming, but no one helped me. I was only two years old!!! "HELP ME! HELP ME! PLEASE SOMEBODY HELP ME!" My older brother HarryHarry and my older sister Eileen were just standing there looking right at me grinning with that complacent look of, "Oh well little skinny baby boy, whiner, special boy, super-child, onion head .... see ya." "PLEASE," in my mind I begged as I threw my arms out to them. "PLEASE! WE HARDLY KNOW EACH OTHER. YOU HAVE TO

HELP ME! WHAT'S WRONG WITH YOU?" They stood there and did nothing. NOTHING!

After an exhausting 30-minute fight for life, on my own volition I was able to grab onto a small root-bound twig and with my tiny, still developing arms I pulled and pulled and pulled trying desperately to keep my new boot on my foot. I pulled until I could no longer hold on and my right foot popped out of the boot. I saw my boot with the bright red sole get sucked into the underworld ..... gone ..... forever. I ran as fast as I could back home across the giant field with one boot on and one boot gone as I heard a horrendously loud slobbering, laughing belch roll out behind me .... "BBBBBUUUUURRRRRPPPPP ..... HA HA HA HA HA."

Needless to say, my mother Betty, who loved me more than anything and more than anybody else in the world was not happy about the loss of the boot. My safety, my mental health, my traumatic, physically challenging achievement meant nothing. "You lost your boot? Oh Jimmy, how could you?"

A few days after my recovery, in that same field we wandered again. Only this time something was oddly wrong. The sky began to blacken. Still silent, we first looked east watching a mysterious shadow grow and the daylight dim. We turned and looked west with our hands over our eyebrows to block the remaining sunlight. What the heck? A few small dragonflies flew by us with amazing speed ..... and then a few more ..... and then by the hundreds and the thousands ..... and then the sky was solid black with dragonflies. Prehistoric dragonflies! Boat loads of them! There was a somewhat overgrown, slimy creek at one end of Lakehurst, the mucky yucky quicksand and the jungle-like moistness always in the Auburn air so they must have bellowed from one end of New York State and were scouring the countryside looking for tiny human prey. I couldn't get these things to stop swooping down at me. My hands turned into baby flyswatters and my baby arms were waving back and forth, to and fro at a million miles an hour. Around and around at supersonic speeds. I almost rose right off the ground. The dragonflies were huge! I swatted and swatted, but they just kept coming. My brother and sister just stood there again like statues and watched. “COME ON! HELP ME! I’M YOUR BABY BROTHER! HOLY MOLEY!” I pled.

Suddenly I was being chased by the King of all dragonflies. He was shiny and pitch black. Its eyes were a bitter, angry yellow-green with red stressed out eyeball veins. Each eye was as big as my whole head. Its body as large as mine. It chased me out into the field trying to poke my eyes out with its hairy front legs or hands – whatever they were. Grabbing and poking, swatting me with its wings. Batting me back and forth back and forth. “You dog!” I thought. “I hate you!”

In my already weakened mental state I was batted back toward the quicksand. Falling to the ground I lay face down gazing wide eyed at the oozing, brown, pus death bowl that ate my boot and almost killed me two days before. The ooze pool sensed my presence and immediately began to extend its tiny little tentacles. The King flew just overhead and didn’t want to risk being entrapped by the roots of the chocolate quicksand. I stood up and ran like no two year old had ever run before. Faster than Tarzan and Jane’s illegitimate kid Boy. Faster than Lassie. Faster than even Mighty Mouse. Faster than that stupid speeding bullet. The King chased me across the field, across the street and kept buzzing, taunting, groping and batting me. I was running and swatting and thinking as loud as I could, “HELP! HELP!” My brother and sister just stood there. There wasn’t a single dragonfly around either of them. I ran and I ran trying to make it to the back door of our house and finally, exhausted, I fell to safety. I had survived. I made it. I lay there panting, bleeding and beaten. Why would my brother and sister just stand there in direct defiance to nature’s most primary compassion rule for siblings? They should have helped me. They should care for me shouldn’t they?

This was my first awakening to the realization that I truly might have to fend for myself and that I, because I had survived, might have some sort of superpower. Some sort of knowhow. An inner reasoning. A peace. A life puzzle-solving expertise. I was different. I was safe again due to my own resilience to outside evil. How was I going to explain this? How would I tell people that I might have superpowers? One thing I knew for sure, it would have to wait until I learned to talk. After all, I was only two.

Chapter 2
The Jeep Ride and the Humiliation that Followed

The following day was as sunny as it could be. The dragonflies were long gone, probably in New York City by now. There were lots of people to poke, push and torment down there. On this morning my father's truck wouldn't start. The final analysis was that the truck had run out of gas. It was the only vehicle we owned so Bob, my dad, decided to hitchhike and get some gas. I was asked to go with him. Can you imagine? Wow. Hitchhiking? With my dad? This is just great. After a short walk to Lake Ave we were soon picked up by a man in an army jeep who was more than happy to accommodate us. The jeep's top was off, I was sitting in the back with the wind blowing. It was a beautiful feeling just me and my dad. I was clearly his favorite. Why else would he take me and leave my dumb brother and sister at home? We had a special connection that he just didn't have with the other two. They never helped protect me. Why should he care about them? I had almost died twice. Did they lift a finger to help? I don't think so. I was the Chosen One. For now and forever. Numero Uno. El Primo. I sittith at the right hand of Bob.

When we reached our destination I stood up in the back of the jeep and maneuvered to get out. I tripped over the spare tire, lost my balance and fell off the tailgate. Using my developing superpowers I instinctively went into a forward flip. Arms out to my side, perfect form, jackknifing, reaching the apex, fingers touching toes, evaluating distance, seeking to land squarely on my feet. I felt comfortable. Looking left and then right. It seemed possible. Nothing was in my way ..... and then I crashed face first onto the pavement. Damn! It wasn't really pavement that I fell on. It was these little silver pieces of crushed stone poured on top of hot, black tar. My face smashed into the stones and my nose began to bleed like a freshly sliced artery. I couldn't move. I wasn't crying, I was just surprised at my landing. My father was in total shock. Probably in fear of my mother's reaction more than anything else. Of course, my brother and fathead sister would be elated, loving it. "Chosen One my ass," they would sing. "Chosen One my ass. Chosen one my ass. You're not the chosen one. You're not the chosen one....."

My dad, seeing his only sure bet on the future lying facedown and not moving or making a sound, tore off his sparkling white t-shirt in Incredible Hulk style exposing his muscular carpenter's build, reached backhanded to the jeep with his right arm and without even looking, literally picked up the jeep by the bumper and simply pushed it aside. It happened so fast and with such ease that no one gave it a second thought. Bob just picked up the Jeep and moved it! I know what I saw! And then he gently picked me up in his arms and cared for me. Rocking me slowly until the bleeding stopped. "Come back to me. Come back to me," he whispered. "Shhhhhh. Come back to me Jimmy. Shhhhhh." Look at this guy. He was in more pain than I was.

I broke my nose in that fall. It hooks hard right. If you take my picture from the right and then from the left, I look like a totally different person. I could have been a CIA agent if it weren't for my one-of-a-kind droopy eyes and eyebrows which look the same from any vantage point. But because of this new broken nose feature my father would sit me down in a chair in our large foyer on Saturdays. Meandering out the door would be a steady stream of family members (some even driving in from out of town), a steady stream of people claiming to be part of our family; talking to others in line like they knew me so well, neighbors, their relatives, friends, friends of friends, and even strangers. All in a line out the front door, across the yard and through the strawberry patch eating *my* strawberries. My siblings and immediate cousins set up lemonade stands.

Gramma Moo was filling pleated candy cups with M&Ms. Gramma Conley was making pigs in the blanket. Aunt Dorothy set up a wine tasting station, and my mom, dressed like a fashion model, was managing the entire affair. "Lemonade? Candy? Pig in the Blanket? Riesling? Merlot?"

My father was in his glory. One by one the curious entered his house. He had an oak pointing tool he whittled from a left over spindle. Instead of the Barnum & Bailey Circus it was the Bob & Betty Circus. I was the star monkey sitting in a kitchen chair, hands neatly folded in my lap at the bottom of the sweeping stairs. One by one the visitors walked up to the six foot stepladder placed directly behind me and made their way to the top. There were the young and the old, the chubby and the bubbly, priests, rabbis, nuns, mothers, lovers, bankers, a knife sharpener, a grocery bagger, a pilot, a seaman, a jockey, a salesman, a mechanic, a maid, a secretary, a milkman, a plumber, a farmer, a policeman, an Onondagan, a diver, the mailman, and even the town historian - all lined up in a row. Once they neared the top of the ladder they would delicately lean forward and peer down over the front of my head. Every one of them gasped with an "Oh my!" or "Bless you young man, bless you," as they bowed their head in prayer. Couples looked starry-eyed at each other and kissed after coming down from the ladder. Most of the men said, "Nice job Bobby!" The women would go right up to my mother, hold her hand and curtsy. Some even kissed her hand.

"This nose," my dad would proudly proclaim, "is the nose of a true Irishman." Glasses would immediately be raised and clinked together, "Here, here," they would say. "To the boy! To the boy!" And of course, it's true. Any real Irishman's nose is smashed, broken, bent and truly is a beautiful sight.

Chapter 3
Caught

On an off day when the Bob & Betty Circus closed due to rain, I casually wandered down to Lakehurst and Throop one block west through the strawberry patch. I crossed the street and ended up in somebody's tent or playhouse or rape house in a cloistered backyard. Kids being kids, or at least I think we were both kids, we were pulling our pants down showing each other our stuff. I really don't know who I was with in the shadowy enclosure so I can't say if they were older, if it was a girl or a boy or some drooling, hunchbacked, one-eyed sniveling troll. I can't recall. Nevertheless, I do remember having my pants down to my ankles when we were suddenly caught by an adult female. She was not happy with the ensuing scenario. In fact, she was quite angry. The incident didn't last long. I can't say that I was fondled and I can't say that I wasn't. I really don't remember looking at anyone else's pee-pee or touching anyone else, but I really don't know. I put my eyes back in my head, pulled up my pants and ran all the way home. I have never told anyone about this before; no one. I never went back there again either.

A bit later, by coincidence I'm sure, my Gramma Moo painted an ashtray in a painting class she once took. It had a little boy and a little girl facing each other looking down as they were pulling their diapers out away from their bellies. One said to the other, "You show me yours and I'll show you mine."

Chapter 4

My Journey to Seward Elementary and the Spy

That fall I began school. I started elementary school when I was four because I was born in early September and that's the way things go in New York. In Texas and other states I would have to have waited another year.

On the first day of kindergarten I ended up walking to school by myself. I have no idea where my brother and sister were or how my mother ever allowed me to leave by myself, but then again she let me play in quicksand, she let me almost be eaten by the dragonflicerososaurous and be humiliated by family members (some driving in from out of town), some claiming to be part of our family, neighbors, their relatives, friends, friends of friends, and even strangers, so why not let the four year old walk to school alone.

I left the grand Murphy home on this cold morning and went back to Throop steering clear of the child molester's house of ill repute. I walked north past Roberts to Crescent, took a left on Crescent, went one block to Lake Ave, took a right on Lake for a long block past Oakwood to Swift. I crossed Swift and walked one block west to Kearney. I crossed Kearney and there stood the William H. Seward Elementary School. It was named after the 12th Governor of New York, United States Senator and the United States Secretary of State under Abraham Lincoln and Andrew Johnson. You know, the guy who bought Alaska from the Russians. Known widely at the time as Seward's Folly. His fellow senators cackled, "Why would we want land at the top of the world you idiot?"

Well, the school named after him was right there on the corner. A little talked about fact is that an assassination attempt on Seward took place the same evening Lincoln was killed. I don't know if you knew that. Seward was stabbed several times while he lay ill in his bed (not in Auburn, of course). There were other murderous attempts made on members of Lincoln's cabinet that same evening. But back to me and my perils. Lincoln's got nothin' on me.

Guided by some indescribable inner body, center focused, directional finding force that few humans possess, I geographically made my way through the Auburn street maze to school. This way-finding power is just another one of the many intellectual tools I would come to realize was a special characteristic that I was born with and would have to manage my entire life. It's similar to Superboy crashing to Earth, having incredible powers and not being able to reveal them to anyone except his new parents. (My dad lifted up and moved a Jeep backhanded without even looking behind him in order to save my life not too long ago, remember?) Even at the age of four, if I had revealed my inner strength I might be locked up and questioned for days, maybe years, maybe forever, under a blinding Secret Service truth-telling silver lamp with water dripping .... dripping .... dripping .... on my strapped-still forehead while being mildly electrocuted every minute while shackled to a metal office chair desperate for the taste of a Fizzie. Oh, I love Fizzies and the magical way they change a glass of water into a refreshing, bubbly soda. All I could think of was fizzies, but there I was, holding my own, refusing to talk. “No! I can’t tell you about any superpowers. I can’t. I won’t!” (drip ………… … drip …..) Maybe the key to the locks that bound me would be thrown away or I might be CHOPPED UP and thrown into the boot-sucking quicksand one slow piece at a time by some oversized galute (with a broken nose!) or held captive and tortured by a fledgling government agency for generations to come. I would be their Irish guinea pig. “You think your nose is broken now? Wait till we get through with you.”

You have to keep quiet when you’re special. This is America, land that I love I’m thinking, but I’m not gonna mess with the Feds. I ain’t tellin’ nobody about my powers under any circumstances.

I made my way to the giant castle-like, super thick brass doors of Seward Elementary. I could barely reach the doorknob. Standing on my tiptoes in my shiny new black school shoes, I placed my tiny thumb awkwardly on the lever, stretching and trying several times to push the darn thing down. After a number of attempts I realized ………….. the doors were locked! I couldn’t believe it! I was the only one there. Wait a minute … there aren’t even any cars in the parking lot. Not a single one. Where was everyone? I was freezing. Man, it was cold. Was it Saturday? Was it a holiday? Why didn’t someone tell me? Especially my pinheaded brother, my stupid sister or my loving MOTHER? I couldn’t believe it. What about my MOTHER??? Where was I anyway? Was this the right place? Was this their plan to get rid of me? I can imagine HarryHarry, Eileen and my mother watching me walk down through the frozen strawberry patch and out of sight, turning to look at each other and simply going back to what they were already doing. “Oh well,” they said at the same time, “Oh well.”

With icy tears falling on my rosy red cheeks from my beautiful light blue eyes, I walked back to Swift and Lake Ave. There on the corner was a single-pump neighborhood gas station/corner store. So I climbed up the steps and went inside. The man behind the counter asked me what was wrong. I told him of my forlorn travels and he assured me that nothing was wrong. Another man dressed in a finely tailored, neatly pressed black suit and tie stood off to the right in the shadows by the basement door; fedora tipped over his eyes, lighting a cigarette, his left shoe sole pressed against the wall, knee bent, left hand moving slowly, perfectly toward the cigarette while he scratched his thumbnail across the head of the wooden match. The flame igniting and exploding into the chilled air. Smoke, fire and sulfur drenched the air. I love that smell. As he exhaled the first breath of non-filter Lucky Strike smoke, he tossed the match out a window that was cracked open. He placed his left hand into his jacket pocket, tilted his head upward just enough to reveal his dark, beady eyes and cold-stare aimed directly at me. I just stood there staring at him.

The gentle old store owner in his white smock and round glasses distractingly coughed breaking the silence; “hack-hack hack,” and continued to speak as he moved his head carefully up and down in a “Listen to me young man and don’t worry about that man in the corner” fashion ….. “You’re just a little early, young fella. In fact, if you turn around outa here and walk back to school right now, I am sure someone will be there.” The smell of Lucky Strikes and death seemed one in the same at that moment. I looked back to the man in the corner, but he was deep inside the shadow by now. There was just a glow of the burning cigarette and a billowing smoke trail. Something was about to happen, but I wasn’t sure what.

I wandered back down the steps and over to school. There were cars in the lot and the doors were open. I did run into my brother and sister and they seemed genuinely surprised to see me. They were standing face to face talking to each other in the hallway rehashing their story, looking guilty like they were keeping some sort of secret. I ignored them, but made sure that they saw me. I didn't tell them about my adventure to the corner store or the spy in the corner or my special way-finding power. Some things are better left unsaid. I did realize that it was now up to me to keep an eye on them rather than depending on them to keep an eye on me.

Chapter 5
The Move to Syracuse

Auburn was a really little town. For reasons I can't remember we used to call it Turkey Town. Later in my teen years calling someone a Turkey was a derogatory term in a joking manner. "You Turkey!" meant, "You foolish idiot, you fell for that?" Or, "Are you gonna do it or what? You Turkey."

My father was a carpenter, making me the son of a carpenter just like Jesus was. I'm not as outgoing and boisterous as Jesus was, no tricks here. None of those magical walks on the water or giving eyesight to the blind. There wasn't any healing of the lepers on my part or turning two fish and five loaves of bread into a meal for thousands. No water into wine, dying and coming back to life, moving of a gigantic rock, change the world type of tricks. At least not yet. Even Jesus waited until he was in His 30s.

Bob the Father, my dad, was in the Carpenters Union for a short while, but for some reason he couldn't take the day-to-day structure of working like a dog for someone else and getting a pittance at the end of the week for your sweat and hard knocks. Oddly enough, I think that's why he left high school for the Navy. High school was boringly structured and the Navy was rigidly structured. Rigid structure versus lax structure suits many lost souls better. They're too smart for informal structure and better off either following orders that lead to perfect order or they work for themselves among society creating their own order. Bob the Father enjoyed working for himself and did so for nearly the entire time he was an adult. Working for yourself is the ultimate responsibility and is a much greater responsibility than just showing up and being a slacker among the droves of like-slackers. First you have to find work and then you have to sell yourself to the customer. How to begin, how to get the ball rolling is time consuming and extremely challenging, and in particular, mentally challenging. Working for yourself takes a lot of organizational skills, logic and a devout determination. Especially when you have a family, a home, a vehicle, not to mention gas for the vehicle, food, clothing and all that other stuff that you have to find money for. On top of all that, you are the only bread winner. In 1958 there weren't many moms schlucking off to work. This great personal responsibility is the key reason so many *do* spend their lives working for others. The brave individual who works for himself in the construction field has to plan the work, price the materials, hire subs to do the work they themselves are not licensed or capable of doing, meet the contracted requirements, deal with the customer and pay everybody off. In the end, you get what's left. Sometimes, or most times, it isn't very much. It's never equal to the time you put into the job.

According to my dad there wasn't enough residential remodeling work in Auburn and there was plenty of work in Syracuse. So after building the most beautiful home next to a wild strawberry patch, directly across from a child-eating jungle muck-hole and prehistoric bugs and stuff, we packed it in and moved 35 miles east to Syracuse. My younger brother Michael was born just before we moved. I remember my mom and dad bringing the little prize home. "Oh good," I thought, "Someone for *me* to torment." I was thrilled! Too bad we were moving. The quicksand would have been the perfect place to start.

My parents bought this mammoth house in Syracuse. I mean mammoth. A gargantuan, two-story, square home on an extra large lot in an area south of Syracuse proper known as The Valley. The Valley was beautiful. Its imaginary boundaries went from Seneca Turnpike on the north end to Dorwin Ave on the south end, Monticello to Sunset on the east side (to the base of the small mountain range running north and south carved by glaciers millions of years earlier), and to Hopper Road to Valley Drive on the west side (the other side of the glacier's carving). It was an attractive neighborhood. Both the Salina Street (pronounced Salīna, not Saleena) side and the Valley Drive side were laced with very tall mature trees, thick New York grass, tons of flowers, bushes, evergreens, oaks and elms and a lot of nice middle class homes. Onondaga Creek came out of the Onondaga Indian Reservation to the south and flowed between Salina and Valley Drive up through the City of Syracuse and into Onondaga Lake.

Our house sat back off Salina Street with giant pine trees to the left and sky-scraping maple trees to the right with a good size front yard. This house was so big it had two stairways to the second floor. One as you walked in the front door in the den and then there was one that went upstairs from the kitchen in the back. There was a two story barn-type garage in the back and probably the main reason my father bought the place. There were apple trees, crabapple trees, grapes and a couple of pear trees in the backyard next to and behind the garage. What a great place for us meandering little Murphys. We had neighbors on both sides. The guy on the left was kind of Italian or Greek looking, a Guido, and lived with his mother. I remember him being about 40 or so with a pencil thin black mustache and thick, messy black hair; the perfect Italiano. It was hard to believe his mother hadn't teamed up with another Italian family to force some little roly-poly thing to marry him and make him happy. They would have 'learned' to love each other. The family on the other side of our house was your by-the-book All-American family. Blond, blue-eyed parents with two tall, handsome boys and a very pretty blond daughter. The Larsen family were graced with beautiful Norwegian genes.

The moment we pulled into our new dirt driveway at 5208 South Salina Street (I know how many feet are in a mile because of that address: 5,280) our dog Prince ran off across Salina and into the neighborhood at like 90 miles an hour. He was gone! My father spent the next two hours chasing him on foot, catching him and dragging his butt home. Prince was a black and tan German shepherd. The dog among dogs.

Statuesque. Ears pointed toward the sky. Standing at attention. Snout slightly tilted upward sniffing for the filthy smell of predators. Ready to rip and tear flesh off the intruder's bones at our beckoning. Tasting the fresh meat and blood, staring directly into your terrified eyes and stating, "Guten morgen. Wie geht es dir?" In other words, "DON'T MESS WITH ME BECAUSE I'LL RIP YOUR FACE OFF!"

Poor Prince was eventually crippled from arthritis. A default in the German shepherd genetic makeup. He couldn't even stand up after a few good years so my parents had to put him down. It was a sad day, but we all understood. Prince was in a lot of daily pain just trying to stay alive. It was best. He was a great dog.

Soon after Prince died, my snarly sister was exploring our new back yard marching through the high grass picking weeds and flowers, making a natural bouquet of freshly picked upstate ingredients. She was skipping and humming some stupid thing like some stupid girl would do .... la dee da .... la dee da dee. Dreaming of Prince Charming no doubt. Feeling her little oats. I was messing around on the driveway picking up small rocks and just throwing them anywhere and everywhere with no target in mind, just playing by myself. I wasn't paying any attention to Dear Eileen. She was invisible, a nonentity, a nothing, a nonexistent twit, a tweedle dumb among the tweedle dees, a rag among the muffins, a wreck among the trains, a thorn among the sides, a dole among the drums, a hell among the heavens. Like my father, I'm learning to hold a grudge too. I went way out behind the barn to do what I loved to do most, look for salamanders under rocks. Is there anything better than lifting up a rock and seeing a salamander underneath hiding from the day's heat and light? Is there anything better than capturing and holding a salamander in your cupped hands and feeling the hustle of slimy little feet scampering across the palms of your hands? Is there? Peering in between your thumbs and seeing that little rascal. This is what life is all about.

Alone and in the middle of my peaceful world, all of a sudden I hear this ultra-high key of 'C' screech like a bald eagle circling and calling for others to join him for the kill. I dropped my salamander and ran head-lowered at Superboy speed to the side of the barn. My lovely sister had climbed up into one of the crabapple trees. She was about two feet off the ground. That's it .... two feet! Half my sister's own height for cryin' out loud .... two tiny feet! She panicked and started screaming and screaming. Yelling bloody murder that she couldn't get down. She was stuck! The tree had grabbed her leg and wouldn't let go! "OH PLEASE," PLEASE HELP HER! WHAT WAS WRONG WITH ME! WHY WASN'T I GOING TO GET HELP! WHAT WAS WRONG WITH ME! "WHY WON'T YOU HELP ME, I'M YOUR SISTER! WE HARDLY KNOW EACH OTHER! YOU HAVE TO HELP ME!" You plagiarist I thought.

I can still see her ravaged face all red, wrinkled and teary. Yelling like she was going to die. It's such a fond memory. No gal in a scary movie has ever scared me since. This was the epitome of scared girls. This was the face that scaredom would be built upon. My sister's face of near death was all I ever needed to get me through scary times. It was my judgment face against all things scary. Scared girls are funny. I just left her there and went back to my salamanders skipping and humming along my way ..... la dee da ..... la dee da dee. Oh what a beautiful morning. Oh what a beautiful day ..... la dee da ..... la dee da dee.

A couple of days later I began learning how to ride a bicycle. A single speed, two wheeler with a heavy frame and big fat tires to boot. The premise of riding a bike is simple; pedal your butt off, you go fast, step backward on the pedal and the bike stops. Step real hard backwards on the pedal and the bike skids. Boys love this stuff. Slamming on the brakes and leaving a black tire mark on the pavement as you lean and fishtail the back end of the bike around is the type of fun you never tire of.

My brother, or maybe even my father, placed me on the oversized bike seat at the top of the Larsen's driveway that slanted gently downward from the sidewalk toward Hansel and Gretel's house; a straight run, perfect. And there I was about to take off into space and be in my glory. I could see myself pedaling super fast, lifting off and flying over my house, circling back over Guido's, crossing Salina, flying up East Warrington to Coldbrook, back down over East Cheltenham just touching the tops of the trees. Two days later after covering the entire Valley I would still hear my sister screaming from that crabapple tree. "Holy shit, you're kidding me!" I would immediately lean forward on the bike and pedal like there was no tomorrow. Pedaling faster while flying still makes the bike go faster. My short cropped brush-cut on my big round head leaning straight into the wind. Goggled eyes searing and focused burning a hole right in her, concentrating and determined to dive bomb her. Here I go. Rrrrraaaaaarrrrr. Just to see her teary eyed swollen face shut up for a minute and morph to a look of wonder as she saw her piss-ant little brother heading toward her at 100 feet per second made it all worth it. I can't explain the silence. Finally, she shut the hell up. Back up into a twisting loop-d-loop. My eyes were wide with a smile from ear to ear. Rrrrraaaaaarrrrr. "Take that you big crybaby!" I shouted. Rrrrraaaaaarrrrr. So far, in the four years I've been alive, I have never had so much fun. It's hard to believe she's been in that tree for two days, but it's the truth.

Back to reality. "OK, here you go. Are you ready?" Boy was I. "Let me go! Let me go!" I exclaimed. "Okay. One ..... Two ..... Three!" Down the driveway I went, barely able to keep the bike upright. I'd never been on a bike before. My arms weren't long enough to reach the rubber handles on the outsides of the handlebar so I was bent over steering from right next to the center post of the handlebar. The front wheel was wiggling and shaking uncontrollably. My legs were so short that my feet were unable to even touch the pedals. Who's idea was this? Down, down, down, faster, faster and faster. And who do I see? There's Gretel Larsen in her wooden clogs, sky-blue dress, white apron, stiff white hat and golden braids with her open arms and young breasts waiting for me. Why would a young woman be in love with a four year old? Maybe that's the way it works in Holland. "I am in love with you too, Gretel!" Faster and faster. "Here I come Gretel!" "Look where you're

going!" they yelled. Gretel? Why do you look so concerned? "Watch out!" "Turn!"
What?

S M A S H !

Right into the back of our Norwegian neighbor's car. Blood and guts were everywhere (not enough for an ambulance mind you). My nose was already smashed so there was no need for a parade of infidels. There were no tears, at least not from me. I'm made of iron. "Gretel? Gretel my dear. Don't cry for me. Hold me if you shall. Yes, right there ….. a little lower. Okay." "Ik houd van u. Ik houd van u," she whispered.

Chapter 6

My Poor Little Brother Michael

Our bedrooms were upstairs on the south side of this big square house. The huge bathroom had two doors, one on our side and one leading to a step down to a stairway landing that led to the downstairs den. If you continued across the landing you took a step up into my parents' bedroom. Their bedroom consumed the whole northern end of the house. This house was great.

Once my little brother Michael was old enough to walk and run, the one thing I loved to do, actually had a duty to do being the older brother, was to chase him around and torment him as much as possible. It's the old 'live and learn about life' concept. I'm going to beat the crap out of you until you're big enough to beat the crap out of me routine.

Like I said, this stairway had a door at the bottom that opened up into the den. The door was usually closed. There was a little brass handle at the top of the stairs on either side so you could pull yourself up from the last step or use it to guide yourself down to the first step if you were going down. It was a little safety thing. Surprisingly, there was no handrail. I used to chase my lovely little brother all over the upstairs catching him and beating him the way I was supposed to. Under the beds, over the beds, against the wall, choking and punching him; basically doing things to him that he was too small to do to me. After all, HarryHarry did the same to me. If you think about it, the first two life-bearing, amebic cells on Earth split apart due to a fight over not having enough of their own space. It really isn't anything new and I don't think anyone is surprised by this normal, animalistic approach. It's just the way life is on all levels.

Occasionally, I would chase little Michael through our bedrooms and through the bathroom. He would be seeking refuge in my parents' room. If they weren't there I would continue to trap and abuse his weaker being. What fun! A few times as we reached the landing he would reach for the cute little brass handle, miss it and tumble all the way down the stairs. "Oh no, there he goes again."

I really did get a sense of accomplishment out of this. I loved it. Not in the mean sense of loving it, but in the sense that I did satisfy my "older brother mission" to seek and destroy my younger brother. I did this quite a few times. I never got tired of it. Bang, Bang, rattle, roll, clunk, mmfff, Ooohhhhhhhhh. My father, being the carpenter of all carpenters, closed off those stairs for good. The rolling and tumbling down the stairs sadly came to an abrupt end.

Chapter 7
The Brass Cane

This detraction didn't stop my brother HarryHarry from acting upon his duties to torment *me* on a regular basis. The cycle of brotherly love didn't miss a beat. I have no idea what Eileen was doing. Crying about something somewhere to someone I'm sure.

On this particular beautiful fall day in the front yard by the driveway, HarryHarry and I were playing like we had an Irish battle spear and we were dressed in full Fighting Irish regalia from the Iron Age. We were tossing a brass tipped walnut walking cane back and forth like it was the last war weapon in existence and we were fighting against the filthy Protestants. This final toss would make or break the war for Irish freedom from English oppression. We were a good 20 feet apart or so.

"Aye laddie, take that ya dirty Limey lover." "And here's to your mother in her Army boots!" Back and forth, back and forth, each time creating a new hate-filled phrase. "Your mother kissed my father's Blarney Stone!" "My father said yer mother's buns was nice and fluffy!" "Thank your mommy for providing milk to the entire English army." The sayings just kept coming. It was brilliant really. One soldier throwing and the other falling in the greatest exasperation of pain. "Aye laddie, ya got me!" "You deserve to die you slimy maggot!" "Thank your dear mother for me."

And then … there it was ……… HarryHarry threw the cane toward me. His form was perfect. Olympian. His right foot was planted firmly in the New York sod, weight distributed evenly, his right arm extended so far back the tip of the killer javelin brushed the rolling tips of green grass. I saw with me own eyes the grass send a message to his hand. That slight reverberation from my homeland's grassy tips were sent through the brass end and through the walnut staff to his perfectly laid finger tips. His eyes were focused on mine. When you fight an enemy, never look anywhere else but in their eyes. This is the wisdom of the Irish. Don't look at the left hand or the right or at the feet. Look in the eyes. You can tell every move prior to it happening if you focus on your enemy's eyes. This is also the way Superheroes strategize.

He thrust his body forward. I tripped over me own feet backward. The Irish battle rod rolled off his fingertips rotating clockwise with zero degree waverance. Soaring through the air like no other spear had ever soared. Not a sound. Not a breeze. The birds stopped chirping and just watched with their little heads cocked to one side. The squirrels stopped shelling, worms stopped burrowing, and all watched. It was the most perfectly thrown Olympic javelin since Greece was built. Both tips glistening, blinking an S.O.S. in the sun. I lay back and followed its flight until I lost it in the sun's glare. I just sat there blinded by the sun with my retinas burning and my pupils shutting down to a mere pinpoint. Where did it go I wondered? The glory of Ireland played before me in my mind. The building of Newgrange stone by stone, the Giants building the causeway, the fortresses, the lovely black haired, blue eyed Irish lasses, the fight for freedom, the Godly intelligence of our people. *Where* was the weapon? *Where* was my brother's scepter? I was held down by the sun unable to move. I just sat there staring at this white light eight million miles away. It was so beautiful. Was this the indescribable white light those nearing death see? I am at peace. I begin to hear the penny whistles faintly gaining ground in the distance. It is here I will stay. Please let me rest here Dear Lord. The knuckled walnut spear harnessed between two brass tips traveled slowly across the sky guided by the message of the grasses and then .... it crushed me as it drove itself into the center of my forehead. My head sank into the grass and soil that lay beneath. I heard my skull crack. I saw horses racing across the River Shannon in full gallop. Hawks twitching for prey. I saw an image of a tall, thin man kneeling over me placing a pewter disc on my forehead. It was warm and very soothing. There was no sound except for the penny whistles and a still, blinding brightness. The skinny man raised the brass-tipped cane toward the sun and a stream of loose energy ran from the sun into the cane's tip. The other end of the cane was placed on the disc against my forehead. Bodhrans. I could hear bodhrans. Marching bodhrans, bagpipers and the whistles. Getting closer and closer, louder and louder. The louder they became the dimmer the light became. It was a reversal of energies. I was out cold, barely breathing.

I awoke on the front lawn by myself. The sun was now behind the house. It was chilly and damp. No one was there but me. My brother probably ran in fear that he had killed me. Or maybe he ran to get my sister and they were rejoicing back by the barn that he *had* killed me. I never did find out, not that I pursued it, but I swear those two are out to get me. Nothing hurt. My head. My skull. I seemed to be alright, physically anyway.

Chapter 8
The Busy Bee Club

A couple of doors south of our square mansion, on the corner of Rosemont and Salina, an open-mouthed, gum chewing, high pitch voiced white woman in a flowered frock with a tall, black beehive hairdo and fake diamond encrusted black teardrop eyeglasses, and her two boys who were our age lived. In order to give my mom and other moms in the neighborhood a break, this lady formed the Busy Bee Club. Every couple of days HarryHarry and I would stroll down to her house and make crafts. You know, special, handmade cards for your mom and dad. Stick figure drawings of the family. We learned that scissors were used for cutting paper and not specifically for piercing flesh (who knew that?). Glue was for gluing and not to be used as icing on cupcakes. And finger paints, well, there wasn't much we could learn from that. The methodology was right up our alley; slop that stuff everywhere. It was great fun for us and got us out of Betty's hair for an hour or so.

Little did we know that the Beehive Lady was searching for information - the goods. Cookies in exchange for private information - the family lowdown. I'm quite certain she was a Russian spy. The fake diamonds were little spy cameras and microphones, and a Wollensak reel-to-reel was somewhere hidden in that doo. It was obvious.

Okay, those of you reading this, do this with me. Make believe you're chewing gum and raise your voice an octave. "Want a cookie?" she would screech. "I saw the Fuller Brush man at your house. Was he there long?" "He was handsome." "What did your mother buy?" "Was that the insurance man at your house?" And we would say, "Yes, and my mother made us hide behind the couch until he was gone because we don't have any money to make the payment." "Isn't your father working?" "He's working, but he lost money on his last job." "Oh, that's a shame. How much did he lose?" "I don't know, but we're eating cream tuna and peas on toast almost every night and we're drinking powered milk." "Oh really? Poor things. Can I get you another cookie, more *real* milk?" "My mom and dad had a big fight the other night too." "Oh really? What happened, tell me more." This went on for quite a while until somehow my mom found out that she was a spy. My mom came by to pick us up one day soon thereafter and pointed for Mrs. Beehive to join her in a private room just off the craft room. Mom picked up a pair of scissors along the way and then proceeded to give the Hive the business. There was definitely some tussling going on behind those doors; punching and slugging, breaking and smashing, gasping and bashing. Lots of begging from the Beehive, not a word from my mom. HarryHarry and I held down the Beehive's kids in a neck choke hold and a move my mom amazingly called the scissors; you placed your legs around your opponent's stomach, crossed your legs, locked your heels and squeezed. It was the Busy Bee Club alright ...... for Ruskies! Oh, and by the way, don't mess with my mom.

The next morning, right before dawn on September 11, 1959, my birthday, the house was surrounded by black limousines. Men in neatly pressed black suits and ties with matching fedoras smoking Lucky Strikes, entered, repressed, dismantled and disappeared everyone and everything from the Busy Bee Club house. HarryHarry and I were hiding in the bushes right next door where Heather the Feather, the first love of my life lived. These guys in black hardly made a sound. It was like quick, super-speed stuff, little movement sounds; ffft, ffft, ffft, wss, wss, wss, ffft, ffft, ffft; no talking whatsoever. Pointing, lot's of pointing. Up there, over there, over there, but no talking. There were no bodies removed, no Beehives that we saw, but we saw it all. They were in and out in 30 minutes. A cement truck pulled up at 10 a.m. and lowered a chute into the basement. They were in and out in 30 minutes. Nobody ever lived there again. We never asked any questions either. My mom and dad acted like nothing happened. They went about their business and us kids went about ours. Parents have a lot of connections to all sorts of people that we never find out about. Were my mom and dad connected to the underworld? The more I get to know them the more it seems possible.

Crossing Rosemont from the Busy Bee Club was our neighborhood corner store, the Jack Lewis Meat Market. And next to that a soda fountain shop. Jack Lewis was a tall, thin man with neatly combed black hair and he too had a thin, black mustache like the Guido. He always wore a clean, white shirt like he worked in an office instead of someone who sliced up body parts all day. He was a pro. Pros who deal in blood and guts don't necessarily wear their jobs on their shirtsleeves. They're clean, precise, make no mistakes, there's no mess and no evidence. The soda fountain was owned by a guy who looked just like George Washington reincarnated. He never said much.

The Jack Lewis Meat Market had every dry good and more that any family needed. Fresh-cut meats (liver, which Bob and Betty loved, but we all hated), bread, canned vegetables, Del Monte canned fruit, fresh eggs, butter, real corn in season, flour, sugar, salt, pepper, milk, powdered milk (mmmm), dried potato flakes (mmmm), apples, bananas; everything. And Mr. Lewis allowed families to run up credit thus saving the entire neighborhood population from starving to death. But the greatest event, the best thing that ever happened to me in my entire life, the bestest gift of all? Every couple of days or so, mostly during the winter it seemed, when it was bone-chilling cold, as me, my stringy sister and mean older brother walked to Meachem Elementary School, a blue Dodge D100 panel truck would pull up in front of the Jack Lewis Meat Market. The rickety, rusty door would slowly creak open and a nearly crippled, bent over old man would cautiously get out. Turning in his seat and placing his fat little legs above the running board with his right hand on the door and his left hand against the gas cap cover, he would get a good grip and pull himself upward and land downward to somewhat of a standing position on the running board; his weight shaking the truck. The three bundled up Murphys would be standing there with our little human tails wagging like crazy. His rough, fat, unshaven face would eventually produce a smile as he struggled making his way down to the ground. He was the friendliest old man. He knew why we were there and he was always pleased to see us.

"Why hello there!" he would exclaim. "It's so nice to see you." He may have been Santa Clause. The Great One, the Feeder of Reindeer, the Keeper of the Book, the Giver of Gifts, the Bringer of Joy, the Eternal Messenger of Hope for Bigger and Better Things to Come. He would mosey his way around to the back of his truck, his weight shifting from side to side. Another inch either way and he might tumble right over and roll down the street never to be seen again.

He would open up the big doors, first the right ….. all the way open ….. and then the left ….. all the way open, and out would waft this instant wisp of freshly made donuts, the likes of which you have never smelled before. Our eyes would instinctively close, our heads would gently tilt back and we would take a deeeeeeep, sloooooow breath of donut heaven. Is there a donut heaven you're wondering? Yes, there is. Donut heaven is right next door to bread heaven. Have you ever ridden by a bread factory? It's the second best smell ever. Donuts, my friend, are the *best* wintery smell ever. The best!

Our friend Santa would pull out a tray of just-out-of-the-fryer plain donuts still warm to the touch. We would willingly take our gloves off and he would give each of us a plain cake donut, "One for you Eileen. One for you HarryHarry, and one for you Little Jimmy." He knew our names just like Santa would. He and his rosy cheeks would then wish us a good day and take the rest of the donuts into Jack's store. These were donuts he made himself. He was the baker *and* the candlestick maker. Forever, from those days forward, plain donuts were my favorite donuts. No frosting, no nothing, just a plain ol' donut, please.

A short while after my biking "accident" at Hansel and Gretel's I got my own bike. A red 20-incher with red and white streamers coming out of the red handlebar grips, a thumb-bell, and the ace of spades clothes-pinned to the rear bike frame revving like a motorcycle over the spokes. It changed my world. I've always loved riding a bike. Plain donuts and riding a bike. Minus the ace of spades, in the early evening, when no one is out on the streets, pedaling down the pavement and coasting at a high rate of speed in complete silence with the wind in your face can't be equaled by anything else that I know of. I'm beginning to see that I'm kind of a loaner at heart or maybe I just like the peace and quiet that comes with being alone.

Jack Lewis's parking lot was the kind of lot you pulled into off Salina Street. There were only four or five parking spaces. You could pull in off Rosemont too, but you had to go around a paved abutment and then pull into the lot. The abutment looked like the perfect bike ramp to me. I could see myself hitting this ramp that was nearly at a 90° angle and 18" high aimed straight up to the sky at full speed on my bike. I'd be performing tricks that the bike world would be blown away by. At least a double back flip I'm thinking. I would change the world of biking forever. I could put The Valley on the map. What five year old can't do a double back flip? I could. I'm versatile, I'm relaxed, confident, and I still carry that very vivid image of Gretel and her assets reaching out to me as she gingerly clogged while awaiting my arrival. All I really need to do is transpose the perfectly timed clickity, clickity, clickity of the ace of spades into Gretel's perfectly fanciful footwork clockity, clockity, clockity. What a beautiful, culturally significant image: clickity, clockity, clickity, clockity, clickity, clockity. "Oh Gretel my love, I can do this first-time-ever double backflip …… for us!"

I performed a couple of trial runs and everything seemed in order. I go back to 5208 and I make a few counterclockwise circles to gather my thoughts and to get my rhythm in sync; clickity, clockity, clickity, clockity. Good. Good. I can do this. I open the circle wider and wider and wider, I start racing down the sidewalk from my house, pumping the pedals faster and faster. My streamers are straight out. The ace of spades humming in the key of A, thumb working the bell ….. ring ….. ring ….. ring, and I blur past the former Busy Bee Club and I swear I see the old bitch standing in the front window with her left hand on her hip, squinting through broken teardrop secret agent eye-frames with her lips pursed, sucking on a cigarette! I don't believe it! How can that be? She's dead! My mom killed her! I heard her gasping from the scissor wounds. I make a screeching right on Rosemont and then a quick left to line up for the perfect backflip projection and .... the next .... thing I know .... I'm waking up on our couch an hour later in our den with Jack Lewis the meat cutter patting my head with a cool, damp cloth. "I think he's going to be all right Mrs. Murphy. He's coming to." What was *he* doing at my house I'm thinking. Staring carefully and directly into my eyes, looking for the truth, he says, "What do you remember? What do you remember Jimmy? Do you remember anything? Did you see anything you want to talk about?" I knew he was talking about the Beehive Lady. "Nothing," I said as I looked away to the left. "Nothing."

Like I thought earlier to myself, I'm not giving up any information to anyone. Jack Lewis may have been a spy too. So the guy back in Auburn at the corner store, the corner store owner, my mom, my dad, Jack Lewis, the Bee Hive Lady and who knows who else, are all in cahoots with or against one another and I am the focus of their actions.

Chapter 9
The Valley Diner and the Trouble that Followed

A football field north of the Valley on the other side of the Turnpike was Campbell's Valley Diner. We were raised in the Valley Diner. I ate breakfast there 500,000 times. It was the best diner within miles. It was super clean with the diner part in the front and a dining room off to the side. There was plenty of parking out back. It was storybook perfect. It wasn't really a diner per se, like the old metal diners, the Valley Diner was a restaurant called a diner. Dave Campbell was the short-order cook. He was a small-framed man, 5' 4" tall or so with his short-order cook's white hat on. His thin hair was cut straight above his eyes. He walked like he was falling forward. Gotta go, gotta get there, gotta get there, gotta deliver the food, gotta go, gotta go. Dave was good natured and always laughing and egging you on; prying was more like it. Dave knew everything because everybody told him everything. My father hated him most of the time, but we still went there every day for breakfast. The food was great and the service was fast. Dave married one of the waitresses after she and her husband parted ways. Dave was a twin to Doug. Doug was in the kitchen making all the stuff that made Dave look good. Dave was loud, Doug was quiet. Without Doug there would be no Dave. Without Dave there would always be a Doug. Doug was the same height, but a little more robust. He had to taste all the food he prepared, right? That was his obligation. He was deserving of a few extra pounds.

Dave would see you walk in the door and he would start making your breakfast. I always had scrambled eggs, toast, home fries, coffee and water. He made the best scrambled eggs ever in a little tiny pan that he was given at birth. He would throw a little butter in there, crack a couple eggs with one hand, pour in a little milk with the other, whip it up, let it sit a few seconds while he worked on everybody else's order, come back, whip it up a little more, grab some of Doug's potatoes (which were the best golden brown, crispy chunks of potato ever), butter your toast and slide those eggs onto your plate in one minute flat. It was awesome. It was also $1.65, coffee included. The waitresses were all cute little girls and they were great also. Taking care of you was most important. These girls were making $100 cash in tips a day in the 60s and 70s. The cute little waitresses were another reason we went there every day. Everyone was in love with all of them. My brother Michael married one of them.

Lunch was just as good as breakfast. The best burgers anywhere. The best macaroni and potato salad anywhere. The Charles Chips were even the best and they were just regular old potato chips that came from a big can. Fish dinner on Friday nights were huge. Haddock and macaroni and potato salad and coleslaw. Every restaurant in the entire city of Syracuse and every surrounding community serves fresh haddock on Fridays. You get an entire piece of breaded fish on a hamburger bun. The fish is three or four times the size of the bun. It's the Catholic way.

We Murphy's were very poor. As smart and as talented as my dad is, he is also as honest as the day was long. Paying everyone he owed money to was his first priority (except for the insurance collector). And then, hopefully after everyone was paid there was something left for his own family. He wasn't being dishonest when we would hide from the insurance guy, he just didn't want to have to lie to someone's face. I can see that logic. Food on the table came before insurance.

We were so poor that one winter I had to wear my sister's hand-me-down winter coat. All our friends and relatives thought it was fine. "It looks great on you." "It fits perfectly." "Let me see. Zip it up." "Put the hood up." "Oh yes, it's perfect." "No one will know it's your sister's."

It was a black and white, small-checked jacket with a matching hood and white fur around the inside of the hood with an extra 'puff' of fur around the edge. It was as queer as it could be for Christ's sake. What the fuck are you doing to me? Why are you fucking doing this to me I'm thinking (using new words). WHY? It doesn't fit and it doesn't look fine, and NO, it won't do! I had no choice in the matter. It was mine to wear like it or not.

In these days you could pay your phone bill right across from the Valley Diner. The phone company had a nice brick office building right across the street. Most importantly, right next to the phone company was the Valley Bakery. Actually, Ballweg Lundsford Funeral Home, Mondo's Italian Restaurant, Campbell's Valley Diner, the phone company, and the Valley Bakery were all right there within fifty feet of each other. You could start your morning at the diner, cross the street and pay your phone bill, have a donut at the bakery, have lunch and drinks at Mondo's, head back to the diner for dinner, die and be buried without ever getting into your car.

On this day my father sent me and my sister over to the bakery while he went in and paid the phone bill. We walked into the bakery and the flour covered baker looked right at me and said, “Oh, what a pretty little girl. You look so cute in that jacket.” Son of a Bitch! Nice going stupid-ass, fat-ass guinea baker. I’M NOT A GIRL, DUMB-ASS! I’m a Superhero God damn it! Unbelievable! You think I want a donut now? How can I eat a donut now? You just called me a girl in front of my gloating SISTER! Do I want a donut? No! I hate your stupid fat-ass donuts! I mean they look pretty good. Oh man. I love the plain and the jelly-filled ..... but no! No, I don’t God damn it!

Soon after being called a “pretty little girl” by the fluffy baker I lashed out and I smacked a girl on the side of her head. I don’t know who she was, but she deserved it. We were both standing on the corner of Rosemont and Salina waiting for a bus or something and I hit her in the face. She cried and cried and cried and then ran home. She sounded just like my sister, looked like my sister too for that matter. I got in big trouble for that one. It wasn’t that I meant to hit her, but more like I had to hit her.

I got in trouble in kindergarten that same week for not remaining still during nap time. There were these railroad tracks made out of wood and I wanted to sleep on the tracks, but we were told not to. I kept getting on the tracks and I kept being told to, “GET OFF THE TRACKS JIMMY!” So I kept pulling myself around the floor on my blankie going, “Wooo wooo. Wooo wooo. Wooo wooo.” I had a fit! What was the big deal, sleep on the tracks, sleep off the tracks. Why does it matter? If you let me sleep on the tracks I will be a good little “boy” and sleep. If you don’t let me sleep on the tracks I will whine like the little girl you all think I am. Take your pick. “Wooo wooo. Wooo wooo. Wooo wooo.” My blankie was taken away and I was forced to sit in a chair facing the corner for the entire nap time. “Big deal,” I thought. I love chairs and I love corners too. It’s where two sides meet in perfect union and agree to continue on in two opposing directions. There’s harmony, perfect alignment, a sense of place and I know where I am. I’m comfortable in a corner. I fit in a corner.

On my way home from school that day I threw a snowball into Salina Street at a car. What harm could a five year old do to a car? How big could the snowball have been? How hard could it possibly have been packed? How hard could it have really been thrown? Did I even hit a car? Probably not, but the crossing guard saw me throw a snowball into the street and reported me to the proper authorities. Caught and reprimanded again, I had to walk to and from school with my squeaky sister for six weeks until winter broke. I was tortured like a common criminal. Squeaky was not happy either. In the first place, I had escaped her criminal acts of depravity in the past and now she was forced to pay attention to me for twenty minutes in the morning and twenty minutes in the afternoon. I wasn't happy because Eileen was a douchebag and I tried not to associate myself with douchebags. In retaliation and in direct defiance of authority for having to walk *with* her, I never walked exactly *with* her. I was always a few feet behind her. In my own mind I wasn't walking with her at all. I was as independent as I always have been. No thanks, I don't need your guidance. Move along little Lassie, move along. It was the longest six weeks of my life. A painful suffocation, a smothering, a sucking of the life right out of me, my skin would shrivel like an old prune every time I was near my sister. I do think I am allergic to her.

I developed one of my favorite sayings as we walked to Meachem Elementary. In an old man's voice I would say, "I used to walk nine-tenths of a mile one way from my house to school. We walked it every day in the rain, sleet, snow, hail, high winds, flooding, high humidity, scalding sun, torrential downpours, and -20 degree weather. And then we had to walk home. You kids don't know how good you have it." Everyone always rolled their eyes.

Chapter 10
Santa

That Christmas Eve I was tossing and turning in my bed. For the life of me I just could not get to sleep. It wasn't that great of a year for me. T-r-o-u-b-l-e was luring me around every corner and I took the bait every chance I had. I'm very intrigued by shadows. The silence of shadows and the unknown world that shadows represent are the life-long puzzle that must be solved. So all year I was busy playin' the tough guy, smashing stuff, throwin' stuff, beatin' up the girls, adding a little of my superpower into the dodgeball games during recess, bruisin' and cruisin', lovin' and leavin', wearin' and tearin', rumblin' and tumblin', kickin' and screamin', yellin' and hollerin', pokin' and prodin', runnin' and jumpin', stealin' and peelin', slippin' and slidin', winkin' and dinkin', shakin' and bakin', hootin' and hollerin', fussin' and fightin', flippin' and flyin', and in general, making a stand against all authority figures. I was six and I was a badass. I was the king of the castle, the ruler of the roost, the ong in the strong, the ow in the power, the eight behind the ball, the cue in the stick, the chalk on the tip, the rail in the road, the hi in the way, the salt in the sea, the beauty in the beast, the apple in the eye, the peachy in the keen, the do in the wah-ditty, the smoke in the fire, the snap in the crackle and pop, the pork in the pig, the light in the tunnel, the dollar in the bill, the whiskey in the still, the beer in the bottle, the bubbles in the suds, the wonder in the thunder .... And then

I heard and felt a loud, muffled .... THUD

Where?

Nothing ...   There it is!

A shuffling .... a sliding

On the roof?

What????

Shhhh .... I lay perfectly still

listening

Shhhhhhhh .... a rustling sort of

Listen

A dull, thumping, shuffling and stomping sort of noise ..... like heavy boots .... a snorting .... a bunch of snorts ..... hooves .... Shhhhhhhh!

It continued for a time and then? ....

there was a lot of rustling ...... movement ..... sliding ..... scraping ..... and a deep voice shouting commands!!!!

I couldn't take it any more so I jumped out of bed and ran to the window just in time to see Santa and his reindeer gliding and falling off the roof. Oh my GOSH! It was unbelievable! It was the most beautiful sight I had ever seen! Look at that! OH MY GOSH! The moon was full, the snow was falling off the roof like a zillion glistening diamonds tumbling in the night. I was blinded, squinting as tears joyfully began running down my cheeks and into the corners of my mouth. It was God's gift to the world. The shining, tiny glimmers of hope and faith. The unwavering commitment to goodness. The symbol of peace and love and goodwill to all. It's so beautiful! There they were: Dasher and Dancer and Prancer and Vixen and Comet and Cupid and Donner and Blitzen. Aw Rudolph ..... I missed Rudolph the beautifully red-nosed reindeer. I just kept crying. I dropped to my knees weeping. Not like a little girl *or* a little boy, but like someone who had just seen Jesus Christ himself. I wept for my new cleansing, for my healing, for the weight lifted from my shoulders by the wings of faith. I wept for the burdens and the obligations that had been lifted from my Holy Spirit. Santa. I *saw* him. I *saw* him! He *does* exist. I'm free, I'm free, I'm free, free, free. I, Son of Bob the Father, King of the Carpenters and the Virgin Betty, Queen of the Underworld, rose from the floor on the third hour, rolled the heavy blanket from the entrance to the bed and was shrouded in everlasting peace. Asleep I fell. Deeply asleep. Visions of sugarplums really did dance in my head. Good night. Good night to all. "Merry Christmas to all and to all a good night," I kept hearing over and over. I felt so good. So light. So saved. Merry Christmas everyone. Bless you. Bless you. I love you. What a great Christmas it was. I was full of joy and goodness for quite some time.

Chapter 11
My First Kiss

By the time first grade rolled around, my first love Heather the Feather had taken her piggy bank and moved out of town. No big deal. I wasn't really in love with her anyway. We only met once for a minute or so. I ended up in her apartment, in her bedroom of all places examining her piggy bank. There was a 2-story flat between the Larsen home and the Busy Bee Club. Heather the Feather lived on the second floor. Maybe I met her at the Busy Bee Club. That could be it. Even if I did, that doesn't mean that I have to be in love with her does it?

I had my first "real" girlfriend in first grade. Her name was Cheryl Hartman; a fine looking ruby cheeked, smiley blond cherub. I was crazy about her. She lived across Salina on Cheltenham. We used to walk to school together once in a while and back home together. And then, in the middle of our make-believe love fest we were caught off guard. Someone accused us of kissing. "Are you crazy?" I said. "Have you lost your mind? Are you sure? Just what did you see? Was I conscious? What the hell does kissing mean? Put our lips together? Ohhhhh I'm getting sick. Why would anybody ever do that anyway? I've seen my parents do it, but they don't know what they're doing. Ohhhhh I'm getting sick."

Needless to say, Cheryl was all bubbly and overjoyed by the news. Proud as a pregnant peacock. Standing tall (as tall as she could) with a look of affluence and prestige about her. Queenly, wood nymphly, bridely, motherly. "Please address me as you should," she would say. "I've been kissed." "You can leave us now. Go!" Oh my God, she's floating! She is floating in the air! She is friggin' floating! Is this the effect that I, Little Jimmy, will always have on women? I can make them float? One kiss and they begin to share my powers? It's like they've sucked part of my soul out of me and that tiny drop of my taste has turned them into the raging, evil Queen that they truly are. This was so not good. I wasn't happy and I denied kissing her. No way would I put my lips on anybody's! "NO WAY!" I shouted as I wiped the back of my hand across my lips feeling slightly weak from the loss of superpower. "Stand tall. Stand tall," I thought to myself. "Gather your strength man. Everyone is watching."

My shallow, cowering eyes met Cheryl's eyes of instant disbelief. Her barrel-chested beauty and pageantry turned into a look of royal embarrassment, hurt and devastation. What had I done to the love of my life? What had I done? I left myself no choice. I had to break it off with Cheryl. Something just wasn't right. It was absolutely wrong for me to have this type of influence over the opposite sex at such a young age. I had to be careful who I exchanged fluids with. Sorry my rosy little chubby cherub. You're not the one. I need to fall in love with someone who understands the strength of my superpowers and understands that the power of a single kiss from me can be, and is, dangerous if ingested in too heavy of a dose or too quickly. My lover has to be pure of any evil thoughts. They have to see through to my soul. They have to know who I am and what I'm capable of, the good and the bad. Cheryl was more concerned about her own reign of power than mine.

We each went our separate ways after that. That was it. Whatever 'it' was, 'it' was over. I never saw Cheryl again. She disappeared. Gone. Just like that. Maybe she changed schools.

Maybe even her last name. Maybe she moved from the county or the state to start a new life and to heal her broken heart. I moved on that's for sure.

Chapter 12

Borrowing a Tareyton

Neither Bob the Father or the Virgin Betty were big smokers or drinkers. My dad was a White Owl cigar smoker. The White Owl Invincible was his choice and was a very nice cigar. They were a mild, machine wrapped cigar. He would gnaw the hell out of the first three inches of those things while he worked to hold it in his mouth. He wasn't allowed to smoke cigars inside the house, much like his mother did not allow his father (my grandfather) to smoke cigarettes inside their Auburn apartment which eventually led to grandpa leaving her and dying alone in an apartment in Elmira, NY so I never got to meet him – thanks a lot! No cigarette smoke in the house was more important than love? It was more important than Grandpa meeting and sharing time with his grandkids? Geez you old bitty.

Outside and around Bob's job sites were the gooey remains of stogies all over the place. Bob *was* allowed to smoke a pipe inside and he did so. He was an avid pipe smoker. He had a couple of very nice carved wooden pipes. One was straight shafted and the other curved downward like Sherlock Holmes'. He looked and probably felt like a professor of carpenterology when he smoked his pipe. He packed his own tobacco and sat back and relaxed in the evenings in the corner of the den under a reading lamp, smoking his pipe and enjoying the Herald Journal; legs crossed and all, jeans, flannel shirt, slippers, white socks; very elegant for a working stiff. The den was walled in a beveled edge, tongue and groove knotty-pine. It was a very comfortable atmosphere like you might imagine a summer camp would be on one of the many lakes throughout New York; quiet and homey.

I don't remember there ever being beer in the house or wine for that matter. There was a fairly stacked liquor cabinet, but I can't say as Bob and Betty were regular drinkers by any means. That being said, my parents were both very good natured and did have people over and did like to party. On those occasions the favorite drink that I recall was the Screwdriver; vodka and orange juice. There were other beverages floating around, some Canadian Whiskey and the like, but never on a daily basis. Betty was a very light smoker, maybe a cigarette or two a day or three once in a while, and again, she too only drank on social occasions. They were both great fun and had a few very close friends who in those early days were mostly from Auburn. Almost every weekend, either my parents drove to Auburn or someone from Auburn drove to Syracuse. It was a beautiful 35 mile ride. The countryside in Upstate New York is unbelievably attractive. From Nedrow you could take 173 to Rt. 175 to 321, grab Rt. 20 and you were there. Another route my parents took a lot was 173 to Rt. 5 and then on into Auburn. That's one of the great things about the Upstate area, there are always two or three ways to get everywhere.

As usual, as any kid would, I stole my mom's cigarettes once in a while so I had to find a secret place to smoke. The first place that came to mind was in my dad's barn. There was an old wooden ladder that led up to a secret loft on the second floor. There was a trap door that you could close, some bits and pieces of broken up hay bales and a little sunlight creeping in between the wall and floor planks. There was also an old window with four weathered and dust beaten panes that the sun barely shown through. It was perfect, nobody would ever find me here. I proceeded to snuggle up into a far corner with my back to the wall and knees bent up in front of me. I got my naturally faded farmer jeans on that were worn and torn at the knees. But to be honest, they were too small for me; gee maybe my sister has a pair that might fit. Assholes. My little black shoes are all worn, my hair's a mess. I'm actually pretty dirty, but it's no big deal, I'm supposed to be dirty.

Matches? Let's see ……. got 'm. Cigarette? Got it. Comfortable? I'm comfortable. Ooooo man. This is great! I'm thinking of that spy guy at the corner store. I put the ciggy in my mouth so it droops just right, tear out a match, light that sucker like it was my millionth butt and take a drag. I'm good. I put the match on the floor and squash it hard with my shoe. I like it. I'm good with it. I'm cool. I am cool. I love it. I take my time. I'm careful with the ashes. Smoke, smoke, smoke that cigarette. I make believe I'm an esteemed hobo ridin' a railcar heading to Elmira. I hear there's work down yonder and I'm gonna get me some.

All of a sudden .....

BANG!

The trap door flies open and slams against the floor. Dust flies everywhere including into my eyes. I start choking and coughing. My eyes begin to water. What the hell just happened? I can't see anything! My left arm is up to my face trying to block the dirt and the dust. I can't see a damn thing ….. except ….. for this shadowy upper body figure. I don't see a fedora. All I see is a back-lit shadow of someone ……. is it smoke, dust or some sort of hot alien steam that I'm looking through?

Holy shit. It's my DAD! Totally pissed off because he could see and smell smoke pouring out of my secret hiding place. His red-veined eyes beginning to glow through the haze were filled with rage, almost bulging completely out of his head. Me, his namesake, the boy who fought and won against the dragonflicerososaurous, the broken-nosed, pure Irish boy leader, the boy who would soon fly, the spy-spotter. "WHAT THE HELL ARE YOU DOING? JESUS, MARY AND JOSEPH!" he shouted. His arms grew in size and in length as they reached out closer and closer to me. Bob was a little guy, but his body and arms were nothing but muscle. The veins in his arms were huge. His heart a fierce blood-pumping machine. His wrinkly, stubby, cut and slivered little cigar-stained fingers were like vice grips getting ready to clamp down on my throat. Look at those hands! They're beautiful. Holy SHIT!

"You *idiot*! You could burn the whole damn barn down in five seconds. You *idiot*!" He picked me up singlehandedly by the throat with his wrist tight to my chin forcing my neck back. His fingers wrapped completely around my throat. "I aughta snap your little neck in two right now!" he growled in a voice I'd never heard before. There was too much blood flowing way too fast through his body; his eyes, his veins, his huge arms, his voice! Bob the Father had turned into a crazy person. He was bigger than life. He was no longer human. He was an entity, the burning bush, the voice beyond reproach, the master of all that existed. I still held the lit cigarette between my thumb and forefinger. He carried me down the ladder with his hand crimped around my neck and my body dangling in the air. With every step down my eyes squeezed together, my face smirked, and my body jerked out of position. He took me outside and dropped me to the ground. I lay there like a heap of old clothes and scuffed shoes. The cigarette fell somewhere out there in the driveway. But I was his favorite, remember? I'm the Chosen One, the true Irishman. I can see things others can't. He was still a shadow standing over me with his back to the sun. Looking down at me, he quietly stated, "Get in the house, now."

I sat in the den next to his smoking chair on the couch waiting for what seemed like hours. And then he came in. His body was back to its normal size now. His eyes were the clear light blue I was used to and pleasingly back in their sockets. His huge arms and even huger hands were way less threatening. He stood across from me and explained to me quietly and thoughtfully about what might have happened had I caught the barn on fire, including the possibility of my death. I think my death would have come one way or the other. Either I would have been trapped in the best hiding place ever only to be discovered days later or I would have escaped the fire only to be caught and killed by my father and thrown back into the burning barn to cover his tracks. One way or another I was going to be found dead. He apologized to me before he slowly unbuckled his thick leather belt with the name Bob Murphy along with a couple of hand saws, hammers and rulers carved into it, and slid it through the belt loops. The removal of Bob's belt looked like Eve's snake slithering down through the apple tree with its tongue deliciously lashing out toward Adam. He told me to stand up, turn around, drop my drawers and bend over. Why would He do this to His only begotten second son? He said He never imagined He would ever resort to this type of behavior, especially toward His own flesh and blood. He told me He was bleeding inside His heart for the pain and suffering the fruit of His labor was about to endure. He folded the belt in half, brought his two hands together forming a big, open loop in the center and quickly snapped his hands outward. The wide belt came together making this incredibly loud slapping noise. He did it again and again and again. The sound drew nearer and nearer. My head hung low, my eyes were closed tight, my face was squished all together, CRACK .... CRACK ..... CARAK ..... CARAK ..... THE BELT CRASHED ACROSS MY INNOCENCE. The thorns dug deeper and deeper into my flesh. Blood and salty sweat dripped, burning into my eyes. My torn open flesh, flesh of the sinner, flesh of the thief, the liar, and the criminal; red, swollen and bleeding, was marked for eternity. This flesh, my thin, perfect, white flesh, was broken. Is this how lessons are taught? How lessons are learned? What exactly can be learned from this? That there must be a better way to steal, lie and to cheat? That planning the theft needs to be studied more in depth? That I need a way to protect myself should I ever get caught again?

My mother didn't even get involved. She was out back under the shade of the old oak tree smoking a Tareyton and drinking a Screwdriver watching Michael dig for salamanders. HarryHarry and Eileen, like two starving child zombies, stood there and watched with a glazed-over, feverish look on their faces. *They* were the root of all evil in every Man. *They* are the combined body of jealousy, covetousness, envy, desire, spite, death and destruction. What did *they* learn? It's okay to beat the shit out of their Holy brother? It's okay to scar the little angel-bastard up? Let 'm bleed! "Chosen One my ass," I heard them whisper and chuckle. "Little bastard! Broken-nosed Fuckhead!" These are not nice thoughts coming from my kindred spirits, but it's true. I could read their minds. They reveled in my despair. This was the first time I ever got the belt. I also got grounded. Neither of which I had ever been before. Lots of tears. Not a good day. Not a good night. At least for Little Jimmy.

Chapter 13

Little League with Jesus

Life is full of lessons taught by everyone we run into and through everything we do. It's hard to keep track of everything. My father spent years teaching the three boys baseball. It was a true love of his and my mothers. We each played in the Valley Little League from the time we were eight years old. First in the T-league, then the B-league, then the A's, and then the Majors when we were 11 and 12. My father coached all of us. He eventually served as president of the Valley Little League while my mom ran the concession stand. Valley Little League was the best league in the city. We had clean, manicured fields, dugouts, properly measured fences, perfect backstops and even bleachers. This was an all-volunteer league.

By this time my parents had made new friends in Syracuse. The Hartmans (parents of my first true love, Cheryl) being among of them. Then there were the Guilts, the Swentons, the Coles, the Delaneys, the Camps, the Martins and others - they all became life-long friends. The Valley Little League always had an opening day parade right down the middle of Valley Drive. All of the teams marched, the sponsors marched, the ladies marched and so did the coaches. Mr. Camp was the police chief so we even had a police escort. The streets were filled with families and onlookers. It was a big deal. Thanks to the sponsors every boy had a complete uniform. The Ts wore t-shirts, but they were still sponsored by a local business: First

Federal Bank, Gannon's Ice Cream, Luigi's Italian Restaurant, Murphy's Pharmacy (not us), Samson's Cement, the Valley Diner, it was very well organized. The concession stand sold popsicles, unbelievable slices of cheese pizza that were made right there on the spot, soda, candy, popcorn and potato chips. It had everything that was good and they made tons of money to pay for the materials needed for the upkeep of the fields. I mean these fields were handsome. We also sold raffle tickets to raise money. All of us Murphy boys were pitchers, infielders and outfielders. HarryHarry was a catcher for a while.

Once when in the Bs I was standing in right field minding my own business, concentrating on the meaning of the words to the Our Father, when everyone started screaming .....

JIMMY! ..... JIMMY! ..... JIMMY!

Our Father, who art in heaven

Hallowed be thy name (oh, His name is sacred, hallowed, to sanctify or consecrate)

Thy Kingdom come

Thy will be done (when I die I will be joining Him in Heaven)

J I M M Y!
On Earth as it is in Heaven (I'm going to be so good on Earth that Heaven is going to be like being here on Earth playing baseball with my dad as my coach)
Give us this day

Our daily bread

and forgive us our trespasses

as we forgive those who trespass against us (thank you for everything Lord Jesus. I am going to be a nicer person and in turn, people will be nicer to me) and lead us not into temptation,

but deliver us from Evil, Amen (Nice)

J I M M Y!

What? ……………….. Are you calling me? ………. What? ………. Is the game over? Praise the Lord! ….. Time to go? The next thing I know, the ball landed directly in the middle of my glove …………….. SLAP! I didn't even move! And it stayed there! It scared the living crap out of me. I thought the FBI had shot me or something. I just stood there scanning the woods and the audience looking for a gun barrel reflecting in the sun or maybe a leftover smoke trail from a snub-nose 38. Nothing! Everyone's hands were up to their mouths in disbelief. I thought my arm had been bitten or maybe broken. I *thought* I saw some dragonflies!

Everyone began cheering, "Woo-Hoo! He caught the ball!" "Did you see that?" "He caught the ball!"

I CAUGHT MY FIRST POP FLY? WHO DID? I DID? I CAUGHT MY FIRST POP FLY!

"YOU'RE ……….. OUT!" WOO-HOO! I CAUGHT THE BALL!

Despite my glorious, golden-boy catch, we lost the game. One of the guys on my team started crying and then somebody else started crying so I started crying too. It was the largest chain reaction crying event in recorded history. Perfectly aligned dominoes falling over weren't synchronized better than this. This whine was heard echoing southward across Seneca Turnpike, through the Valley to Dorwin Ave. It made the local news. Birds stopped feeding their young, squirrels stopped looking for buried nuts from the previous winter, ants stopped their impeccable, never ending mobilization, snakes stopped snaking, bees stopped buzzing, cows, well, we know what they did, milkmen stopped milking, bakers stopped baking, and hit-men stopped aiming.

The following year I moved up to the A's. During one game the coaches got into a big fight over a call. My father was right there in the middle of it. It was brutal. The women were screaming and yelling, "STOP! STOP! WHAT ABOUT THE CHILDREN?" It was something else. Bare-knuckle fisticuffs. It wasn't as if we all didn't know each other, everyone knew everyone. I don't remember what set it off. We weren't instigators, but then again we were Irish and didn't take any shit either. Actually, almost everyone was Irish. Another thing about the Valley Little League, there was no drinking alcohol on-site. Flare-ups among the adults were very few and very far between. This is the only time I remember anything like this ever happening. Somebody must have really messed with somebody.

When I was in the Majors I hit back to back home runs with Dickie Guilt two different times. I batted 3rd and he batted 4th (clean up). Dickie was a gangly, tall, muscular boy for 12 years old. He either hit a home run or he struck out. As for myself, I'm pretty sure I was a decent, but probably not a great offensive player. I just couldn't read the pitches. If I got on base I was somewhat lucky, but I really wasn't all *that* bad. Once on base I did have this one trick up my sleeve. When I got to first and sometimes even second, I would keep track of where the ball was. Usually the first baseman or whoever caught the ball would throw the ball back to the pitcher. The pitcher would take his glove off and rub the ball or something. Maybe take his hat off and wipe his brow, general fidgeting around the mound. In the mean time the first and second basemen were away from their bags with their backs facing me. This was perfect! These guys were sound asleep, maybe contemplating the meaning of the Hail Mary. More than once I would steal second or third while this lackadaisical, cool stuff was going on. If you weren't watching me I was gone, nearly invisible. I was never thrown out. I did exercise my superpowers to a very small degree. I wasn't a blur on the field or anything, but there was no way they could throw me out even if they were looking right at me.

For the longest time I played shortstop, not a traditional position for a left-hander. Why is it nontraditional? Because if there is a runner on first and the ball is hit to the shortstop, a right handed player scoops the ball up with his gloved left hand, takes the ball out with his right hand and simply underhands it to the second baseman or he can just whip the ball in motion to him. A lefty has the glove on the right hand. He has to catch the ball, turn and then throw to the second baseman. That extra second it takes to turn can be crucial. It never bothered me. I was a great shortstop. I eventually made my way to first base where a lefty should be. I loved playing first. I loved stretching for the ball. One foot on the bag, a giant stride toward the ball, the glove stretched as far as it would go – GOT IT!

At the end of our stay in the Valley, when we moved to Nedrow, we were out of the district, but they still snuck us in there because my parents were an important part of the organization. We were very lucky to have this privilege. It was on the QT. Like I said, the Valley Little League was the best league in the city and everyone was trying to sneak their kids in there.

Chapter 14
My Sister Begins Love Training

My parents, being parents, once in a while would go out with their friends and leave my responsible sister to babysit us. She would immediately invite some guy over and they would make out on the couch all fricking night long. I don't know what the hell was going on really. I would just watch the little black and white TV set with my cowboy hat on and they would be lip-locked and whatever else behind me. It was uncomfortable to say the least. I think she was with Joseph MacCollom. It was gross.

Chapter 15

Move #2, Nedrow

The Swarm

When I was going into the 4th grade we sold the Salina Street home and moved to Nedrow, NY. A one-square-mile town of 2,200 residents one mile south of 5208 bordering the Onondaga Indian Reservation. It was a smaller house. More like a normal house. The house in the Valley was just, "too expensive to heat during the winter," I heard my father once say. The first day we were in Nedrow, HarryHarry, a friend of his from the Valley named Danny and I went hiking in the woods a short way from the house behind the sprawling Clooney mansion. There was a little creek running through the woods and a tree fort way up in this tree right next to the creek. It had one of those ladders that was nailed to the tree trunk. You've seen them. Each step is a board about 18" long and each board has a couple of nails driven into the tree. Well I decided to climb up to the tree fort. It was really high. When I looked at it years later, it was still way up there maybe 50' in the air or so. I start climbing up to the fort and I am a little scared because I'm only nine years old, but what the heck. I almost get to the top and I don't want to go any farther because now I'm really scared. My brother and Danny keep shouting, "You're almost there, just keep going. You're almost there!" "Chickenshit!" "Keep going!" "Panzy!" "Pussy!" Shakingly, I continue up, but I'm not comfortable, and to be honest, I'm sort of afraid to go back down. I'm afraid to go up and I'm afraid to go down. I could freeze right here forever and just hug the tree and let the bark grow around me, hold me tight, keep me warm and feed me. It would protect me from the elements of life and no harm would ever come to me. I would never move again. I would be encased in the everlasting womb of the Tree of Life. In the spring, warm sap would run along my young body massaging me all over every day. Running between my toes, tickling the bottoms of my feet, up my long legs to my tummy. It would be a gigglefest every day. Wonderfully warm sap would be flowing around my penis and my nipples, in and around my fingers and over my shoulders, neck, ears and face. The sap would become my blood. I would become the tree. In the summer, the inside of the bark would be nice and warm in the daytime and perfect in the evening. I would be floating in the tree's embryonic fluid; the fluid of Earth's life. I would be all that the Earth could give. I would have no more and no less than all I needed to have as all living things on Earth have had every single moment since Earth's gasping first breath. I would be everything among every thing. I would be all consuming and all consumed. There would be no "I" for I would be a part of all for all to be a part of.

When my warm summer would show signs of waning and my hemisphere began to lose favor with my Sun, the ever courageous gift of fall would incrementally arrive with each echoing tick of time as my tree began to sleep. The warm sensational giggle-fluid no longer brought the glee it once had. I would fight to move, but the protective life-shell would harden to keep Mother Nature's fierce winter winds and biting cold away from me and I would sleep … and sleep … and sleep … and be so comfortable inside my womb. Dreaming of my brook below and the daisies and daffodils, and making wishes upon the flight of the dutiful dandelion helicopters, and I would chase the firefly, borrowing its light for my own personal glowing bracelet in the night. I can't think of anything better, anything at all. I do want to stay right here. My eyes are closed. My breathing has slowed. God's strong, able hand is reaching out to me. Not to catch me, but to take me. To carry me. To save me.

Unfortunately, I have to wake up. I have to move on. My stupid brother wants to see me fall. What an idiot he is, and his stupid friend too. Why am I even listening to them? I'm my own man. I can make my own choices.

After what seemed like a lifetime I get to the top of the nailed-to-the-tree ladder and pop my head over the edge anxiously looking inside the fort. There, sitting before me, were at least a thousand honey bees. It was like walking through the doors of the Cotton Club. Thousands of finely dressed black and yellow bees seemed to be just waiting there for me in tiny little bee rocking chairs with their legs crossed and smoking cigarettes. Just rocking and waiting. For me? Upon closer inspection, some sat at tables with white linens and had little mixed drinks in their hands while others were standing and dancing in the back far-right corner. I'd never seen bees dance before, or rock in rocking chairs for that matter. They were good dancers! This was very impressive. One bee, back in the corner, sat at a piano playing some barrel-house blues. The beauty, who must have been the Queen Bee, was singing, "Roll me Daddy. Roll me one more time. Roll me Daddy. Roll me one more time. If you roll me Daddy, then all of your love will be mine." She was friggin' really good, and gorgeous to boot.

Scanning back across the room I very slowly lower my head so that my eyes were peeking just over the doorway edge .... looking right .... looking left .... looking right .... the Queen abruptly stopped singing. The Piano Man stopped playin', the rockers stop rockin', the glasses stop clinkin' and the joint got deadly quiet. Even the breeze stopped breezing. The leaves stopped rustling and the trees stopped their harmonic swaying. Deadly quiet. Down below me the brook stopped babbling and the minnows stopped minnowing. The hummingbirds stopped humming, the crows stopped crowing, the robins stopped bob-bob-bobbin', the owls stopping asking and the cardinals started praying. The Queen graciously raises her little microphone to her lips (I guess they were lips), and pointed to the doorway. Every bee in the house looked over at me. "Well," she says. "Look what we have here. You have a big-ass head my friend. Everyone ..... everyone! Look at the size of that thing!" The audience gasped and then laughed crazily like only bees can. "You poor, gigantic-headed thing," she continued. "How do you carry that monster thing around my friend? Talk about baring a burden for your entire life. *You* have been fucking cursed!" And then, the Queen rose slowly from the stage and the deadly silence returned; her wings humming a perfect low E.

“ENOUGH!” she shouted. “ENOUGH!” “Today is a day of rest and thoughtful togetherness. We have gathered here to celebrate the work of our hive and to enjoy each other’s company in song and dance in the comfort of our home. And then this fat-headed, crooked-eyed dwarf pokes his broken nose into our business and frankly it has ruined my day.” “ENOUGH!” “ENOUGH!” she shouts. She stares directly at me.

“Be done with him.”

They look at me, my eyes widen, my left eyebrow rises up in curiosity, my big head shrinks just a bit lower, but I’m still peering over the edge .... my eyeballs shift left .... right .... I look left .... they were all looking straight ahead, right at me. Every tiny little bee eye is staring at the huge head.
THEY ATTACK!

Turmoil is everywhere. I’m stung immediately. Again, again, and again! The Piano Man starts banging out Little Richard’s “Tutti Frutti, Oh Rudy! Tutti Frutti, Oh Rudy!” Little tiny beer glasses are smashing everywhere and wings are buzzing like chainsaws. It’s deafening! I have no choice but to turn from the fort .... jump off the ladder .... and tumble and fall and fall and tumble, slowly rotating through space finding my point of balance. Belly first, feet together, arms out to the side, arched back. It’s too bad I wasn’t diving off Niagara Falls or somewhere, anywhere where there was a chance of landing safely because I felt pretty good about my form ..... OUCH! ..... and I’m still getting stung again and again and again, and I’m falling for like a minute and a half slowly collecting my form for the perfect landing, thinking of covering as much water area as possible to break the fall ..... and finally ..... I largely splashcrash into the shallow creek with the most awesome belly-whopper .... ohhhh shhhhhhiiiiit ………. and just lay there, eye to eye with a thousand minnows sitting in little minnow chairs. MINNOWS! "AAAAHHHHHHHHH," I blub under water. "No Way!"

I jump up and look around. HarryHarry and Danny are clapping and screaming with laughter. "That was unbelievable! That was the best dive ever!" "A 10! A 10!" they shout, "A 10!" I start running out of the woods down the street and toward our new home, but I don't know where it is and I keep running and running and I can hear HarryHarry yelling, "It's back here! It's back here!" So I turn around and follow him home screaming and crying, stung and swollen, lost, wet and feverish. My mom was there to comfort me and pat me dry. HarryHarry was sent to the back yard to make mud with the hose and then bring it in and give it to my mom. She made small mud patties and placed them over the stings. As the mud dried it sucked the bee venom out of the holes in my body where the stingers pumped their poison. I was stung a total of seven times; four on my face and three on my body. Broken, bruised and battered, I clung to life. What a beautiful dive though. The next day while playing in the back yard I was stung two more times. This time by wasps.
Welcome to Nedrow ……….

Not too soon after we moved to Nedrow (Skid Row we used to call it, or Deadrow), before Interstate 81 was completed, all of the semi-trucks and every other truck on Earth would travel Route 11 (Salina Street). It was the main thoroughfare north to Canada and south into New Orleans. From lower Nedrow north to Roswell Ave, Salina dropped for a rolling mile or two downhill. Nothing extreme, but nonetheless a bit downhill. It's hard for me to think of a road that's heading north sloping downhill, but it did. It's like something M. C. Escher would think up. You look north and your mind thinks uphill toward the north pole, but you're actually going downhill. I'm not sure I can explain this correctly so I'll move on.

One typically lazy evening us boys were playing in the lot between the church where the Jehovah Witnesses danced and highly praised the Lord, and the Nedrow Firehouse where a select group of men drank, rescued people and put out fires (occasionally in that order). Sometimes we would hang out on the church steps looking for new cars, cool cars and fast cars cruising up and down Salina. Other times we would just be lying in the grass among the dandelions chewing on a stem doing pretty much nothin', blindly loving life at its fullest.

Off in the distance we could hear a truck horn blowing, coming closer and closer from the south. We really didn't pay much attention to it until it got a lot closer and became annoyingly loud. It was a fast moving, medium-sized flatbed carrying 4' x 8' sheets of ¼" steel going north on Salina Street down that gradual slope beeping and beeping and steadily laying on its horn. Salina was a straight run so there shouldn't have been a problem. The driver must have lost his brakes and he was warning everyone to get the hell out of his way. As he gained speed past Orchard heading fast toward West Roswell, the driver yanked the wheel left across the oncoming southbound traffic lane, down an embankment and disintegrated the cinder block basement wall of the corner house. We ran like crazy over there. It was just down the street for crying out loud. We got there before the volunteer firemen did and way before the ambulance did. It was like a bomb had exploded. Broken and snapped trees lay scattered to the sides of the path the truck cut through the woods. You could taste the dust from the decimated block wall. It was everything a young kid dreamed of.

Lots of Nedrownians were gathering. The fire department didn't take long to arrive and begin assessing the situation. We were crouched down in the bushes trying to see inside the truck, but the cab was so far inside the house there was nothing to see. We made our way back to the corner of Salina and Roswell and waited. The sheets of ¼" steel were like razor blades slicing through the wind. They flew off the truck bed with a number of them going through the backside of the cab. One of them chopped the driver's head off right at the neck. A volunteer firemen paraded the head out in a soaked white towel ripe with fresh human blood. He stopped to talk to the police and when he did we snuck up and hid behind a bush. The towel was right there in front of us. He placed it down on the sidewalk and made a half-assed attempt to keep it covered. There was a slit in the towel and we could see inside. I think the fireman saw us hiding out of the corner of his eye and placed it down just so we *could* see inside. There it was ….. looking straight at us ….. an eyeball ….. wide open like it had just seen a ghost. The talking head was pleading with us to save him, to help him before he died. I don't think he knew that his body was even missing. It was like he was saying, "Shit, fuck, this fucking hurts, man. What the fuck happened?" "What are you looking at you little piss-ants?" His eye was falling out of its socket hanging on only by the optic nerve. It was beyond scary. We were all in shock. In fact, our eyes were as wide open as his fallen eye.

Us guys talked about stealing it and hiding it in the loft over my garage. That would have been so excellent. Put it on ice 'till Halloween. We could have done it if we had really wanted to. We could have staged a fight to distract everyone, taken off my shirt, grabbed the head by its hair, removed it from the towel, put a dumb rock in its place, wrapped the head in my shirt and run home. Or we could have gotten caught and ended up in juvie. Being the cowards we were we settled for hiding in the bush and being happy with the fact that we saw a talking bloody head. Whenever I smell blood or taste it I think of that guy and his begging eyeball and missing body. We should have snuck into the basement and seen what his body was doing. There isn't much a body can do without the head though. It can't look around. It can't wonder. So the body was probably just lying there dead.

Chapter 16

Turf Districts 1-7

Even though Nedrow was a small town of one square mile and 2,200 people, it was still divided turf-wise into seven neighborhoods. Kids pretty much stayed on their own turf right into their teens. Each had their own creeks to play in, their own woods to play in, their own hills to slide down in winter and their own streets to ride bikes on in the summer. Section 1 was the Dorwin Ave to Leonard Ave neighborhood which was the border at the south end of the Valley. This area was a collection of regular American homes, two long blocks deep from Salina St. to Onondaga Creek. It consisted of the south side of Dorwin and then Stonefield, Ruhamah, Everingham, Hoover and Lindberg with Ida splitting them down the middle and Brookside Drive running along the creek. There was a little cul-de-sac neighborhood tucked into the southwest corner.

The next two streets going south, Section 2, were Leonard and Elton, somehow apart from their neighbors to the immediate north and south. Leonard was a little shaky especially toward the end of the street, but they were still nice little homes with very nicely kept yards. That's one thing I can say for Nedrow, almost all of the yards, despite the oldness of the house, were very nice. Flowers hanging from the porches and planted throughout the yard. Everyone may have been poor, but they still had a sense of pride. Elton was okay and then it kind of fell apart towards the end also. Next to Elton was the P&C, Ned's Drugs and the Nedrow Laundromat.

The next neighborhood, Section 3, ran from West Roswell, Orchard, Wendell and Meredith to Dutton. Most of this neighborhood was pretty run down. Nice families lived there don't get me wrong. It was just a little run down. These long blocks were cut by Midland with Riverside following the old creek. Part of Section 3 was the drug neighborhood when I was a teen. Tons of pot were sold out of one basement for years. A few of the people I knew made their living from selling drugs and never really held a job their entire lives. They were really talented and smart people, just untrusting of nearly everyone and extremely paranoid. I know one of them was afraid to go to the dentist because they thought the dentist would place them under the gas, interrogate them, and turn them and all of their sources into the police. No dental work for 30 years.

One time when I first began to play the guitar I was jamming at a party at Fritz Kringle's house (no relation to

Kris). I wasn't very good I admit to that, but there came a point where I just didn't feel welcomed anymore. I was embarrassed by my playing so I left, leaving behind my stolen 1963 Guild Starfire III, my Montgomery Ward amplifier and everything else. I walked up Roswell toward my house. I noticed that a few of the partiers were following me. I didn't do a lot of drugs so they thought I was a narc. Actually, I was just a kid who liked my friends, but didn't like drugs. I walked real fast to Clooney's and climbed up this huge fir tree in the front yard. I could see and hear them, but they had lost me. They were talking about me. I don't remember what they were saying. Maybe I've blocked it out over the years. It was depressing. I wasn't narcing on anybody. I was just me you idiots! Fuckers.

After the drug neighborhood there was a huge empty property owned by the Bailey's. It was known as the Bailey Farm. And then there was Edward Parkway, Farm Road, Bailey Drive, and West Conklin making up Section 4. Farm Road only had the old Bailey farm on it, but at the top of Farm Road was Bailey's Ice Cream. The best ice cream ever. Their Spanish Sundae was my favorite. Conklin was a little shaky except for Rene Debrow's place, Rene was a bubbly blond cheerleader with basically the same physical makeup as my loverly Cheryl Hartman. Rene had a pool and a trampoline, nice cars, clothes, a summer camp, the works. They owned the local trash business. They were rolling in the dough compared to the rest of us po-folk. Edward Parkway and Bailey were nice streets. There were a few smart kids that lived on Edward and Bailey. Fucking Shaver (F.S. as I called him - Fucking Shaver!) lived on Edward. I think we were in the eighth grade if I'm not mistaken, maybe the summer between 8th and 9th. F.S. was growing pot that summer and he went on to work for various pharmaceutical giants and the like after graduation. Yes, one of the brainiest people in OCS was growing weed right in his house, sunning it in his backyard under his parents' nose. I had a fairly well-known reputation for always being in trouble, and here's the school braincell angel growing weed and smoking it with the other class braincells. I campaigned against F.S. for student president our senior year. Naturally he won and I lost.

Can you imagine me as class president? That would have been a complete disaster. I was probably running on the free drugs, long hair, no shoes and shorter mini-skirts ticket.

On to Sections 5, 6 and 7. If you crossed Salina Street you had East Conklin, Randall, Kenneth, Cedric, Worden (Nedrow spelled backward), and Hudson, all one block deep running into Smith. Hudson became Smith and Smith went around the corner to Rockwell Road. Rockwell Elementary sat in this corner nook. These homes were a little run down but it was okay. There were nice homes in every section of Nedrow, just not very many of them. Nedrow, if you haven't guessed already, is an older, mostly poor town. That's why we moved there.

Then we come to my neighborhood, Section 6. Rockwell and E. Roswell to Laursen, but not including Laursen. Thompson Road (where I lived) cut the streets in half and Macon ran behind them. The Clooney mansion was on Macon. These two blocks ran north and south while the blocks on the other side of Salina ran east to west.

Section 7: Laursen, Pembrook, Coldbrook, Kenyon and Brae Burn Lane, even though we were linked, they were kind of on their own as far as kids went. Brae Burn had five extremely nice homes up on its dead-end hill. This was a great street to ride or walk your bike up and then ride down. I don't know who lived up here. At the very top, I think Mr. Dole, an OCS teacher rented a room, but I didn't know anyone else. There were a lot of families and a lot of kids in each of these neighborhoods. Nedrow was great.

Chapter 17
Our New House and the Case of the Stolen Donuts

Our house on Thompson Road was your standard two-story home back in 1962. A basement with a dirt floor, window for the coal chute, a coal stall, a coal shovel, a fruit cellar and an octopus furnace. My parents paid $14,000 for it. On the first floor there was a kitchen, dining room, living room and a nice front porch the width of the house. Upstairs was the only bath, and three bedrooms. As you came to the top of the stairs my sister's bedroom was first on the left and then my parents' bedroom, both facing the front of the house. Across the hall we three boys shared a bedroom. HarryHarry had a twin bed and Michael and I slept on a bunk bed. Michael was on the top. The bunk bed, HarryHarry's and Eileen's beds were made of solid cherry as were the matching dressers and night stands. My parents' bedroom was of a different ilk. A little more of a modern ash maybe. The bath was a regular bathroom, no big deal. My dad cut a hole in the hallway ceiling and installed an attic ladder. This is where we stored mostly Christmas stuff.

Eventually my father tore down the back porch and built an addition on the back of the house to enlarge the kitchen. He installed new cabinets, countertops, vinyl floor; the whole works. Soon he remodeled every room in the entire house. New maple paneling in the den and a darker (I can't remember what wood type) in the living room. This was the best paneling money could buy at the time; a solid quarter inch thick, real wood paneling. Bob also made a beautiful 6" crown molding valance around the perimeter of the dining room that reflected the florescent lighting upward and off of the acoustically tiled ceiling. It made for a softer light. Both rooms had oak flooring that eventually shared an off-white Berber carpet that also ran up the stairs and down the hallway. Bob didn't install the carpeting. He did make the valence around the windows in the living room, hung the curtains and everything else. The front wall of the living room was wallpapered ….. by Bob. He loved hanging wallpaper even though at that time, hanging wallpaper was becoming a lost art. He poured a concrete floor in the basement, built an office, a half-bath, and had a new furnace put in. We had a two car garage that was used for his shop and for tool storage, never a vehicle. We now had a car and a truck. My dad was a Chevy man. My mom still never drove much. The yard was fairly deep with that thick New York grass everywhere, two decent maple trees in the front yard and two good size pines in the back, one against the house and the other in the center of the back yard. A combination of regular vines and purple grape vines grew along the back and side fences. My dad and the rest of us boys kept the lawn mowed and washed the car and truck regularly. Mowing the lawn and washing the vehicles was a way of life for us. Clean and neat (but not whacky clean and neat, regular clean and neat). That was my mom and dad's order of the day, put things back where you found them. Simple enough rules to follow. How else do you know where something is if you don't put it back where it's supposed to be?

The yard changed as time went by thanks to my father who had the big trees cut down and replanted new trees, bushes and flowers. We rebuilt the porch too. It was clearly the nicest porch on the street and Bob and Betty spent many hours on that porch every summer. There were two wicker rockers, two wooden folding chairs and a couple of small tables. Is there any place better than Upstate New York? I'm not sure that there is. My mom kept the house in near-perfect order. Keeping a house clean is tough when you have four kids and a husband. Sorting, washing, drying and ironing the laundry, making meals throughout the day, cleaning the dishes (we all did the dishes), making the beds, vacuuming, mopping, cleaning the damn toilet, wiping away the tears, breaking up fights, washing faces and entire bodies, listening to tales of woe, paying the bills, hiding from the door-to-door collectors, baking, listening to your husband - none of this is easy. It's a skill that few men will ever possess. There would also be an above-ground pool about 4' high by 20' wide installed way back next to the garage. Eventually the driveway was paved and a full-size 'Made-by-Bob' ¾" plywood basketball backboard was hung on the garage face. This served as our basketball court for years. We also practiced our pitching along side the house. My dad would play catcher to us boys. One-on-one. He taught us separately, giving each of us his personal time. In the wintertime my Dad nailed some 2x6s together and drove stakes into the ground to form a 20x20' square on the sleeping grass. He would line that with a plastic sheet and fill it with water.

Within a few days the water would freeze and we would have our own ice skating rink. Bob wasn't rich, he was clever.

The most important thing about the garage was the loft over the garage. Miscellaneous items were stored up there like a sink or two to be used on a future job, fiberglass insulation, scaffold planks, ladder jacks, 50# boxes of nails, all the stuff we used, but would get in the way if it was downstairs. In the summer the boys would get to sleep up in the loft with friends and naturally roam the streets during the night. We never did anything dangerous that comes to mind, we would just walk the streets. There were a couple of girls that ended up up there. My brother and his gang probably had a little more girl action than I did ... because I never had any.

My sister pulled off the greatest heist in the history of the family and used the loft's excellent feature as a hiding place to store the illegal items. She and some of the 3-legged dogs, I mean young men in heat; let's see … Francis Align, Rick Benois, maybe a VanPelt and a couple of other guys, I'm not sure of everyone involved, but they robbed a store. Let me create the scene shall I? Every other morning or so a huge delivery truck would drive up to the P&C Grocery just a block away from us across Salina St. and drop the boxed goods off in front of the store. No one had ever stolen anything up to this point. Among these fresh items were donuts. Boxes and boxes of them. All types - plain, sugar, glaze … well, really there weren't that many types delivered to stores back then.

One night my sister and her slew of boyfriends stole about 30 grocery bags full of donuts and stored them, where else? In the loft! The entire neighborhood ate donuts for weeks. Donuts for breakfast, coffee at 10, lunch, for dessert after dinner, and then for a bedtime snack. My parents weren't real happy with the Make-Out Queen. Stealing was a sin and we were Catholic. This is a very difficult dilemma to be faced with when dealing with a conglomerate like P&C Groceries. The possible consequence of living with the Devil for eternity after you die, or having a somewhat overwhelming supply of delicious Hostess donuts. What's a poor working class man and a stay home Catholic mom to do? You can't hide the sin from God.

What were the legal ramifications? Having to pay for the damaged goods and your daughter and her friends doing some sort of community service? You're barely surviving as it is, how are you going to pay a fine? Your blessed son James was already becoming known for his mishaps and shenanigans, and now your daughter was going to join the filthy den of iniquity? What kind of parents are you anyway? You could sneak down there in the middle of the night and return the donuts, but what if you were caught? What if the police pulled in and thought you were stealing more donuts and then you had to explain to them that no, you were "returning" the donuts, and that you spotted bees flying east over your house with grocery bags filled with donuts. You followed them into the woods behind Clooney's and you sent your second youngest son to climb up into the tree fort by the creek because he already knew the Queen and sure enough, he found the donuts, and that you were just being a good citizen and returning them. Or, you could call a meeting with your closest neighbors, explain the fiasco while you laugh and laugh and all the little Murphys would laugh with you … hahahahahahaha ... hahahahahahaha "Here, take some donuts with you. As many as you want. Really! Go ahead neighbor. Help yourself. George, take some donuts. Chuckie, Diane, Sue, Mrs. Belton, Mr. Soure, help yourself. Mr. Goldfield, Bobby, Mr. and Mrs. Wurner, please. Donuts are good for you! Healthy!" So we fed the neighbors donuts by the dozens. Debby's accomplices took donuts to their neighbors as well. It took three weeks to empty the loft.

The donut-eating Section 6 population gained an accumulated 500 lbs. This wasn't a light haul. There were boxes and boxes and bags and bags of donuts. We didn't feel right about inviting the Rileys, our Jehovah Witness neighbors over. We didn't think they were allowed to eat donuts first of all, and we didn't need them to have one up on us to the point where we would have to invite them into our home for donuts and listen to their convertatious conversations. "Did you know Jehovah made donuts? And His donuts, like your donuts, were spread among His people. Jehovah, our Lord above all, once turned five gallons of apple cider into 10,000 mini-donuts to provide for His community. He turned the tears of His children into a sweet glaze and sand into Little Jimmies (what a coincidence) to sprinkle on top." Blah, blah, blah, blah, blah. No, no donuts for the Rileys. And the Grahams? They probably made their own donuts from wheat and sugarcane they grew in their garden and made their own icing from milk from their goats. The Grahams grew everything and were the nicest people in the neighborhood. Cute little girls; Cindy and her baby sister Linda. They grew tomatoes, potatoes, corn, lettuce, berries, summer squash, wheat, rye, peppers, onions, beets, roosters and hens and everything. The Graham's donuts were probably the second best donuts ever in the whole world. They would come around door-to-door selling their fruits and vegetables every season. My folks would always buy something. We kind of felt sorry for them thinking they were doing this to make ends meet. Actually, they were sharing their wealth by providing fresh fruits and vegetables to their community. They were more Jesus-like than the rest of us would ever be. But the Murphy's were *giving* the stuff away. We were thieves, but we were sharing thieves. That's uncommon no matter where you're from.

Chapter 18

My First Fight (with a boy)

The fourth grade was my first grade at Rockwell Elementary on Rockwell Road a block from our house. My bee stings were healed, the donuts were gone. Everything was on track to begin our new life. My older brother and I were the new kids in town. My sister was a sophomore in high school. I don't think Michael had started school yet. Nedrow is a nice little nondescript town as are many New York towns and villages. They're everywhere. Every few miles there's a Sentinel Heights, a Lafayette, Jamesville, Pompey, South Onondaga, the Reservation, Homer, Fabius, Apulia, Navarino, Otisco, Tully and many, many more dot the map. As soon as you drive into one little town you drive out of it. Bam! Then you drive along a meandering road or two surrounded by the tallest, most gorgeous trees in the world and soon you enter and leave the next little burg. The one thing they all have in common is that they are very competitive high school-wise, and yet very friendly otherwise. Most communities are poor, middle class, somewhat educated farming communities leading simple lifestyles. A bit of the backwards (or backwoods) mixed with the attempt to adjust to modern times. It's funny on one hand, but not so funny on the other because it's real. Of course, modern times in the 50s and 60s meant a home, a car, a black and white TV, a radio, a refrigerator and a washing machine. Ninety-nine percent of moms would still hang their clothes out to dry on the clothes line. They did this mainly because there is nothing like putting on clothes that have been dried by Mother Nature. The smell and feel of these clothes is like no other. An electric drier is just that; heat generated by electricity. Great during the winter, but during the spring, summer and fall your clothes can dry on a line in minutes.

Not long after moving to Nedrow we were playing field football on the front lawn of Rockwell Elementary with Gerry Mulligan and a few other neighborhood kids when Mulligan picked a fight with my brother HarryHarry. Mulligan was just re-marking his all ready pissed all over Nedrow turf and letting my brother know who was boss. Who the neighborhood badass was; the Skid-row King, Lord of the Slum; the Big Dick. I don't think my brother really cared, but he had to fight or forever be deemed a coward. I'm not sure my brother was ever in a fight before. Our family wasn't like that. Gerry kicked HarryHarry's ass and that was that. Any questions?

The Mulligan's were raised by their mom. Mrs. Mulligan was very nice and tried her best to raise the kids damn near all by herself according to my recollection. Hopefully I'm right because I'm sure Gerry is still kicking someone's ass and I don't need for his next victim to be me. Although I would like to think that HarryHarry would come to my aid and just rub Gerry out and put an end to the bullshit. We might have to plan some sort of mystical Indian burial and make Gerry disappear only to be found years later tied up in an elm tree down by the creek near the Nedrow/Reservation border wrapped tightly in rope stolen from the Bailey farm with hawk feathers from some dead hawk laid between the rope and his naked body to mummify the flesh and bone. We would carve a message into his body with an ice pick stolen from the Red & White Grocery that would say, “This guy was a prick.”

But let’s see, in the Mulligan family there was a rough and tumble, ready to kick anybody’s ass, fowl mouthed, pigeon toed, somewhat good looking, but mostly manly looking and completely lacking in self esteem oldest child, Jeanette. Gerry, the next oldest, was also a mean, foul mouthed fighter. He had to be, he was the family dog. The other side of Gerry the Dog was extremely talented. He was a phenomenal school yard basketball player. Actually, he was exceptional in all sports. He was really fast and was a very quick thinker. He would look one way and move the other or look one way and go that way. You never knew where he was going. That was his gift. On the basketball court, few, if any, could match his quickness and agility. Unfortunately, he dropped out of school so I don’t believe he ever played school sports. Too bad because he would have shined. But as usual, in the Nedrow ghetto, there was no support system to keep many of us in school.

Sports weren’t all Gerry was good at. He could also sing the parts of entire doo-wop bands all by himself. He was the entire band rolled into one. The tenor, the bass and magically, the harmonies and dance moves all at once. This was his finest gift. He was very funny and brilliant, but bound for nowhere. Being bound for nowhere in Nedrow wasn’t all that uncommon. We simply were never shown where to go or how to get there. We were pretty much all on our own.

Flip Mulligan was next in line. Flip was the best of the family. He was level headed, smart, good in sports as well, but not much for the ruthless ways of the older siblings. My mom used to say, “Flip is a very nice young man.” And there was some little brother I never knew. The Mulligan’s were regular Nedrow ghetto kids left to their own devices. In a familiar way, we all were close-ranked, learning from our mistakes and the mistakes of others rather than learning from the tools that a formal education might teach us. I forget where their mom worked and I never met their dad. He drove a tool truck or something like that. Let me note that not all Nedronians were doomed for the poorhouse. There were a few families that had their shit together like the Shavers, the Mobergs, the Gilberts, and well ..... that's all I can think of.

I was in the 4th grade now as I've mentioned. Second and third grade just went by and left no etched memories at all. My belief is that I was under government hypnosis at this time attending a special hyper-brainiac intelligence removal training center in the Adirondack Mountains. They could enter my brain through my forehead in the precise spot where HarryHarry nailed me with the brass-tipped cane and the skinny dude placed a pewter healing cap over my forehead. There was already a scar there. It was perfect. All tied up in a neat little, "Super Jimmy's Superpower Combination Brain and Gigantic Muscle Drain Package." They tried to suck the intelligent life and superpowers out of me for two solid years. Under the out stretched tentacles of that shadowy spy from the Auburn, NY corner store, the take-all-prisoners-leave-no-traces black suit, black tie team who swept in and buried the supposedly warm body of the Busy Bee Club Lady and her entire family, the Santa/Donut Man with his mesmerizing plain donuts, and Jack Lewis's phony meatloaf affiliates. They were studying me, trying to make the best out of what they couldn't understand. Two years away from my family, blindfolded, tied up, kicked, starved and left for dead month after month after month and yet ..... I survived. Somehow, all of a sudden, one day out of nowhere I'm in the 4th grade at Rockwell Elementary face to face with Freddie Sowers.

Freddie was adopted by the Bertolo family; more Jehovah Witnesses. The Bertolo's lived on Orchard Ave pretty much directly across from our house, across Salina, and down Orchard's hill, across from us as the crow flies. They were as pure as the driven snow, saintly almost. There was an older sister I didn't know. I knew the two older boys Markie and Don. Don mostly. Both were straight, tall and very well mannered. I don't know how many kids were in that house, but it seemed like there were a lot. Irma was another adoptee.

Freddie, dear little Freddie, was nothing like the Bertolos. He was the devil incarnate. The devil lives in fucking Nedrow people! For real! I don't think anyone should be or ever will be surprised about that. And it's fitting that Freddie lived with the Bertolos, that they adopted him, that he was their pet project and just what their head-held-high, poor-as-a-church mouse and Glory be to God life needed. And, the fact that they should be stifled by the evil that shared their dinner table was perfect. He was their Judas. It is also fitting that Irma lived there too. Irma was the balance between the all powerful good that the Bertolos oozed and the ugly, molten filth that we see in ourselves that the devil chides us with as seen in little Freddie. For all I know, Freddie may have been their torture toy. Someone they kept in their lair to burn, abuse, not clothe and not feed. Freddie was there to keep the Bertolos' personal demons in check. With Freddie around, their sins were palatable, at least to them. Religion is a whacky thing. Jehovahs, if you do not know, are not allowed to dance, celebrate any holidays like Christmas, Easter, or Thanksgiving, any birthdays, the 4th of July or anything. Especially Halloween. They are not supposed to recite the *Pledge of Allegiance* or join the military, sing *any* national anthem, salute *any* flag or run for *any* political office. They're not supposed to do anything but multiply like little fucking rabbits, adopt prisoner kids and go knocking door to door sticking their face into everyone's business while they preach the life that they themselves can never lead. We had Jehovahs living two doors down right on the corner of Rockwell and Thompson. I mentioned the Riley's earlier. They had adopted kids too. What the fuck is that about?

Aaron Waters was one of them. He was a scrawny, beanpole of a kid (like Freddie come to think of it) with a huge head (like Freddie's, and both heads being bigger than mine if you can imagine that) from India or somewhere. Maybe he was Native American. He was some type of Indian that's for sure. Aaron was more like a girl than a guy. I had my problems, but I don't think Aaron saw his faggie ways as a problem. His favorite saying was, "Each man is the builder of his own future." You're kidding right? Can you hear him saying this? Pucker up!

There were two sisters, Harmony and Serenity Riley. They were God's gift to humanity. There is beauty and then there is Harmony and Serenity; one defines the other. Harmony, according to herself, was a "Touch of Honey." Is that a nice thing for God's witness to call herself? That's like something Eve would say to Adam. You can't tell a kid in 4th grade that you're a touch of honey. I wasn't stupid. Serenity, on the other hand wore glasses, but they didn't hide her beauty. Now she, according to herself, had a, "Wise and willing heart." While the phraseology seems different, being a taste of honey means the same thing as having a wise and willing heart. These chicks were horny! They should have both said, "Hi, I'm Harmony and I'm horny. Hi, I'm Serenity and I'm hornier." Throughout time it has been proven that overly religious chicks are the best sex partners and the subliminal message that Jehovah's little girls were relaying openly to anyone who might listen was clear: I TASTE LIKE HONEY isn't so subliminal, but WISE AND WILLING HEART is the same thing as saying you have a wet and willing pussy.

Super religious chicks all have like a dozen kids. You can't have a dozen kids without fucking your husband's brains out for 15 or 20 years. That's why religious people stay religious. The wife is thanking the Lord for her children and the husband is thanking the Lord for one of the horniest women on the planet. There was a whole church of them there Jehovahs in Nedrow right next to the firehouse. I secretly loved both sisters equally. If I were smarter, I would have changed religions immediately.

As luck would have it, since I was the new kid in town and deranged Freddie was the tough kid in the 4th grade, Freddie and I got into a mean-ass fight on the playground. It really wasn't much of a fight. He hit me in my already broken nose and it began to bleed like a sieve. Fight over. I cried like Aaron would have. Later that evening, a chosen Bertolo family member adorning their sacred Robe of Crucifixion for the Sake of Jehovah, and beat the crap out of Freddie in the fruit cellar for his own good. (In Jehovah's church it could be a male or female who does the beating. Punishment coming from a hand filled with religious passion provides an equal opportunity for all).

Chapter 19
The Magical Birth of Charlie Moore

Up to this point in my life, before moving to Nedrow, I don't think I'd ever seen a black person. I don't remember any in Auburn and I don't remember any in the Valley. The black people in Nedrow all lived at the end of Roswell, Orchard, Meredith and Dutton on the other side of Salina down by the creek. They didn't have to live down at the end, they just did. Maybe they fished suckers out of the creek, I don't know.

Soon I was roaming all over the streets of Nedrow. Once in a while I would hang out at the end of West Roswell by the creek. For being nine or ten, the end of Roswell and the creek was a ways from home. I never did see anyone fishing down there come to think of it, but that doesn't mean they didn't. I even fished there. You could wade into Onondaga Creek and catch big ol' suckers with your bare hands. They would be hiding in the rocks on the edges of the creek in the weeds. It was easy.

Three-quarters of the way down Roswell there was a black boy by the name of Charlie Moore. Charlie's brother's name was Gimmie. We used to call him Gimmie-some-moore. Gimmie was cool. Every time I'd see him he would say, "What's up, Bud?" I would say, "Nuffin."

Me and Charlie used to wrestle every time we saw each other. Our bodies were the exact same size only his head was long and skinny like his mamma had trouble gettin' his head out while he was being born, and my head was big and round like a basketball (my mom might have had trouble too!). His head was probably normal size before he was born, but his mamma got totally exhausted just as his head entered her birth canal. She passed out from a combination of summer heat and the physical beating birthing induces. All of a sudden her eyes rolled back in her head like she was under some sort of voodoo spell and that was it - she was out cold.

The Nedrow African Tribal Women with their animal skins covering all but their naked breasts were the birthing mothers for the poor black and the poor white community down by the creek. They were natural doctors trained by generations of black birthing mothers who originally were trained by Mother Nature herself a few thousand years ago along the Nile River. They were prepared for anything. In Charlie's mom's instance, having her son's head stuck in her birth canal and being in a coma, the birthing mothers' intuition directed them to pummel only yellow flowers like the buttercup, daffodil, yellow rose, dandelion, sunflower, and tulips that they gathered from around the lower-forty creek area into a medium size rock bowl with a small hourglass shaped rock that looked like it was the only rock that ever pummeled anything in that bowl; they fit perfectly together. It looked like a bowl Native Americans might use as well. Indian mothers and black mothers have a special relationship with Mother Nature that other cultures don't share.

In a larger wooden bowl they threw in at random, non-measured increments of dried sucker head, bullfrog head, salamander head, crayfish head, garden snake head, milk snake head, beaver head, and field mice head. These specific God's creatures all lived a hidden or submerged life (like Charlie's head was at the moment). The sucker hid in the tall weeds of the creek's embankment, the bullfrog hid in the muck of the old creek, the salamander hid under rocks in streams and damp, earthy areas, the crayfish hid under rocks on the rushing creek floor, the garden snake hid in holes in the ground, the milk snake hid in the barn with the cows, the beaver hid in underwater shelters, and the field mice hid in tunnels they bored under fallen grasses from the previous fall season. The yellow herbs were mixed with fresh breast milk provided by the youngest birthing mother and placed on the nipples of the catatonic mother to be. The yellow paste was also placed on her lips, her closed eyelids, the very tips of her eyelashes, on the tops of her ears, and the edges of her fingernails and her toenails. The glossy mixture glistened and sparkled rays of light that broke through the shaded window. It was almost as if the light rays were actually coming from Charlie's mom's nipples themselves. She was spawning rays of fresh, golden light from her own source of natural goodness. Golden streams of light were illuminating and deflecting off the odd-shaped birthing room. Beautifully, as if the room were designed in this manner, all of the light made its way back to the birthmother's body and she herself began to glow a golden yellow.

The women formed a distant circle around the mother so as not to block the dancing light, and held hands with their left hand facing upward and their right hand facing downward. This is the universal symbol for the give and take of nature's way. They then slowly moved to a silent rhythm they all felt together. Every eighth measure they would raise their clasped hands upward over their heads, lean inward toward Charlie's mom and then outward and upward toward the breaking sky to symbolize a vaginal contraction. Charlie was all out but his head. The birthing mother whose milk was used, tightly wrapped little Charlie's body from his shoulders down in a clean white cotton cloth that was handmade by the Holy Roller Deacon's wife and blessed by the Holy Roller Deacon (we had Holy Rollers in Nedrow too). The ground up, dried heads that lived their life in hiding were also soaked in fresh breast milk and mixed into a brown mud. This was rubbed on the inner thighs of the entranced mother, on top of her thighs and around her vagina. Charlie's head just sat there for a while all soft and mushy waiting patiently to be pushed out. He probably should have been dead by now, his mom too, but the radiating yellow herbs stimulated Charlie's mom's body like the sun stimulates the Earth. Everything takes notice when the sun comes up. She was still incoherent, but she was now warm and comfortable. You could just tell she was holding the hands of both Jesus *and* Mary. The sleeping, crushed-head mixture became warm to the touch from the golden light generated by the herbs. The heads began to warm and smoke like the dew rising from the early morning fields. Charlie, like all of these wondrous creatures who hide their head, had no choice but to slide his head out and greet the day.

POP!

Charlie Moore was born.

As instantly, Charlie's mom began breathing gently and more deeply as the yellow light beams danced upon her pretty face. Her eyelashes were accented with a glistening pollen. It was a beautiful, magical birth. Charlie was born and his mom was fine. The only thing was, Charlie had this long, pencil-necked head with little curly black hairs on it. He wasn't ugly or deformed to any *great* degree, he just had a super elongated football shaped head like the early Egyptians did. He was pretty cool looking. So out in the street you had a big fatheaded white kid fighting an elongated, squish-headed black kid.

Charlie and my battles for dominance were simple. Either he would hold me in a headlock and scissors or I would hold him in a headlock and scissors. We would lie in the middle of the street for hours just choking and squeezing each other till it was time to go home. A headlock is when you place your arm completely around the opponent's neck and squeeze. This cuts off air to the throat and blood flow to the brain. I mentioned the scissors earlier. This is when you placed your legs around the opponent's stomach, locked your feet together, squeezed the breath out of your enemy and tried to damage their internal organs. I used this hold on the Busy Bee Club lady's kids.

I think me and Charlie both had good fun. No harm ever came out of our matches. I was sure to moderate my super strength because I could have just picked him up and thrown him across the creek, but I had tremendous self control. When it was time to go home we just stopped wrestling and went home. Our matches weren't racially motivated even though the country was in racial turmoil at the time. Maybe that's why the blacks lived where they lived in Nedrow. Maybe they thought they were better off just living the quiet life by the creek among themselves. The creek was beautiful. Lower Dutton and this area where the blacks lived was a bit poorer than the rest of poor Nedrow, the houses were a bit more run down, but as a kid it didn't matter and as a parent I think they were just trying to survive and reach for that American dream. Blacks were living a different life than whites were. The black kids most definitely knew more about the racial war than white kids did because black parents were in the middle of the whole thing. Whites were free to do as they wished. Blacks had been fighting for rights Lincoln promised them 100 years earlier. Blacks were free in Nedrow. Nedrow was the Land of Salvation. God's gift to the Free Man, the Holy Land, the Promised Land, Mecca. There were no railroad tracks running through Nedrow. The school bus picked up everyone. The white kids and the black kids and the Indian kids all got along. Indian boys were dating white girls. White boys were dating Indian girls. I don't remember blacks and whites dating, but I am sure it must have happened behind somebody's back.

OCS (Onondaga Central School) was a very small school system. There were about 700 kids in kindergarten through the twelfth grade. Out of maybe 85 to 100 kids graduating each year, there were two, three or four black kids. So what I'm saying is this; we all got along. Nobody cared about the rest of the world. Headlocks and scissors were the common fight for all races. Charlie and me were fightin' the struggles the rest of the world was fightin'. We were solving racial differences at the end of West Roswell Ave. During the fight we would be discussing our troubles, our pains, our hopes and our dreams for freedom from the clutch of the enemy. At dusk we would release each other, dust ourselves off, shake hands, laugh and go on our way. Socially, we were examining our strengths and weaknesses coming to the early evening conclusion that we were equals. After all that fighting and bickering we were equals. We were humans divided only by Route 11. We walked the same streets to the same elementary school and we rode the same bus to the same high school. Nedrow was the center of peace and harmony in the known universe. No one had to scientifically prove this. How could they? And besides, once the outside world starts examining what's right or wrong about something, the losing faction will be sure to destroy that which is good. It was like Gerry Mulligan. He didn't give a fuck that he was beating up a helpless kid, he just gave a fuck that he won. No matter what the physical or mental consequence he imposed upon my brother, he had to win. It was like Freddie Sowers. He didn't care to talk, he just wanted to break my nose. Fuck you Freddie! It was already broken you stupid fuckhead! You lose!

Chapter 20

The President and My Best Friend

That same year, in 1963, I got my very own pet. A hamster with fir as white as snow, pink feet and cherry-red eyes. I named him Whitey. I loved Whitey. We used to play together all of the time. I taught Whitey to play cops and robbers. I was the cop and he was the robber. We always played on the landing of the stairs so I could keep an eye on him so he wouldn't have the chance to run away like a robber would. Amazingly enough, when I pulled out my western six shooter with the plastic mother of pearl handle out of its carved leather holster and pointed it at Whitey and said, "Hold it right there or I'll shoot!" Whitey would stand up on his hind legs, lift his left front leg (we were both left handed), point his hand at me in a gun-like position and pretend to shoot back. We were like a Vaudeville team, he never let me down and I always took real good care of him.

My beloved Whitey died suddenly on November 22, 1963. The same day President Kennedy was assassinated. I remember Mrs. Miller coming into my 4th grade class and telling everyone to settle down and listen carefully, that President Kennedy had just been assassinated. All of the girls in the class started crying left and right. The Traylor sisters, who later became regulars in the Mulligan boys' bedrooms, were balling like they knew him personally or something. "Oh my God! Oh my God! Not the president!" Tears and crying and almost choking. "He was so handsome .... and Catholic!" "John John. Little John John," they cried. Their behavior was alarming to say the least. Why would you do that to the rest of us dummies? I don't remember any of the boys even grimacing. "What happened?" I was only in the fourth grade. I was new to the neighborhood. I had already been stung several times, beaten up, and now my president was dead? "Wait, What happened? We're being let out early? What's a president? What happened? What does assassinated mean?" Home we went whether we had parents there or not, school was dismissed.

When I got home my mom was in shock too so I went to get Whitey. Mom was watching Walter Cronkite, Morley Safer and everyone else stumble through their words as they tried to get the latest news from their connections in Dallas. Whitey, I thought, was asleep in the corner of his cage all rolled up in a little ball just waiting for me to come home. What a nice little buddy. When I reached in to get him he was as stiff as a board, hard as a rock and ice cold. Whitey was dead! I was devastated! My president and my best friend were dead? That brought tears to my eyes for sure. Now I got it.

In the following days, there was a lot of coverage on TV regarding the death and the funeral march plans for President Kennedy. In Whitey's honor I felt he should have the same trip through our living room as the president was going to have on his way to Arlington National Cemetery. I already had a little military wagon and some toy horses. I set buildings, plastic trees and military figures throughout the living room. I wrapped Whitey up in a silver death cloth made of Alcoa's finest aluminum foil and laid him gently in the wagon. It was very distinguished and honorable. As Kennedy rode through the streets of Washington, Whitey rode through the streets of our living room. I lay awake for hours reliving our days together. It was a very sad time. Fortunately, as a nation, we mourned Whitey's death together as one. After Whitey's funeral march and after the president had been laid to rest, I placed Whitey on the back porch to be buried in the backyard on top of my sister's dog who was already buried out behind the garage. Bright and early the next morning I woke up ready to bury Whitey, but I couldn't find him. I looked all around the back porch and I found nothing. So I stopped, stood in the center of the room and slowly turned in a circle around the entire room looking in every crack and crevice .... up .... down .... slowly .... nothing. I did it again, this time in reverse. Still nothing. I ran inside screaming, "Has anyone seen Whitey? Has anyone seen Whitey? I had him wrapped in his silver death cloth on the back porch and I was going to bury him this morning along with the president. Has anyone seen him? Has anyone seen him? Did you move him mom?" My mom said no she didn't. HarryHarry and Michael said no, and Eileen said no. My Gramma Conley, who was staying with us at the time, spoke up. "Where was he Michael, HarryHarry, Erleen, Lizbit, Bobby, Jimmy?" (She always called you everyone's name before calling you your own name). "Come with me Gramma and I'll show you!" Off to the back porch I dragged her. "He was right there on the window sill. I left him right there! I know that's where I put him because I was going to bury him today! He was wrapped in his silver death cloth!" "A silver death cloth?" "Yes, he was right here." "Do you mean that ball of tinfoil?" I looked at her with heavy eyes, but I couldn't say a word. I just stared at her. My dear grandmother, who was a roly-poly renegade, pocket picking gypsy stowaway from the Ukraine, looked at me rather plainly and said, "Michael, HarryHarry, Erleen, Lizbit, Jimmy ..... Bobby, your father, was going to the dump this morning and I wasn't sure what it was so I threw it in the trash and gave it to your father." "Holy macaroni Gramma! My heart and soul! My one true friend. My love. My pink-footed furry friend. The Gangster. Lefty. My mentor. My confider. My partner in crime. The robber. My life! In the trash? Gone to the dump? Of all places, in a trash can? Dang Gramma, the dump? He was a national hero!"

I'd experienced devastation before so it wasn't new to me. My shoulders were slumped and my neck was bent forward on a regular basis. In fact, so far, my life was one big ball of tinfoiled grief gently picking up steam rolling downhill north.

Chapter 21
The Hitchhikers

When I was in the sixth grade some of us Catholic kids would get bused from Rockwell Elementary to St. James Elementary down in the Valley for catechism classes every Tuesday from noon to 2:30. Sometimes on the return trip I would hitchhike from St. James back to Nedrow. Sometimes I would hitchhike with Patrick MacCollom. He lived about half way to Nedrow in a new subdivision across from James E. Heath Park. He was about my age, maybe a little older than me, definitely more street savvy than me. Patrick moved into a real nice neighborhood in the Valley called Valley Oaks. His parents were clearly spies. They had to be because all of the MacCollom kids were trained munitions experts. They were building bombs and tapping phone lines from the day they were born. The eldest son Joseph was a serious underground anti-U.S. master technician. You have to remember that during this time, 1965, Lyndon Johnson was president, U.S. troops were beginning to be sent to Vietnam, 14,000 national guardsmen were called to quell the riots in Watts, miniskirts were in, Joe Namath signed with the Jets, the *Beatles 65* album was released, *Love Potion #9* peaked at number 3, Alan Freed died, Winston Churchill died, Martin Luther King was arrested, there was a U.S. nuclear test in the Pacific Ocean, Malcolm X was assassinated, Stan Laurel died, France performed an underground nuclear test, the *Sound of Music* opened, the Temptations' *My Girl* reached #1, the USSR performed a nuclear test, Jeff Beck replaced Eric Clapton in the Yardbirds, Rembrandt's Titus sold for $7,700,000, the first atomic powered spacecraft was launched, in one day 40 tornadoes ravaged the U.S. midwest injuring 5,000 and killing 272, an earthquake hit Seattle, Cassius Clay became a Muslim and adopted the name Muhammad Ali and in May KO'd Sonny Liston and in November TKO'd Floyd Patterson for the heavyweight boxing title, Willie Mays' 512th home run broke Mel Ott's National League baseball record, the Rolling Stones recorded *Satisfaction*, the Campbell Soup Company introduced SpaghettiOs, *Supercalifragilisticexpialidocious* hit #66, Sonny & Cher made their first TV appearance on *American Bandstand*, Casey Stengel resigned as manager of the NY Mets, Folk-rock began, Dylan played the electric guitar at the Newport Folk Festival, Morley Safer reported that the U.S. was losing the battle in Vietnam, the Beatles played to 55,000 crazed fans at Shea Stadium, Great Britain performed a nuclear test, *Lost in Space* premiered, Charles Linster did 6,006 consecutive push-ups, Pope Paul VI proclaimed that Jews were not collectively guilty for Christ's crucifixion, the U.S. government sent 90,000 soldiers to Vietnam, and finally, *A Charlie Brown Christmas* premiered. These were troubling times to say the least. We needed people like Joseph doing the work we didn't know how to do.

Patrick's older sister Jennifer was a master technician and a fortune teller. When I was a teenager she read tarot cards for me. We were in her apartment with incense burning and a single tiny light glowing in the corner. It was dark. No music, just me and her. Jennifer was a super skinny thing, maybe 5'2" tall weighing in at 85 lbs with a bit of a rough complexion and alcohol and drug symptoms. That's the way I saw it. I could have been totally wrong, but I was always afraid of her. She was a part of the local underground culture where drugs and weapons were the norm. At least that's the way I saw it. She and Sean, Patrick's other older brother, and Joseph were steeped in underworld crime. How do you get there? Why do you choose to go there? What's wrong with just being a kid?

So there we are, just the two of us. How did I get in Jennifer's apartment? What the hell was I doing there? I don't know. I was just a bored kid looking for something new to do. I'm sure I could have fallen into the underground world that they lived in and I don't know why I didn't. My upbringing was baseball, washing the family vehicles and mowing the lawn. Do these menial tasks really mean that much? Is it the simple life-lessons of starting a job and finishing it that leads you away from the underworld (not that tracking and killing an intended spy target isn't starting and finishing a job, but come on!). Parents take note, innocent household chores might be a more powerful training tool than ever.

Jennifer, after shuffling the cards several times, asked me to cut the deck. She laid four cards in a diamond pattern in front of me face down and asked me to ask the cards a question, first about romance. I wanted to know if I would someday find true love. She flipped the card over and it was upside down – facing away from me, meaning that no, I would not ever, in my entire life find true love. "God dammit," I said. The next question was about fame and fortune. When the card was flipped it was facing me, but Jennifer told me that my fame and fortune would not be found in Syracuse, that I would have to leave town in order to find it. The next card signified health and happiness. It too was facing me. That was good news. The final card was the financial card. It was upside down, facing away from me. I was disappointed, but the cards are the cards. They don't lie. I think Jennifer thought I was part of a narco squad anyway and just wanted to get rid of me so she was telling me to get out of Dodge NOW while the gittin' was good.

Sean, the middle child, was a crazy technician who just blew shit up all the time, laughing, snorting and twitching his eyes as he went along. Laugh, laugh, laugh, laugh, laugh, snort, twitch, twitch, laugh, laugh, laugh, snort, snort, twitch ..... twitch. And then there was my friend Patrick. Patrick was fun and not so technically inclined but still inclined only because he grew up being surrounded with illicit inclinations. And finally there was Shannon the younger sister who was perfectly normal with no aspirations to kill and maim. She was their Marilyn Munster. The gorgeous, the pretty, the book smart younger sister who had to find the right mix in her mate for life. Somewhere between her brothers and sister who could protect her should the commies actually attack, and someone who might provide a normal life for her. Shannon wanted the picket fence lifestyle. Not the electric fence, cattle-prod lifestyle.

One day on our way home from catechism, Patrick and me decided to hitchhike to Pennsylvania, 70 miles south. We started hitchhiking from St. James and made our way to the entrance to Interstate 81 South in Nedrow. It must have looked rather bazaar to see two little kids on the highway with their thumbs out. I have no recollection of anyone picking us up in either direction except for this one elderly Alfred Hitchcock looking guy in an old, rusted 1950s Plymouth sedan. Patrick got in the backseat and I got in the front. We were riding along talking about whatever it is eleven year olds talk about to adult strangers, and this guy starts leading the discussion toward nudist colonies. What do I know? I'm eleven. "We don't wear clothes you know. Everyone, even the girls, are completely naked." This sounds great! I notice there are magazines strewn on his front seat right next to me. I ask him if he minds if I take a look at them. He says, "No. Go right ahead." So I flip open the magazine and stare blankly. I'm like frozen. I come out of my frozenness enough to turn the page. I turn the pages one after the other, one after the other, turning slower and slower, and there it is - page after page of naked people. This is great, but there is one thing in common with everyone in this magazine; they are all stark naked young boys.

HOLY FUCK! I don't know what to say or what to do. I just keep staring at the pages. Young naked boys Patrick's and my age. I am in fucking shock. Frozen I tell ya! Patrick sees this and fortunately for both of us, his years of spy training kicks in. He starts screaming as loud as he can at the old fart to, "PULL OVER AND LET US OUT! PULL OVER RIGHT NOW OR I'LL BUST YOUR FUCKING FACE IN YOU FAT OLD BASTARD! PULL OVER OR I'LL FUCKING KILL YOU! I HAVE A FUCKING GUN! PULL *OVER*! I'LL RIP THE SKIN OFF YOUR DEMENTED FACE BEFORE YOU KNOW WHAT THE FUCK HIT YOU. I'LL SLICE YOUR FUCKING THROAT IN TEN FUCKING SECONDS. PULL OVER OR I'LL KILL YOU!"

The old man slows down and pulls over immediately to the side of the highway. I don't know what the hell happens, but we're let out somewhere near Scranton. I can see the *Welcome to Scranton* sign just up the road. We run across the highway and hitchhike back to Nedrow. I'm home in time for dinner. Nobody knows nothin' and Patrick and I never speak of it ever again. Fucking Faggot! Chester the Molester! Jerkoff! If I were by myself I would have been killed. Thanks Patrick. Thanks Sean for teaching Patrick. Thanks Jennifer for teaching Sean. Thanks Joseph for teaching Jennifer. I think I owe all of you my life.

Chapter 22
The Teacher

Being from Nedrow, first we never had money to go to the movies, and second, we hardly ever went downtown for anything except to see the model train go around the ceiling at S.S. Kresge Company's Five & Dime around Christmas time.

Not long after my memorable trip to Scranton, at a movie theater in downtown Syracuse in the summer between 7th and 8th grade, me and some friends made the monumental trek by bus downtown. There was this teacher from OCS named Mr. Few who must have taken the summer job of being the ticket-taker guy at the theater. You paid at the window, got your ticket, stood in line, gave it to Mr. Few, he ripped it in half, kept half for the theater count, and gave you the remaining half. One of the Kreslin boys at OCS had recently accused Mr. Few of sexual misbehavior – which at the time was more or less unheard of, but clearly part of a rising, underground epidemic. I saw Mr. Few standing there at the entrance to the theater and had no choice but to go to him with my ticket. His beady eyes in his triangular, flat-topped head stared coldly right through me. He was quietly sniffing like a jungle cat lying in wait. When he placed the torn ticket into my tiny little hand he slowly rubbed his wrinkled old middle fuck-finger back and forth into my palm. I was scared to death to look up afraid the he might mark me with his spit or something. He actually looked just like the gnarly child-killer driving the old Plymouth to Scranton. I sheepishly moved on and went into the theater with my head bowed low. I felt ashamed. I can see his finger as clearly as if it happened yesterday. It's just not right. There should be a secret squad of child molester killers out there. Maybe that's what I'll do when I grow up. If there's solid proof, I'll kill the fucker. My nose bled through the entire movie.

Chapter 23

Caught #2

The next evening my parents got a tip from an unknown source that my sister was out with Jonn Tarrow whose nickname was "Sparrow" (for his quick and fleeting moves) and whose favorite quote was, "The wrong way seems the most reasonable." My parents didn't want my sister going out with the Sparrow. I don't know why. He was incredible. Tall and muscular with Murphy-blue eyes and perfect hair. He was an above average, totally suitable male specimen. Every girl wanted this guy and yet he was dating my well-trained sister. I didn't say he was smart, I said he was good looking. His parents lived in this awesome house, probably at the time, the finest house in Nedrow, up on a hillside buried in the woods and built like a villa in the Alps. I never went there, but rumor had it that it was unbelievable on the inside. Eileen and The Sparrow were in the same class, but he seemed older to me. My sister's favorite saying in high school was, "Life is a dream in the night." The Sparrow's saying is perfect for a guy and my sister's is perfect for a girl don't you think? He'll fuck anything that breathes and she'll believe anything anyone tells her. A match made in Skid-row heaven; for The Sparrow anyway. Eileen was a real beauty. Irish-white skin, pitch black hair flipped along the bottom, forehead-length bangs and those stunning light blue eyes – the ideal 60s look. Being experienced and beautiful like my sister just adds to your market value among the Sparrows, the Albinos, the Behms, the Bertrands, the Bolands, the Brunells, the Clarks, the DeOrdios, the Hourigans, the Kanes, the Kenyons, the Langs, the O'Herns, the Shenfelds, and the VanSlykes. They were all lined up in alphabetical order panting like our new dog Humphrey.

Anyway, my parents, acting on an anonymous tip, maybe from one of my sister's disgruntled suitors, get in the car and they take me with them (again, the Chosen One ... no HarryHarry, no Michael. I am back my friends. I'm back! I am the One. I am He. There is no other for I am, I shall be, forever and ever). I'm in the rear seat in the middle sitting forward with my elbows on the front seat-backs between my parents. I have no idea what's going on. They drive up to Make-Out Lane which is not too far from our house and pretty much right below Sparrow's house on this particular night, and we see Jonn's fancy convertible parked on the side of the road with the top down. My dad, not being born yesterday, flashes his brights and beeps his horn a couple of times. Low and behold, cute little Jonnie's messed quaff attached to his handsome head pops up from the laying on top of someone position in his back seat and stares directly into our headlights. Oh my God! It was fucking (no pun intended) perfect! This was a tactic I'm sure my dad learned while in the Navy. Sneak up in the dark on the enemy, get within firing range, give a visible signal of friendship and a familiar greeting, and when the enemy shows their head, decapitate it. We drove by slowly. I am sure the two lovers realized it was us. Home we went.

I just couldn't get to sleep that evening. My sister eventually came home. I'm really not sure what went down. My parents weren't much for yelling and screaming. They were good folks trying to make life work for everyone. They were just regular folk. Later that evening I got out of bed and I peeked into my sister's room while she was sleeping. I don't know why, I just went ahead and wandered in. She was lying on her back with her face turned away from me. It was a hot night so the covers were mostly down. The windows were open and the sounds of a typical upstate summer night swept in and around us as the moon shone its light through the front yard's maple trees. She had a white nightgown on .... and there before me .... like the Glory of God .... lay her uncovered milkless breast. Since seeing Santa Clause, Dasher and Dancer and Prancer and Vixen and Comet and Cupid and Donner and Blitzen, I have never seen anything more beautiful, more Christ-like in my life. How could something so simple be so important to the continuance of life on Earth?

Men and boys of all ages go crazy over the breast. Unless you are a male, it might be hard to understand the reason why. I can't even explain it, but among all of the world's gold and the mighty, untrainable wild stallions, the necessary killings, the absolute conquering, futile destruction and all that Man needs to do to satisfy themselves, all Men drop to their knees when a bare breast walks into a room. They start whimpering like little babies. A Man will do anything to suck on a breast. Hundreds if not thousands of Men have literally taken another human life for the promised opportunity to suck on a breast. Man has traversed the globe looking for a woman who will bare her breast without question. Man doesn't care if the breast is the tiniest uncupable breast, or the perfect breast, or God's gift to the world of breasts. Man simply needs a woman's breast from birth to death. Interestingly, sucking on the breast is also the women's greatest weakness and it provides access to the uncontrollable relaxed flowing of the juices that normally stand at strict attention hiding in her secret pussy chamber. The breast is the female's Achilles' heel. For all the begging and pleading we little Men do for the luscious, life-giving nipple, we don't do it without the hope of future cause; the insatiable quest for the Glory Hole. While we are completely dizzied, almost drugged by the soothing nipple, once we have the nipple secured inside our lips teasing it within our teeth, our knees begin to lose their tremble, our eyes dry and we stand erect to a Herculean power stance while at the exact same moment the woman's knees just as quickly begin to quiver. That's why most Women can't even bare the thought of talking about their breasts. The slightest mention of the word breast and most Women stop the conversation dead in its tracks. This isn't because they think of it as a dirty word or a violation of some sort. It's because they know they will succumb to the quest for their pussy just by engaging in the conversation. In my studies, the nipple is directly wired to the thigh muscles; suck on the tit and the thigh muscles automatically open. It's like a single-pole light switch. Flip it on and the pussy flows like a dam that has been forever holding back the Vagina River. It's an involuntary motion. It's simple. Don't complicate it. Suck on the nipple and both the Man and the Woman become blinded from the mind-light shining in their sexual organs. This light is the brightest light known to the sexes. Every coherent thought and sensible social training the entire world has been through for centuries stops for sex. That's why people have sex everywhere. Once they start talking about sex and the Man is allowed to touch the breast, you can forget it. You could be standing in the Presidential Palace and if a Man can get a Woman to talk about her breasts, he can fuck her right there. There isn't anything wrong with this. I'm just telling you like it is. We all know it. I can see it now. All the Men reading this are shaking their heads yes and all the Women are just reading this, thinking about it, considering the options and loving the thought of it. FREE AT LAST! JUST FUCK ME!

That would be GREAT! But as we know, and as I've mentioned before, Women do rule the world so they have to be quite a bit more sensible than us guys. My sister's breast confirmed this. Her moonlit breast was staring me right in the face. I had never seen one before. It looked so soft, so delicate, so incredible. All I did was stare at it. It was glowingly beautiful. Greater than any Santa and stupid Reindeer ever was. I love breasts. I quietly turned and went back to bed.

Chapter 24
The BB Gun

After the late night excursion to Lover's Lane with my parents, my father, thinking I deserved something that would take my mind off of things, bought me what every boy dreams of, a new Daisy BB gun rifle. It was part of Daisy's Spittin' Image line, model 1894. An exact replica of the world famous

Winchester 94 carbine. I had already been up in the woods shooting a real rifle with Kelly Fitzpatrick. Like the idiot I am I pointed the loaded rifle out of the woods and shot it down into Nedrow somewhere. Fitz wasn't too happy about that. It happened so quickly I'm not really sure I did it on purpose, but I did do it just the same. We walked out of the woods immediately. He went home and I went home.

The Fitzpatrick's were real hunters. They packed their own shell casings with gunpowder, melted down and poured their own lead bullets and then crimped the finished product into the casing. They were pros. They made bullets in their basement; shotgun shells, 22s, 30-30s and 30 ought-6s.

The first day I received my Winchester, HarryHarry was running around the side of the house dancing and shouting, "Bet you can't hit me! Bet you can't hit me!" So I shot him. Nailed him in the thigh. It sounded painful even from where I was about 20-yards away. He let out a moan, turned and ran into the house. I thought I was in big trouble. But no, HarryHarry went up to our bedroom and poked his head up over the window sill and shouted, "Bet you can't hit me! Bet you can't hit me!" So I carefully took aim at the window while waiting for his little freckle-faced head to pop up so I could take his eye out or maybe crack a tooth or repay him with a shot to the center of his forehead. There ….. he ….. is ….. BANG! I missed. What I didn't realize was that the BB went through the window screen and it was powerful enough so that my mom, who was in her room, heard it ricocheting off the bedroom walls. My BB gun was taken away the first day I got it.

I did eventually get it back. This led to a solo journey that would of course get me into trouble once again. As you may begin to wonder, what's happened to my superpowers and the guys in the black suits and ties? I don't know. We may have moved to Nedrow to get away from all the spy business after my mom killed the Busy Bee Lady. My parents might have decided to live the quiet life like the black folk did down in Section 3. Mom simply wanted to go to Mrs. Gleason's house on Fridays and get her hair done, go to Enrico's Italian

Restaurant for dinner, continue to hang her clothes on the line and sit on the front porch with Bob smoking the occasional Tareyton while sipping on a screwdriver and watch the world go by. This would not be a bad choice for a retired undercover agent. As for my superpowers? If you don't use 'm, I guess you lose 'm. And besides, I'm too entwined in growing up humanly normal. I'm having too much fun as a regular old kid. The chances of surviving in this world are slimmer if you are normal, and that creates a greater challenge from within to succeed. Let the chips fall where they may, address the challenges, solve the puzzles, and fight as a human would fight. The only way you can learn about another species is to live among them and do your best to become one of them.

Here is what I think will eventually happen. I will someday lose my powers all together. It's like anything else, you have to keep actively training or your mind and body will refocus to whatever it is your new main focus might be. Only if you maintain a "forever" focus on a single, or a few life-long projects, can you exceed your own expectations. Most humans just can't do this. It's no fault of their own. They simply aren't trained to do this. I do keep this conundrum in the back of my mind and hope that someday I will have learned all I need to know or care to know about humans and continue on my real quest of superpoweredness and save those poor souls in less fortunate positions than myself. Okay, back to my journey.

I took off one day with my BB gun and went walking through the lower forty at the end of Roswell (no Charlie Moore in sight. Good for him 'cause I might have shot him too) and I made my way across the creek. It was flowing pretty fast and was more than knee deep. The creek is about 40' wide. It ain't no hop, skip and a jump. I had to catch my balance a few times. It wasn't that big of a deal I guess, I'd done it several times before, but not by myself. I made my way to the half-moon swim hole surrounded by, and most likely filled with toxic runoff from Samson's Concrete. There are tons of a white caustic something or other smothering the Earth out behind Samson's. There are also some dirt roads back in there and a great old spring fed pond where maybe thanks to beavers damming up the area, all of the trees in the water are dead. This water is crystal clear. The plant life in the water thrives and fish and beaver are everywhere. I tried to shoot a few of them to no avail because BBs don't travel all that well in water. If the water were deeper it would be a perfect place to snorkel or even scuba dive. As tempting as it is to step in there, it might be bottomless, and as luck would have it I would pop up back in Auburn across from my old house in the chocolate muck-hole, child-eating quicksand. That would be funny.

This pool of fresh water reminds me of a land where dinosaurs might still roam. It truly was a time forgotten, an undiscovered wetland hidden in the reserves of Nedrow. It was also kind of creepy being there by myself and I began to wonder what I was thinking when I started out on this journey. I did have my gun for protection, but just the same. I walked along the bank and followed the power lines up to Rt. 80 and headed south toward the horse barns where regular city folk would come to the country and ride a rented horse for an hour or so. Almost all of the workers at the barn were beautiful young country girls spending their summer hours on the farm. I don't think there is a finer sight in the entire world than an Upstate country girl working on a horse farm.

My plan was to hide in the woods not only to spy on the pretty girls in their country cowgirl boots, short shorts and pigtails, but maybe to shoot a horse or two in the ass just to see what we would see. They might not even feel it because horses are huge, muscular beasts unlike my scrawny older brother. A BB shot from a considerable distance might just hit the horse and fall to the ground. Boink! But on the other hand, our little horsey friend might just whiney like they were hit in the balls (now there's an idea) with a baseball bat and throw those fat-assed, cityfied, nose-in-the-air snobs on their puffy Mercedes Benz asses. It might cause a chain reaction, a domino effect. One horse might scare the next and those two would scare another. I could shoot another in the balls. I could cause a friggin' stampede with two BBs! City folk would be flying everywhere! A Mercedes ass, a BMW ass, a Corvette ass, a

GTO ass, a Porsche ass, asses would be flying everywhere! Shoot for the balls it is then.

Being the great explorer that I was, I got sidetracked before ever reaching the barn. I saw some old glass windows leaning against the side of a house. It didn't look like anyone was using them. They were pieces of junk. Half of them were already broken. My chubby little schoolmate Gary Nielsen lived there. He was gay before anybody knew what gay was. Here's a question. Are child molesters who prey on the same sex considered gay? I guess they might be. They should be if they aren't. Men fucking boys, men fucking men. I wonder if child molesters ever think of themselves as gay? They should if they don't. If you have a penis and you're playing with penises and thinking of penises, you are gay. You can't have a penis and want to play with other penises if you're straight. If predators knew they were gay maybe they would reconsider being predators and just be gay. Being referred to as a predator has a certain empowerment to it. Being referred to as gay greatly lessens the evil implication. Referring to a predator as a gay guy really sounds awkward. That's what the news should report these guys as, "A gay man has just been arrested for raping a male child." This would really piss the predator off. They would shout, "I'M NOT GAY. I'M A PREDATOR!" And then the interviewer says, "But you are a man and you raped someone of the same sex. This makes you gay." "SHUT UP! I SWEAR I'M A PREDATOR. I'M NOT FUCKING GAY!" "Yes, of course, but you preyed on a same-sex individual. You are gay." Nothing against gay people. Like I said, it's 1966 and we don't even know what gay people are yet. But don't you agree that a guy who wants to be with a guy is gay? So a predator who wants to be with a guy is gay too. To clarify; a predator is a stronger entity attacking a weaker entity. The "prepared" attacking something unprepared. Something "known" attacking the unaware. Maybe not all of the time I guess, but in my mind that's what I immediately picture. The dark predator towering over the fallen victim. Does that make all gay people predators? The dominant gay figure towering over the weaker, insecure male. See how easily I get sidetracked? It's a wonder I made it to Gary's house at all. It's a wonder I left my yard to begin with.

Gary, my poor little chubby gay friend, unfortunately died of AIDS before anybody knew what AIDS was, but that's beside the point. I'm standing here in front of these broken, paint-peeled piece of shit windows with my new BB gun. What's the harm in breaking a broken window? So I shot out the rest of the windows. The next thing I know Gary is screaming at me through one of the open, but not broken, house windows. "Jimmy Murphy! Is that you? Is that you?" "Holy shit! Gary? Is that you?" He runs away from the window screaming, "Mom, mom ….. mo-o-o-o-m! Jimmy Murphy has a gun and is shooting out our windows!" You asshole, I'm thinking. You fat little fuck. I took off like a bat out of hell. As soon as I crossed over Rt. 80 and got into the woods I took one giant leap, and another, and another ..... my feet were lifting right off the ground higher and higher with each step and soon .... I was low-level flying. Oh man, I've never flown before. I've dreamt of flying. I've always felt that I could fly. I had visions of how calming it might be. Could I hover like a hummingbird or would I have to keep moving? Maybe because I was just a kid I might have to keep moving. Hovering is like wading in water I'm thinking. Move your arms and your legs and you can stay in one spot. I should be able to do that. But instead I circled the dinosaur pond a few of times. It was an amazing sight to see the pond from above. It was crystal clear and loaded with fish, turtles, a beaver family and reflecting the clouds in the sky. I could even see myself. In my reflection I could see that I actually had wings and tail feathers. And another thing, I wasn't full-size, I was about the size of a crow. Wow. I didn't know that. I always thought that if I flew, I would be me. I thought I would be Little Jimmy Murphy, full-size with my blue jeans, flannel shirt and old shoes. Instead, I look just like any other bird in the sky. So here I was hanging with the hawks, robins, sparrows, barn swallows, hummingbirds, orioles, bees and bugs, doin' what comes naturally. I *love* flying. After a few minutes I flew south following the creek through the reservation, gained some loft and circled back toward the old creek where it dead ended when the military straightened it out in the 50s. This is where even more beaver thrived. Birds are incredible creatures with amazing control, unbelievable hearing and excellent eyesight. Then I decided to come down at the very end of Roswell right where I began this trip. I didn't want to be seen transforming back to my human self by anyone. That's a silly thought. I can't believe that I really just flew. It just happened. It happened because I *needed* to fly. So this is kind of comforting. Perhaps my superpowers lie dormant until they are called upon by my inner voice. In some cases I will probably *have* to call them forward to stop a bullet for instance, but even then maybe not. Maybe to pick a car up like my dad did. Otherwise, they lie dormant ready to come forth whenever needed automatically. This is friggin' great and a comforting relief. I ran back home. I put the gun in my closet and hung low the rest of the day. That evening at dinner there was a knock at the front door. It was Gary's mom. Gary nailed me. My parents had to pay for the already broken windows and the additional windows I broke. That was the official end of my gun. I never saw it again.

A couple of years later I called a telephone operator looking for some information and this voice said, "Operator, may I help you?" "Yes," I said, "I'm looking for the phone number to the Remedy Tavern on Seneca Turnpike." "Is this Jimmy Murphy?" "Yes," I said. "This is Gary. Gary Nielsen." "Oh, man. How are you?" "I'm fine and you?" "Good. How long have you been with the phone company?" It was a nice social visit and we let bygones be bygones. Sometimes life isn't as evil and foreboding as I tend to think it is.

Chapter 25
The Madras Hat

To go back and prove my point about Nedrow being divided into seven different turfs, and while we are talking about guns and stuff, here is a perfect example of both. There was a tall, gangly, skinny weakling that lived up on Bailey Drive (Section 4) named Ian Edwards. He was friends with Liam the slave hiding Spanish landlord (more on this later). Ian was a little wanna-be nerd. Actually, he was a nerd, I take that back. He was smart and very attentive to detail. He fit right in with the other nerds in his neighborhood, the Mobergs, Clevelands, Beckers, Sheas, and the Debrows. Not the Debrowskis. They were another story. The Debrows used to be Debrowskis, but they changed their name so they wouldn't be looked upon as Pollocks anymore (and probably so they wouldn't be associated with their cousins).

Ian was the only child of Mr. and Mrs. Edwards, the mean, bitter Scotsman and his tougher-than-nails wife. Cross them by mistake or not and they'd sooner crucify you or openly sabotage your way of life than ever talk to you and try to settle your differences. Why did they move to the U.S.? I don't know. There were plenty of relatives and other Scotsmen to fight with in Scotland. Maybe they were banned from Scotland. "Get out of here Laddie and take the brood with you. Here's a boat and a paddle Patty."

I was about 12 years old at the time of this most unfortunate mishap. This was back in the day of the Madras clothing fashion craze. Madras, if you are out of the loop, was a large checked pattern in pastel blues, greens and whites and maybe even a little pink. Everyone was wearing Madras hats, pants (with a white belt and white shoes), Madras shorts (with a white belt, white shoes and white socks), Madras shirts, skirts, dresses, purses, scarves, every damn piece of one's wardrobe could be Madras. You could be a complete Madras Man or Madras Madam if you wanted to be. I think the first item to hit the streets was the Madras hat. It was sort of like a fisherman's cap or a rain hat – a soft, cloth top about three or four inches tall with a 2" soft brim all the way around. They were quite fashionable. It was the kind of hat you could roll up and stick in your Madras pant pocket. It was a lovely item.

Let's see, this incident took place around the 4th of July. Back in these days every kid, at least the kids in my neighborhood, had M-80s (quarter sticks of dynamite), cherry bombs, Black Cat firecrackers, ladyfingers and bottle rockets. It was the norm. We would throw the M-80s and the cherry bombs in the drain pipes that went under people's driveways or blow up cinder blocks with them. An M-80 would blow an 8" cinder block to smithereens. The bombs were waterproof so we could toss them in the creek too and mess with those pesky minnows. People started exploding things three or four weeks before the 4th. The Indian Reservation was filled with trailers that sold fireworks. They were a sovereign nation so no U.S. laws applied. Making money off White people over the 4th of July holiday was one of those Indian laws. People would literally buy trunk loads of fireworks. Indians and the Italians. Let's not forget the Italians, they both had all the fireworks.

Well, somehow, skinny Ian ended up wandering around in our neck of the woods with a brand new Madras hat on. He was probably over to Liam's. It was a fine looking hat. It must have been a children's size because Ian was a pinhead. Fine looking or not, brand new or not, what the hell was he doing hanging around my neighborhood? After taunting him a while with the standard degrading language twelve year olds are so good at using, and poking him and pushing him around a bit (I don't know who I was with) we grabbed his nice new hat. This really pissed him off. He was on the verge of tears. He would have fought back, but braincells like Ian can't fight. They don't even know how to fight with words. I called him every name in the book and he never said a word. He stood there like a scared little tittie-sucking baby Scotsman in a big tartan baby diaper.

Eventually, the poking fun of my Section 4 friend had to come to an end. Enough of the bullshit already. I wish I could have strapped him to a chair, tortured him some more and forced him to watch with his head tied to the headboard and his eyelids stitched open. The whole thing happened way too quickly. I placed a cherry bomb on the road, lit it and then threw his hat on it. The hat landed perfectly over the bomb. Needless to say it was the most fantastic explosion since the beginning of the universe. That son-of-a-bitch flew about twenty-five feet in the air, straight up like a Madras Rocket. We were all speechless, but Ian in particular was really speechless.

The look on his face was like no other look I had ever seen on a human. It was as if I were the anti-Christ and I had just pushed the A-Bomb button that was hidden in my undershorts to end the world. Thanks to Murphy-the-Fuck-up's undoing, Ian's pleasant little fairytale life had just come to an excruciating end. "Houston, we have lift off." Up, up and up it went into the outer stratosphere, tinged with fire and filled with a smoldering green smoke, twisting and turning until it ran out of steam and then it sauntered and waffled back to Earth. It was ruined ..... big time. Holy Shitski. That hat was now a rag. A very used rag. Indistinguishable really. Not a member of the neat and tidy Madras family any more that's for sure. It was officially part of the blown-to-bits, fire-and-smoke-ravaged, what-the-fuck-is-it family. It really wasn't funny.

Ian's biggest fear wasn't that the hat was gone or that we tormented him, it was the fact that he would have to tell his parents, Mr. & Mrs. Attila the Hun, that he had lost his hat. That it was taken from him after his being pushed around by an *Irishman*, and then blown up.

Little, wimpy, skinny Ian, with tears in his eyes, grabbed the remains of his still smoldering, once new baby-blue hat, dropped his head, hunched his shoulders forward, scuffed his sneakers and whined all the way back home. I could hear him a mile away. I can still hear him! No matter what the outcome, this was a great experiment at so many levels. It was a beautifully thrown hat, a beautiful explosion, a beautiful liftoff and a beautiful landing.

It was around dinner time that the doorbell rang. It was the Scots, Mr. and Mrs. Edwards, fit to be tied, screaming and gesturing all over the place. You couldn't understand a thing they were saying. You really didn't have to. This time my dad was speechless and not a happy camper to say the least. Both my parents took the brunt of that verbal beating. My father ended up gladly paying for a new hat and deeply apologizing. I think my dad thought it was funny, but knew it was dead wrong. There was no laughter when the door closed.

Chapter 26

The Holy Rollers

Life is full of learning experiences and as you can see, I try to learn more and more each and every day. Even scary, frightful experiences teach us much about life and its do's and don'ts. Over by the Nedrow Lumberyard, a block from my house, sat this fifteen foot by twenty foot white clapboard-sided building with a single, thin, white entrance door. It isn't necessary to have a back door in a fifteen foot by twenty foot house. There were three little windows and even the little window panes were painted white so you couldn't see inside. But the practitioners, the Holy Rollers, had to crack the windows for air. Otherwise they would all die in one night. The church was just dropped there in the middle of a small parking lot like Dorothy's house was dropped into the middle of OZ. Poof! Out of the sky one Sunday night, God's hand came down disguised as a ray of shimmering light breaking through the clouds. When the ray disappeared there was a House of Holy Roller Worship in the middle of the Nedrow Lumberyard. It was a block away from Jehovah's House of Worship only it was seventy-five percent smaller. There was one other difference. Oddly, Jehovah's witnesses were all White and the Holy Rollers (Pentecostal Christians) were all Black. There was another difference too. Jehovah's peoples were somewhat crazy; loving their God, crying for forgiveness, crying because they had been saved by Jesus' own touch. The Holy Rollers on the other hand were caarazy! There was nobody communicating with the Lord like the Holy Roller. Nobody!

Catholics like me don't ever dare shed a tear in church. We don't cry in public for anything. You can get banned from the Catholic church for openly expressing your feelings. They'll stone you to death right then and there. "GET OUT! ONLY JESUS CAN CRY FOR YOUR SINS. YOU'RE ONLY CRYING FOR YOUR OWN SELF PITY!" Well, that's probably true. People are whiners and Catholics are people. Catholics though, are the essence of stodginess. If you say your prayers louder than anyone else in church, you will be talked about at breakfast after church about how annoying you were and how rude that was and how that type of behavior is hated and they wish you would move to another pew or be excommunicated, banished, beaten, flogged and then burned at the stake. Don't fucking speak up in the Catholic Church you rude bastard. And say the prayers in the same monotone, low decibel drone as the rest of us. And don't fucking sing too good. We all hate that perfectly-in-tune little birdie voice you have. You're not a fucking bird, you're a Catholic for Christ's sake.

There could have been an "I Love the Lord" contest right there in Nedrow. If there were, everyone would have converted to Holy Rollerism. The poor Indians can't beat their religious drums fast enough to keep up with the Rollers. And besides, smokin' seasoned herb through the peace pipe speaks a totally different language to the mind of God. I can see the Indians sitting cross-legged, elevated, seated in a circle floating around the outside of the Holy Roller congregation during mass, but there would be no sound coming from the little white church. Indians can't hear anything when they reach the true state of Indianism. They absorb all unnecessary sounds from within their floating circle, and, their power of silence extends about 100 feet above, behind and beneath them. The Earth is their Mother. No one person or any single or combined religion will ever come between the peace of the Indian and their relationship with Mother Earth. It's impossible. They are Mother Earth. They are the Earth, Wind, and Fire. They are all that good represents on the Earth. Except for when they drink, and then they're just another bunch of drunks.

The Holy Rollers would meet every weekend in the early evening hours in their sweat box. Nedrow would begin to hear this raucous, hell-raising, screaming and shouting going on. Wow man, there is nothing like the Holy Rollers praising Jesus for hours at a time. You could hear it all the way from my house. Some swore you could feel the Earth moving. It was frickin' scary. Me and the other kids would always walk over by there, but never get too close. It was just so interesting to listen to. What the hell is going on in there? One time, and one time only, me and my next door neighbors, the Cronk boys and girls, we did sneak over there and peak through one of the cracked open windows. The place was packed wall to wall with finely dressed Holy Rollers. There were like 50 people in that tiny place rolling on the floor one-by-one when they were seized by the Holy Spirit, screaming some unknown language, clappin' and singin' and makin' the Lord's joyful noise. They were in a blessed Holy Trinity Trance. There were shiny black snakes in there with them winding over their bare feet and up their legs. One man held two snakes up in the air while he was jumping straight up in the air like tribal Africans do. Holy shit, they weren't snakes at all. As quickly as lightning strikes, the man with the two snakes flashed and fell to the floor transformed into a snake! He had transported himself to the other side. That's the power of the Holy Spirit my friends. You have to be willing to let yourself fall into wild abandonment. You have to! You have to free yourself of every inhibition. You have to accept the fact that you are emotionally vulnerable. You have to give 100% of yourself to the Lord Jesus Christ. I'm not sure you can proclaim the faith of the Lord *without* rolling on the floor, screaming, shouting, sweating, and crying. How can the Lord accept you if you're mumbling in a group monotone like the Catholics do? Jesus is like, "Uh, excuse me. What did y'all say?"

The next time you go to your Catholic Church, stop for a moment and listen to the way the congregation says their prayers. You can't understand a thing anyone is saying. "Hail rumble, full of rumble, the rumble rumble with thee, blessed rumble rumble, amongst rumble, and blessed rumble rumble fruit of thy rumble rumble." And then everyone says 'Amen' at a different time. The last person to always say Amen is always the loudest and always seems to be standing right behind you. Catholics sound like robe-wearing monks in a monastery. In truth, there are only about fifty people who actually know the prayers and the other 350 people *are* mumbling. And don't forget my friends, Jesus knows you are mumbling. All of the Holy Rollers will be in Heaven way before any of you. They are the prayer of the Lord. They have truly given of themselves. They have allowed the spirit of God to take them. They speak the same unintelligible language as the Lord. Jesus and God don't speak English, they speak a combobulation of all languages. If you're English, then you understand Him in English. If you're Chinese, the Spoken Word is clearly in Chinese. But if you were to write out what Jesus and God were actually saying, it would be like a kindergartner trying to write words. It wouldn't make any sense. That's what speaking in tongues is. All of the world's languages rolled into one. It's only the Indians, the Holy Rollers and those whacky Anglo snake worshipers from the South who got their shit together. Nedrow had a bit of it all. We were culturally significant.

Chapter 27

The Girls Down the Street

The guys in Nedrow, after all of their giving to God religious ceremonies were through for the day, were fortunate to have the lovely Krone girls living right down the street from us. Shelly was a couple of years younger than Sandy. Sandy was my age. Samantha Walsh was part of the naked gang too, but not so much with me, not that I didn't try. Samantha had huge breasticles for a 12 year old girl. But we all know size is relevant. To a 12 year old boy or girl, little breasts, or any breast for that matter, are huge. Me and the Krone girls started kissing and playing sex games when we were twelve or so. Mark (we called him Tony – his real name was Robert), their brother, would act as the circus ringleader and we would do whatever Tony told us to do. Really it was just innocent, sometimes naked, playful fun. I did have sex when I was 12 and had plenty of sex playtime. Sometimes there would be three or four guys in line waiting to do the nasty with an available neighborhood girl. It wasn't any big thing. It was just something to do. No harm came of it. It wasn't mean or abusive. I don't remember anyone every making fun of the girls or belittling them. I would have to think sex among the young is going on everywhere all of the time. The Mulligans were doing it on their turf with the Traylor sisters and we were doing it on ours.

Mary, Jesus Christ's mom, was twelve or thereabouts when she was pregnant with Jesus. I've always thought of Eve, Adam's partner, as being a few years older than twelve. At first glance her portraits make it seem like she's in her twenties, but under closer examination she does look like she's in her teens. Both Adam and Eve, when created, were physically ready to have children. God couldn't create Man and then spend time raising Man. God is friggin' busy. He's like, "Okay, let's get some dust together, a little wind and whip up someone in my likeness, only with 10 fingers instead of eleven, a penis, curly blond hair, muscles and everything else." And then, after being created, Adam was roaming around like a lost little boy stuttering trying to make up words and discover things while playing with his penis, but poor Adam didn't have anyone to splain the words to and their deep meaning. So God, after watching this for a couple of days, probably the longest two days of His eternal life, gave some morphine to Adam and knocked him out. He then proceeded to perform a miraculous surgery taking out one of Adam's ribs (leaving no scar) and turned it into this beautiful, naked girl just as the sun was setting so He named her Eve. Adam finally came out of his stupor and there is this unbelievably beautiful naked blonde holding his head in her lap with her breasts dangling right in front of his face. He's like, "Holy Shit!" This is the first time anyone (of course, they were the only two people on the planet, but nonetheless) - it's the first time anyone had ever used foul language. And placing the word "Holy" before the word "shit" didn't really help matters. God, being who God is, doesn't make wincing a habit, but upon hearing Adam's choice of words, this also marks the first time God ever winced. And because of this, God Himself, thinking of the mess He has created says, "Holy shit! What have I done!" So these two people were sinning and causing others to sin before the evil snake ever came into the picture. This is the Word of the Lord.

When discussing Shelly and Sandy we have to remember that there was no Mr. Krone, no father figure. I think he died in

WWII or something. Mrs. Krone worked all day and sometimes into the night downtown at the Golden Spike. A classy hangout for the shadowy, underground type figures hiding in Syracuse's semi-political world. Please don't misunderstand me, the Krone kids were all really nice kids and probably got into less trouble than I did and I had two parents around all of the time. Tony did have trouble attending school, and one year, maybe it was in the fifth grade, he *never* went to school. Never! I don't know how he pulled this off, but I am pretty sure he never went to school the entire year. I'm not sure what happened. He had to make it up somehow.

Kids being kids, nosey and all, one time we found a pair of fine French, black laced panties in Mrs. Krone's dresser drawer that had a black silk glove sewn into them with the middle finger .... well .... right where it should be. I mean how cool is that? A pair of undies with a glove sewn into them? That's creative genius!

Mrs. Krone must have sensed that there were extracurricular activities going on while she was at work. One day she came home early and found me upstairs with her daughter Sandy. This was not good for neighborly relationships. But Mrs. Krone was no dummy. She got back at me a couple of years later. She had a Christmas Eve party. None of the neighbors were invited because she worked downtown and had her own friends. I wasn't really invited either, but ended up there because of her kids. It was the first time I was in the house since I got caught with Sandy. My parents were out on the town with friends of their own. Being the boy-man that I was, I drank some beer and some shots and whatever else came my way. No one even stopped me. It was great to be treated as an adult until I fell on the floor drunk as a fucking skunk; dead weight in the middle of the dance floor. I can hear Mrs. Krone now, "How's that you little fucker? That's what you get for messing with my daughter. Get this piece of shit off my floor!"

Here's the story I was later told. I did fall drunk on the floor. It was snowing outside like there was no tomorrow. The Krone kids tried walking me the few blocks home to sober me up, but like I said, I was dead weight. There was a priest visiting his sister who lived on East Roswell. I guess I gave him the business as we walked by. He couldn't hear me because it was late, it was snowing, and he was locked inside submerged in prayer for me and the rest of the disintegrating Christian world. There was only one thing left for the Krones to do; they took me to my front porch, dropped me at the door, rang the doorbell and ran like snowshoe rabbits. Gramma Conley (of throwing my best friend Whitey the Gunslinging Hamster into the trash fame) opened the door and immediately called my siblings for help. They dragged me in and laid me up on the couch. I was dead, gone to the world. I have heard that I was calling poor Gramma every name in the book. They cut my boot laces off with a knife and left me there. My parents came home and my father dragged me up to my bed. I have no memory of anything whatsoever. Late the next morning I remember waking up and coming downstairs. I remember someone saying, "Shhhh, shhhh, here he comes." That was another very sad day. The worst Christmas ever.

Chapter 28

The Other Naked Neighbor

One of the great things about the Nedrow house, at least for me, was the stairway to the second floor. Especially after our new neighbor Vanessa Erekson moved in. She was a blonde bombshell. Vanessa was in the eighth grade as was I. She was a trained ballerina. She was built like a brick shit-house. As my father used to say (not about Vanessa, but in general), "She is the cat's meow."

Our staircase went up about twelve steps, hung a Louie, and then there were about five more steps up to the bedroom hallway. There was a window at the landing (where Whitey and I used to fight). If you sat in the middle of these final five steps, my graceful ballerina's bedroom was right across the way. Vanessa had legs of steel, was stunningly over developed for an eighth grader and had perfectly pointed breasts; a naked

Nedrow goddess living right next door to me. You can't make this stuff up. This is a true example of the luck of the Irish. Vanessa, my personal Goddess, would try on her clothes at night and study herself in the mirror. I would be sitting on the steps with my Wolfman eyes popping out, salivating from my paralyzed mouth, and like Quasimodo, I too would be snorting and feeling so misunderstood. I would almost be crying with inexplicable joy and uncontrollable appreciation. Vanessa was the first girl I ever saw totally naked. She too was Cheryl Hartman reincarnated; the rebirth of my first true love. My queen. My everything. My mourning dove. My Loretta Young. My breath of fresh air. I would climb any mountain, swim any sea. She was the ski in my daddle. The ship upon my shore. The skip to my loo, the wang-dang in my doodle, the sauce on my noodle, the peanut in my butter, the mud in my puddle, the French in my poodle, the ring around my rosy, my pocket full of posie, my dosie in the doe, the knick-knack in my paddy-whack, and the one-two in the buckle my shoe. I loved her.

Everyone wanted that thing. To quote an old blues man, "She had a great big top, a skinny little middle, the hips on that girl they sure like to wiggle, she's all right, she's alright, she's alright. She had long, long legs people were singin' 'bout, a curvy shape everybody's talkin' 'bout, she's all right, she's all right, she's all right." All the guys in the entire school were an exact replica of the guys who used to follow my sister around, a bunch of three-legged dogs in heat. But for me, I was lucky. She was my neighbor. My naked neighbor looking at herself in the mirror was thinking of me I'm sure. I did get to play with her perfectly formed, A #1, thumbs up, best of the bunch, pick of the litter, two of a kind, visions of joy that brought eyesight to the blind breasts once, or should I say, almost played with her love breasts. One steamy summer afternoon we were in my other next door neighbor's garage behind our house lying down on some old grungy, wrinkled rag discussing life's finer things, gently kissing each other and laughing and talking. I had a dangerously loaded rod in my pocket. I was trying to politely dry-hump her while gently playing with her tongue while trying to take her bra off while trying to get her to spread her unbelievable ballerina legs a little bit. It was beautiful. She was beautiful. A virgin Goddess in a white tutu. Vanessa was hoping for slow, unfolding movements performed by her ballerino balletomane; movements with fluidity and elegance. "Adagio, adagio, adagio (slowly, slowly, slowly)," she whispered. Vanessa, my love, wanted to improve on her ability to control one leg and increase her extension with her other leg. "Adagio ….. adagio ….. adagio," she kept whispering. It was so hot outside I wished we were some place other than the filled-with-junk, rotting, cockroach-filled garage, but you are where you are when love strikes. It's very difficult for a teenage boy to be patient when it comes to sex. Actually, it's impossible. Even if you don't know what the hell you're doing, time is of the essence. "Adagio …………… adagio …………… adagio," she kept repeating.

As all Swedes are, she was so beautiful with long, shoulder length blond hair, just a gorgeous face, soft, innocent lips, a thin, kissable neck and the most exquisitely white, untouched skin ever. Unfortunately, I was into allegro, allegro, allegro! "Just open up your fucking legs will you? Jesus Christ, I'm sweating like a fucking pig here!" It's hard to be a ballerino, people.

Actually, some would say it was the perfect outside temperature. The time was right. Sweat was dripping over the both of us. Nobody was around. Her hands were rubbing my cock on the outside of my jeans. She wanted to be fucked. It was perfect, but I just couldn't wait. If I had just taken my time with her I could have fucked her right there that day. I became too frustrated and broke her concentration and she remembered where she was, in our neighbor's garage lying on a bunch of old rags. Fuck! She stopped me, à la seconde. Écarté! Damn! All this work and effort and I was really only trying to get to her extra large, softer than soft, never-been-fondled, never been licked or sucked on tits that I happen to be wildly attracted to. What's the big deal? Jesus! I'll admit that it wasn't the most romantic environment and that I was more involved in the rabid, emotional, sweaty encounter than trying to create the perfect environment. But that's what we young colts do. Jump and run. Once me and my throbbing, about to burst cock rolled off of her in total, sweaty frustration, I came to my senses a few moments later.

"My darling," I said to her, "we can work on getting your cloths off and fucking your pussy to death as time goes by. You can teach me. I'm yours Vanessa. You can mold me to do what you want me to do and then I will do what I am going to do anyway. I'm here for you. I can concentrate on every physical attribute you bring to the world. I can be your first and only for a while. You were placed on this Earth for a reason. To bring joy to those in need like the hungry, the thirsty, the horny and the impoverished. You have peaked the interest of mankind. You have turned the heads of those with stiff necks. You have straightened the backs of those poor men with osteoporosis. You have given a robust breath of air to those with lung disease. You have provided an inner feeling of youth to those whose wives are too old to provide that essential manly need. You have given hope to the crippled who move more nimbly in your presence. You are the universe of love's emotion delivered to us, those of us, black, white and Indian, who live in God's chosen vacation land, Nedrow. You have the apples in our eyes, you have legs that can be stretched and bent, twisted and turned, opened and then opened even wider. You can touch your palms to the floor. You can do splits. You can hold one leg parallel along side your body opening up a vast new region for exploration. You are the deliverer of a ballerina's goodwill to a poor country town in Upstate New York. You give us hope. You can deliver us from evil ….. amen.

Vanessa, my love, spent her entire junior high and high school years desperately in love with some jealous Dennis the Menace looking creep with a caveman brow and beady eyes in the next grade up. Besides having pleasure, I'm sure, with my Nedrow Goddess, I just didn't like the guy. HarryHarry didn't like him either so maybe that's why I didn't like him. Naturally, as you might have guessed, they broke up during his senior year. She wasted her entire junior high and high school years with one guy and he was an idiot! I never had another opportunity to impress her with my glorious words of Shakespearian wit.

That shoulda been me with that real fine chick. That shoulda been me with that real fine chick. That shoulda been me ….. drivin' that ..... Cadillac.

Chapter 29

Clooney's

Time moves on with haste and even as a child the seasons change more rapidly every year. I lost track of Vanessa changing her clothes and examining herself while she dreamt of me, and I think she caught on to my viewing stage. Winter in Upstate soon blew in. The winters are long and hard in Upstate NY. Buffalo gets all of the credit, but Syracuse and the surrounding areas get nearly twice as much snow as Buffalo, and in some cases, a littler farther north, three times as much snow. The largest snowplow in the world is at Syracuse's Hancock International Airport. The blade is 32' 3" wide. It's 48" tall and can clear 8,500 cubic yards of snow per hour. It's attached to a pay loader. Buffalo has nothing on Syracuse.

You've heard me mention Liam Clooney before. This is the story of the Clooney property and how we made the most of it as kids. Behind my house on Macon Street lived the Clooney family. They had a four-story mansion on the hill. It was a beautiful Spanish style, slate roofed home that dated back to the 1600s. Is that possible? Its official name was Oak Crest. The legend told that there were many hidden treasures (even a trove of silver and gold) in and around the house. I had heard that the Spanish explorers originally designed the home and had it built for themselves. It had slave quarters and horse stables in the basement. There was a work shed and a carriage house (another pretty big house) at the south end of the driveway where the lower ranked soldiers and the staff stayed. In the basement of the staff house there were also horse stables and an underground tunnel that ran up to the main house.

Clooney's great uncle Seamus Brennan, a member of the Irish Mafia, purchased the house as a gift to Liam's grandmother and grandfather. Liam was in my class. His uncle Tom owned a tobacco company and ran a nearby pub called the O'Malley Club. After Liam's grandparents and then his father passed away, the Clooney's found one of the secret rooms with all kinds of depression-era gambling stuff, but no gold. There were also servant's quarters way up on the 4th floor of the main house. You have to see this place to believe it.

I don't know why, but I was never one of Liam Clooney's close friends. I think my fledgling reputation as a bully and a criminal preceded me and his mom made hangin' with the Murf a no-no. I did stand in their expansive foyer once, but that's as far as I got. Clooney's had an enormous multi-acre lawn with a nice size hill serving as the front yard. The entire Section 6 and 7 neighborhoods grew up sledding on this hill every day of every winter for hours on end. Cliff Six and others from District 7 practiced their downhill skiing technique on this hill. They would build these mounds or moguls down toward the bottom and ski jump. I never did this. We weren't a skiing family. But everybody in Nedrow had sleds, padded toboggans and metal flying saucers. This was before the days of mass produced plastics. By the way, behind Clooney's is where I got stung by the bees my first day in Nedrow.

You could start your sled ride at the top of Clooney's hill and sometimes make it all the way down the hill and across Macon Street probably 150 yards away. As if it were planned by the God of Sledding there was a huge maple tree planted two-thirds of the way down the hill directly in the center of the yard and a gigantic pine tree to the right. It was easy enough to avoid unless you were on a toboggan or a flying saucer. That's what made sledding at Clooney's so much fun, trying to miss this damned maple tree. As we grew a little older we would go sledding with the neighborhood girls. Ahhh yes, pure, innocent adolescent fun. We would get on a toboggan with the young lady in front and one of us on behind. As you raced down the hill you would play with the girl's boobies. Even though she had 6" of padded clothing on over her boobs, it was still a thrill for all involved. Crashing into the tree was even more fun. Then you would roll over and over into the snow with this pretty girl, end up on top of her and maybe steal a kiss or two. I remember making out on that front lawn under the full moon with Mindy Ordino, a blue-eyed, neighborhood redhead. Yikes! I loved her. She was a year older than me and a grade ahead of me. We were lying in the most beautiful snow you have ever seen. Each flake glistening in the crisp moonlight. Kissing and rolling around in the crunchy snow and just lying there in the stillness of a cold winter's evening. Dreaming, wondering, sharing, holding gloved hands and being still. Mindy was a beautiful young woman with a greater capacity for life's zest than anyone I ever knew. She was probably one of the girls that visited the loft with my brother HarryHarry, but that didn't bother me. When you're fifteen or sixteen anything is possible. I think Mindy liked me too. But so much goes on during this period of life that actually connecting with someone for the rest of your life is next to impossible. So we capture these moments of bliss and keep them forever in our memory. The naïve love we share with someone has as much meaning throughout our life as it did when it first happened. Nothing can compare to that night with Mindy on the front lawn of Clooney's. We were both in Heaven as it is on Earth.

When Mindy and I went our separate ways that snow-crazed evening, I was pulling the toboggan toward home on Rockwell Road when I threw a freshly made snowball carelessly up into the air over my head. It never came down. I stopped .... and I looked and looked .... and then I found it .... to match this wonderful evening, the snowball was balanced perfectly on the power line overhead.

Kids are the greatest inventors of things to do when passing the time. On real snowy nights when there were four or five inches of packed snow on the roads and continuously falling fresh powder, my friends and I would walk from our neck of the woods down to where the city buses turned around at the corner of East Conklin in Section 5. Nedrow was the end of the city-run bus line. The drivers would almost always sit there for a few minutes until their scheduled leave time and then take off nice and easy up Salina back toward the city. Since it would be snowing like crazy, the bus would take its time getting up to speed. We would run up behind the bus, grab onto the bumper, squat down in a sitting position and get pulled all the way to the Nedrow Tavern maybe a mile away or so and sometimes we would go even farther. But the farther you went the farther you would have to walk back so you had to keep this in mind. Our boots would act like skis. Quiet ……………. peaceful ………………….. smooth …….................. a gentle mixture of snowflakes and bus fumes ... truly a great time.

On other boring, snowy evenings four or five of us would hide next to the P&C parking lot on the West Roswell side, next to Ned's Drugs in the woods and wait for that same bus to go to the end of the line. We would nail it with as many snowballs as we could until it was out of reach. It must have scared the shit out of the driver. Then we would wait for its return and nail it again. We would kill that bus. Me, Tony and Dean Krone, Jack Clawson, Manny and Chuck Hayford, Fritz, Bowl-a-rama Bob, whoever happened to be out that night. We would murder it. One lovely evening upon the buses return trip, instead of being in the woods where the trees shielded us from the driver's view, we stood right there in the open P&C parking lot. The bus was moving at a snail's pace, purring up Salina. It was as if the driver was providing the most perfect target for us on purpose. What a great guy. Bus drivers are the best! We pummeled it relentlessly with 30, maybe 40 direct hits. BAM BAM BAM BAM BAM BAM BAM BAM BAM BAM BAM BAM BAM BAM BAM BAM BAM BAM BAM BAM BAM BAM BAM BAM BAM BAM BAM ………. BAM … BAM BAM! The bus was in the passing lane closest to us. In the cruising lane on the other side of the bus, out of sight, purring along with the bus was a New York State Trooper. The bus sped up, the Trooper slowed down, dropped behind the bus, turned his lights on and came flying into the parking lot. Holy Snowball! We all ran as fast as we could down the lot, down the truck delivery driveway next to the

Nedrow Laundromat that was next to Ned's that was next to the P&C and we disappeared into the darkness and the tall grasses behind the P&C. We were golden.

We finally end up over by Jack Clawson's house near the corner of Elton and Salina on the other side of the P&C. We catch our breath and have some great laughs retelling the story over and over. "Oh man, we killed that bus!" "We were set up, man!" "I've never seen Tony run so fast. You were like lightning, man!" "That was fucking awesome!"

After about fifteen or twenty minutes the coast seemed clear. We break up and go home. It was an excellent time. Dean Krone stayed behind or decided to take the side streets home. I walk back to Salina Street, take a right and start to walk home. The Trooper immediately pulls up behind me with his lights on and tells me to get in. How stupid was I? The guy chased us down the alleyway. He obviously knew what we were wearing. It was Johnny Law (his real name), the famous NYS Trooper. He knew all of us by name and where we lived. He takes me home, knocks on my front door, tells my parents the story, gets back in his car and leaves me to suffer the consequences. Damn!

Chapter 30

Changing Direction

Everything changed when I was fourteen. During the summer between 8th and 9th grade I stopped hanging around with the kids I grew up with, the good kids, and turned to an older group more HarryHarry's age, but not the type he would hang out with, the more adventurous type. HarryHarry was a simple country boy. These folks were all 16, 18, maybe even 20 years old and into drugs and drinking. I started drinking when I was fourteen years old over at the half-moon across the creek with Fritz, Randy Ducane, Burt, Bowl-a-rama Bob, Neuman, Dean Krone, Peter Farrington, Don McCluge and a couple of the older girls. Miller Genuine Draft was my first beer. It was just a beer. I didn't start drinking every day craving a case at a time or anything. I also started experimenting with pot, smoking banana peels, oregano, and various wild weeds. We would cook them up at Mark Roth's house in his mother's oven, roll 'm up and smoke'm. We even sold some of that crap to other dummies like us. These were the days of nickel and dime bags. A nickel was a quarter ounce of pot that sold for $5. A dime was a half ounce for $10. A full ounce went for $15 or $20. Pounds went for $165. Nickel and dime bags were a good deal. Everybody had $5. In these days it was all Mexican reefer. I wasn't a big smoker and again, it wasn't a daily quest of mine to get high, I just wanted some more excitement in my life. I quit playing Babe Ruth baseball that summer too. I was bored to death playing with the same old boring kids, walking the streets picking our noses, watching the cars go by as we sat on Jehovah's steps across from the Nedrow Tavern. I'd been doing this for half my life now.

Chapter 31

Running Away To Strawberry Fields

In 1969 the famed Woodstock Music Festival was taking place right down the road from Nedrow. My new group of friends were all going to Woodstock. We were listening to Hendrix, Zeppelin, the Beatles, Eric Burdon and the Animals, Ten Years After, The Who, Sly and the Family Stone, the Rolling Stones, Joplin, Baez, Blind Faith, and Bo Diddley over at Chuckie Haines' house, Kurt Schneider's house, the Walters' and the Cronk's house; everywhere and anywhere we were welcomed. Music was alive, a real part of our lives. Totally different from the soapy stuff my sister was listening to like Roy Orison, Gerry & the Pacemakers, Donovan, the Temptations, Herman's Hermits, the Supremes and so many others. Don't get me wrong, this was great stuff too, but where is the comparison between the cool, soft rock of '65 and the raw rock of the late 60s and early 70s? There isn't any.

I really, really wanted to go to Woodstock, but my parents refused to let me go. To get my revenge, when I was fifteen in

1970, I ran away to the Strawberry Fields Festival a few miles north of Toronto, Canada with this same group of much older friends. It's hard to believe they took me with them. I must have been somewhat cool or they would have blown me off. I don't remember much about the trip except for the fact that at one point, somewhere where we were spending the night, there was a lake nearby and my old elementary school nemesis Freddie Sowers came walking out of the water soaking wet with blood-stained ivory horns protruding from either side of his forehead. He *was* the body and blood of Satan and everyone refused to go near him. Of course we were all stoned or tripping, but nonetheless, the unanimous consensus among the Flying Nedrow Fellowhood was that Freddie *was* Satin. He scared the shit out of me that's for sure. A year later, Freddie would crash his car into a tree by Clary Middle School in the Valley and kill his passenger Peter Farrington. Peter was everyone's best friend. He was a skinny, real hippie kid that lived up next to Samson's Concrete. I don't know where he came from, somewhere in Fayetteville maybe? His parents seemed to be quite well off and Peter was a spoiled hippie kid. He knew everything about drugs and had access to all kinds of stuff. His parents were fairly old so he did what he wanted to. Once, in the middle of the long hair craze someone offered him $20 to shave his head ….. and he did it. It shocked everyone. Peter was who he was. He lived his own life. He was a leader. I drank so much beer at his house one time that I threw up. It was the first and last time I ever threw up from drinking. After Freddie the Devil got the shit beat out of him a few times by Peter's friends, Freddie disappeared never to be seen again. Back to Hell I guess. Payback again for beating up Little Jimmy Murphy in the 4th grade you fuckhead!

Just prior to running off to Toronto I had my wrist in a cast. I was in gym class one morning and while everyone else was doing what they were supposed to be doing I was gonna high jump. Why the hell can't I just go along with everyone else? Why can't I just do what I am told to do? What the hell is wrong with me? I don't know. I don't think I'm doing anything wrong. I really don't think I am breaking any rules. I think I'm fine. I'm not an instigator. I'm not a trouble maker. I'm actually very shy and reserved, quiet and careful, calculative and aware. I just need some place to fit in. Some place to keep me interested. Some place to welcome me and teach me things that will bring out my hidden potential. I have absolutely no superpowers any more either. They've gone into remission deep within my subconscious. I'm as visible and as vulnerable as all others. I am heavy and grounded. I can still jump humanly high. I'm fast and quick and capable to move among other outcast athletes like myself. It isn't that I'm not learning from my mistakes because the mistakes I make are all new mistakes. I'm not rehashing or revisiting the same smoke filled rooms or getting drunk every day. These small instances are little stepping stones toward the creation of the nurturing, caring being I will develop into. My inner glow has only begun to shine its light. I have overwhelming potential, I just don't know how to get to where it is that I want to be. No clue as to how to get there. I am one lost mother fucker.

This particular fine day though, in gym class, the grass was slippery from the morning dew out in South Onondaga and like I said, I was goofing off. I lined myself up for the high jump, got into my stance, right foot out front, knees bent, shoulders forward, head down, breathing steadily, everything seems fine. I take off toward the pole and right as I am about to release into my jump my feet slip out from under me. My legs go awkwardly out and up. My arms are flailing as my body was just beginning to twist in the air. My entire weight falls on my right wrist and I crush it; dislocating it. The bottom of my hand where my pinky is was level with the top of my wrist where my thumb usually is. It was one strange looking thing, man. It looked impossible, unimaginable, like some freak monster drawing or something. It wasn't painful because I had gone into some sort of shock. Coach Fletcher was pissed, but not surprised and disgustingly told me to go inside to the nurse. One fucked up moment after another seemed to be my M.O. There isn't really anything one can do about these things. Life is life. Life's paths for the most part are created for you by circumstance and you chose the path you want to follow. It's a simple, "Okay, yeah I'll try that," or a simple, "No, that's not something I want to try." It's pretty clear cut.

Off to the hospital I go with my father driving and my mother going along for the ride. I'm a coward as you know so even the sight of a needle going into someone's arm on TV much less the sight of a needle being inserted into *my* arm can induce a coma-like state of consciousness. I pass out as soon as the doctor begins to twist and yank on my wrist ....

When my eyes open I'm in complete blackness. I have no idea where I am or what it is that I am looking at. My superior inner calculation estimates that I'm 800 million miles tall and just sort of almost lying down on my side, but still sort of standing. I'm floating, but stuck in an invisible black gel-type material. My eyes can barely even blink. I can see through the blackness, but can't move. Everything seems to be pinned up and just hanging there. As my eyes gain more focus I can see that there are distant bright and not-so-bright lights; stars I think ... a gazillion, gazillion, gazillion of them and there are these spiral cluster type things all with extremely, almost blinding bright centers. I can't shade my eyes because of the black jelly stuff I'm stuck in so I slowly squint. My arms are stuck where they are. There are bazillions of these spiral things in every direction. I feel like I'm a million years old and not the innocent age of 15 that I really am. I am wise, filled with a common knowledge, a perfect sense. This vision is more impressive than anything I have ever seen or even dreamt of or considered before. It's like I'm standing on Earth looking skyward except for the fact that I'm just hanging here suspended in space. I feel like I'm invisibly nailed down like Gulliver.

My surrounding's massiveness instantaneously makes me wonder about God. All Gods. I mean really, if I'm suspended in the middle, or suspended somewhere, it could be anywhere because it's impossible to tell where the middle is, where was God suspended when he created all of this? I'm recognizing the fact that these spiral-armed pinwheels are all galaxies that Earthlings have not yet seen. Earthlings are still contemplating whether or not our galaxy is the entire universe. I now see that this contemplation is far from the truth. It has me wondering where can God be? A better, more pertinent question is, where was God when this whole universe thing began? What is the true relationship between the Universe, God, Jesus and Man? I have this inquisitive need to know where God was when He created the universe and where He is now.

It dawns on me that in order for me to find where God was at the time he created the universe, I need to place a finite parameter on the universe and map it out. I need a level playing field in order to do so. This simple, searchable, level plane I envision I will call the Universe. To keep it simple, the playing field is 100' long by 50' wide and 1" thick. It could be anywhere, in a desert, in the middle of the woods or in the middle of grazing land or even in the middle of New York's concrete jungle. Let me explain what I'm going to do for you, my people. From somewhere near the center of my finite parameter I will pace off in a single direction to the best of my ability twenty-five regular steps and then stop. Ready? Come on, here I go .... one, two, three, four, five, six, seven, eight, nine, ten, eleven, twelve, thirteen, fourteen, fifteen, sixteen, seventeen, eighteen, nineteen, twenty, twenty-one, twenty-two, twenty-three, twenty-four, twenty-five. Okay. Now I'm going to pace off to the left ten steps (it could be to the right, it really doesn't matter). Ready? One, two, three, four, five, six, seven, eight, nine, ten. Stop. Now I'm going to reach down. This isn't as an exact of a science as you may have thought, but the final outcome *is* exact. I'm going to pinch my field on the surface and take that piece of Earth and whittle it down to the tiniest single grain that I can. This is silly I know. We've been led to believe that the universe is endless in all directions. It isn't 100' long by 50' wide by 1" thick. This section we have chosen to examine is a simulated, minute piece of the overall universe. That's easy enough to grasp. This is the power and the knowledge I have within Me. Listen to what I'm telling you. I know, you think you've heard this all before, but you haven't, so listen to Me. That one grain I have on My fingertip doesn't represent Earth, it represents the Milky Way, our galaxy, the one I can view because I'm 800 million miles tall, but you can't because you are inside of it. The Milky Way, by my estimation is approximately 110,000 light years across. This should be easy to understand because we are familiar with the number 110,000 and you have heard the term light year before. Light travels at 186,000 miles per second, 1,116,000 miles per minute, 669,600,000 miles per hour, 16,070,400,000 miles per day, and 5,865,696,000,000 miles in a single year. The grain in your hand actually represents 645,226,560,000,000,000 miles (this is how far light travels in 110,000 light years). That's six hundred forty-five quadrillion, two hundred twenty-six trillion, five hundred sixty billion miles across. This is our single galaxy among an uncountable number of other galaxies. Even though I am 800 million miles tall, I am nothing compared to our single galaxy. I am 806,533,200 times smaller than the width of the Milky Way. It's just unimaginable. Note: The distance between one galaxy and another, from where I'm standing, is much greater than the size of any single galaxy. Hang in there, don't let me lose you, be patient.

This measurement 645,226,560,000,000,000 miles is something our mind has to ignore because there is nothing on Earth to measure it against. It is impossible for us to know what this measurement is. We can only justify measurement that our eyes can see or that our mind has previously captured. For instance, from mountain top to mountain top. From the front door to the car. From the shelf to the grocery cart or the butter knife to the bread. These measurements we can easily understand. On Earth we can see the pretty stars in the sky and playfully imagine their distance, but we would rather see them as the Big Dipper and Orion's belt than really concern ourselves with their true distance from us and what that really means. And that's all fine until you ask yourself this important coma-induced question. Where was God standing when He created the universe? Where *was* He? Was He standing close to Earth like I am or was He eighteen jazillion million light years on the other side of wherever this is? By the way, here's another question. How big is God? Is He our size? Maybe 6' 2", 5' 8" or 800 million miles tall like I am? Reasonably now, how could someone 5’ 8” tall or even 800 million miles tall create an immeasurable entity like the universe?

I love it out here, but I’m the only person out here so even though I am the Light of Every Shining Thing, I wish there were more of my kind. Was God alone or is there a whole otherworld of magnificent Gods? We might find the answer to this in a moment or two, let’s see.

If I took that 100’ long by 50’ wide by 1” thick parcel and made believe it was our Milky Way, not the universe, but our own galaxy, and again I pick any grain of dirt. Now let’s say that grain represents our Earth within our galaxy. That’s reasonable. Okay, so within the immeasurable universe and the nearly inconceivable Milky Way lies the speck called Earth. We know that’s true because that’s where we are, on Earth. Within that speck called Earth is the seven mile wide by twelve mile long Sea of Galilee. This is where Jesus performed many of his miracles. He walked on water there. He calmed the Sea. He turned water into wine. He made a few loaves of bread feed an entire community and He healed the broken and the sick. Now listen. The Universe is so massive from where I am, I can’t see the end in any direction. It goes on and on and on and is filled with stars and galaxies and blackness as far as my gigantic eye can see in every direction. Now that I’m standing next to our Milky Way, I see that it too is loaded with billions of stars and who knows what else, and the center of the Milky Way is this beyond blinding white light. I have no friggin’ idea what might be in there. I’m a Super Star and I can’t even stare at it. Where is Earth in all these stars? I couldn’t begin to tell you. Here is a question I can answer. Do I believe in Jesus? Yeah, I guess I do. I can sort of see these miraculous things taking place. Something did happen with Jesus for sure because word of these events spread to everyone on Earth and changed everything. Jesus did give people something to believe in that has brought comfort to millions of people wandering the Earth who need some comfort. That’s okay. Here is what I find impossible to believe after being tied to the Universe. That God, the being who created the entire, unfathomable universe, the universe so large that we humans simply cannot even begin to understand its size and expansive depth, how could God possibly know where the Milky Way is, much less where Earth is, much less where the Sea of Galilee is and who Jesus is? To me, now that I have a view that no one from Earth before me has ever had, I see the believable improbability of their ever being a God. And I'm good with this belief. It's simply not feasible that within this 645,226,560,000,000,000 miles, the width of our single galaxy among an uncountable number of other galaxies and an immeasurable amount of distance between the uncountable number of galaxies, that God knows where the Sea of Galilee is and knows that there was a Jesus roaming around the Sea taking care of business. In closing this dream segment, I hate to be the one to tell you this, but there is no God.

I say this because as I float here above you, I know, that as a people, as strong individuals, as strongly defined cultural groups, with the realization of this fact that God does not exist, the fact that we *are* all alone here on this tiniest grain of dirt, that with this "all alone" factor, we will gain a new respect for ourselves as a whole, as a combined unit all staring into space wide-eyed in disbelief that we may actually be here by ourselves, that we really *are* responsible for our own fate, that without equal help from all of us we will destroy our home, and that we alone are responsible for our destiny, that perhaps now we will be at peace with each other's beliefs and each other's cultural differences and truly meld together to form the union of our species as it should be.

But even with this new and clearly defined revelation at the age of 15, that there is no God, I can assure you that on my day of reckoning, on my death bed, at 104 years old, I will be crying like an Irish Ukrainian baby and will be begging for God's forgiveness.

"Wait. What happened? Dad? Mom? Oh man. What's up? What happened? What the heck am I doing here?" There's nothing quite like awakening from a slight coma because your fear of needles is so great that you pass out at the sight of them. And the fact that from a simple pain relief injection, the entire truth about the Universe, God, Jesus and Man is revealed to me is an even greater revelation than me having supper powers; supper powers? What the heck are supper powers? What I meant to say is, a greater revelation than me having superpowers ever was. It's even worse. At least with superpowers you can prove something every once in a while and secretly save a life or something. Knowing that God doesn't exist can land you in the loony bin with a half-ass frickin' lobotomy after being sexually assaulted by some hunchbacked, one-eyed, foot-dragging mongrel in the sanctuary basement.

While it's interesting to discuss God, Earth, Heaven and Hell with my compadres, it kind of loses its luster when you actually know the truth instead of spouting off your religious "belief of the day" which is what most stoned dudes do. Now I'll just have to shake my head in agreement, "Yes, oh yes, you're right. God is blah, blah, blah." "Wow, that is brilliant! Did you think that up yourself? That Fritz is sure smart. Blah, blah, blah, blah, blah. Let's smoke another joint and get even smarter." I decide never to tell anyone the truth about God.

After I was released from the hospital I painted my cast like the American flag and had people sign it. It was cool. It drew attention to me (not that I needed attention). I got my cast off the day before running away to Canada. Here's my account of the Strawberry Fields Festival. First, we had trouble getting into Canada. We tried the Peace Bridge because it had such a friendly name and there was a rumor that this would be our best bet. They refused to allow us in. I was on the down-low because I was just a kid. So we drove west to the Rainbow Bridge (named after a Jimi Hendrix album) and got in. The crowd at the festival was huge. Many more than the stadium where the festival was being held could hold. Being all peaceful and loving hippies we banded together and started to rip the chain link security fence down so we could get into the concert for free. I, being a teenage toddler with a limp wrist, was up on a roof watching all of the action. I saw hundreds if not thousands of revelers try taking down the fence. I saw policemen on motorcycles get kicked over by the maddening audience. I saw Canadian Mounties on horseback raising their steeds up in the air like Roy Rogers on Trigger and stomping the peace-lovers. It was unbelievable. I think John Lennon was either scheduled to perform or was performing there with Yoko. This wasn't long after Woodstock so people expected or were *demanding* the concert be free. This riot went on for a good couple of hours at least. I don't think it worked out well for either side. I was up on the roof by myself. My traveling companions were down in the heart of the fighting-for-freedom crowd. None of us had tickets. Eventually the riot was quelled and the people returned to a park near the stadium where we were promised that some of the bands would make a presence the following day to perform for us.

Early the next morning the entire mob of scraggly-haired hippies awoke to the crisp Canadian air. This must have been what it was like at Woodstock only without the rain. For me personally, at least I was experiencing something. I wasn't blowing someone's hat up. I was experiencing life. I was living! "Ow! Watch the arm." I was also coming to the realization that I loved the hippie chick. The barefootedness, the long colorful dresses, loose hippie blouses, no bras (maybe no underwear), long wavy hair, free, intelligent, philosophical, caring, nurturing hippie chick was right up my alley. They were the American version of the Gypsy. My love for them clearly came from Gramma Conley. I would have been a good Ukrainian lover, a real swashbuckler, a good thief, a great conman, but only for the sake of the survival of my family I'm sure.

Before noon on this fine day there was this extraordinary homemade reefer bowl being passed around. It was a 3" pie tin filled with pot sitting on top of a 3" cast iron plumbing elbow attached to an 8" long straight piece of cast iron pipe. That's the great thing about pot smokers, they really know how to improvise. They can make a pipe out of anything. A Bic pen, a corncob, plain old tinfoil, the cardboard inside a toilet paper roll, soap, soap stone, brass fittings, any type of plumbing, tree branches, anything! We used to take a piece of hash, a pin, a piece of shoebox cardboard and a drinking glass. This was great. You'd stick the pin off-center up through the cardboard, stick the hash on the end of the pin and light it. Then you would place the glass over the hash depriving it from oxygen. The glass fills up with hash smoke. You move the glass to the edge of the piece of cardboard and suck the smoke from underneath, emptying the glass. Now that's a fucking toke hombre. It'll knock you right on your ass.

But about the large plumbing fixture. People placed the heavy, monstrously burdensome pipe against the bottom of their chin and over their nose engulfing their entire lower face and toked with their mouth wide open and in their nose at the same time. Everyone was gagging and stumbling all over the place. It was so much fun. I'm sure if the plumber pipe maker had more time he would have used a torch to cut out an opening to fit around the nose and the chin. But since when do stoners have time for such perfection? They barely have the wherewithal to brush their teeth or bathe. Now eating, that's an essential. Ooo man ... gotta eat, mother.

The police and the Mounties seemed to leave us alone. We weren't hurting anyone and at least we weren't damaging the stadium. Before too long the festival organizers sent a flatbed truck out among the wild banshees and set up a small PA system. Delaney & Bonnie with Eric Clapton played a couple of sets to sooth the intoxicated beasts. That's all we were asking for. "Give us some free stuff will ya?" When I went home three days later, I was across the street from my house at Ron and Melinda Richenbacher's home. I snuck in their back door and was talking to Ron about my experiences when the phone rang. It was my mom asking for me. Totally surprised, I asked her how she knew I was there. She said our beagle Humphrey hadn't been over to Ron's for three days and he was now sitting on the front steps.

I can't say as I remember being punished for running away or even talked to about it. I think my parents were just glad I was safe and back in Nedrow. I was glad too.

One time when I was a bit older I went over to Ron's house and there were about twenty people sitting cross-legged in a big circle in his living room. They had a 30 lb canister of the gas freon on a 4-wheeled dolly. Freon is a refrigerant. It's very dangerous if inhaled. It can easily be deadly. Well these idiot friends of mine were passing around the canister. Rolling it back and forth across the room. First of all, it's even more deadly when it's shaken. They were taking turns inhaling it and holding their breath for as long as they could. And then they would fall on the floor and go, "WEEEEEEEEEEEEEEEEEE, WEEEEEEEEEEEEEEE, WEEEEEEEEEEEEEE." What the fuck was this? And then they would just lie there on the floor and recover. Bullshit I thought. So I took the canister off the dolly, walked out the front door, put the canister in my van and drove off. Fucking idiots.

Chapter 32

The Young Adult Years

The Greatest Fights

A short time later after settling in from my trip to Canada I was walking home one night and ran across a party in the falling down house next to the falling down Red & White Grocery Store across from the Post Office at the top of Dutton Ave. I was way too young to be at this party. These guys were all in their mid to late 20s, I was fifteen or so. I knew most of them because, well, Nedrow is Nedrow and everybody knows everyone. You can guess who is from what family without ever meeting them before and you would probably be right. There were some tight older girls there and that's what I was trying to check out.

In no time I was upstairs in the bathroom with about six other people. There wasn't anything going on that I hadn't seen go on before. Everybody was drinking, listening to music and just partying. It was pretty late in the evening, somewhere around midnight. I just rolled in uninvited. One of the guys, it was Abraham Madison Jefferson, told me to go and get him a beer downstairs in the refrigerator. I told him no, who the fuck was he? He insisted that I leave and go get him a beer downstairs in the fridge. "No!" I said. "Who the fuck do you think you are, God?" After a few more discouraging words, old Abe leaned back and threw his big-ass fist toward my face and landed a direct hit on the side of my mouth ……. "OK!!!!" Oh SHIT that hurts! So, being the little punk that I was, I began to spew out every complimentary word that came to mind.

"ASSWIPE!

MOTHER FUCKER!

PRICK!

DICKHEAD!

STUPID FUCKING ASSHOLE!

FUCKING COCK SUCKER!

PIECE OF SHIT!

CUNT!

JACKASS!

FUCKER!

FUCKWAD!

DUMB FUCK!

COCKBITE!

JERK-OFF!

SHIT FOR FUCKING BRAINS!

FUCKING WHOREBAG!

BITCH FUCKING CUNT!

ASSHOLE MOTHER FUCKER!

FUCKER!

Okay!!!!! I'll get your fucking beer!"

So I walked slowly down the stairs bleeding like a stuck pig. On my way down I drooled, spit and wiped blood everywhere I could. All over the walls, on the handrail and the stairs, the furniture and wherever else, and then I walked out the front fucking door. "Asshole! Get your own fucking beer!"

Not long after that peaceful encounter I was once again walking up Dutton Ave one lovely evening (what is it with Dutton Ave?) from the Durochette house or at that time Howdy Edwards had an apartment on Dutton. I might have been coming from Howdy's. There was this drunken Indian standing, if you could call it standing, in middle of the street. He staggered over to me, stopped me, stood right in front of me and wouldn't let me by. I'd go to the right, he'd go to the right. I'd go to the left, he'd go to the left. Right, right, left, left, right, right, right, right, left, left. I wasn't getting by.

I was just a little guy who was used to wrestling a little black kid whose head got stuck in his mother's vagina down on West Roswell. I was a lover, not a fighter. I was the fresh water that kept the salt water from coming upstream. I was the full moon that lit the way for wayward travelers and those who run in the night. I was the light wind that air-dried the clothes hanging on the line. I was the first breath of air that entered a baby's lungs. I was the voice of reason when all else had failed. I was the one four leaf clover that every human finds and treasures. I was the new wool socks you got for Christmas. I was the five dollars you found in your old pant's pocket. I was the shiny pennies in your new loafers. I was the patch you put on your bicycle tire. When you were in need I was the friend indeed. I was the Hoo in your Hoody Do.

The drunk Injun drooled and sloberly asked me who I was. I told him Jim Murphy. He asked me if I had a brother named HarryHarry. We were the only Murphy's in town. I said yes. He said he hated my brother. (Oh great!) I was trying to negotiate my way out of the situation. "Look, he's not really my brother. I just said he was. I don't even know who he is. What did you say his first name was, Gary? I know a Gary but his name is Gary Nielsen. What's his name? Jerry Murray? No, I don't know him. Why? Did you say Jerry or Barry ... or Gary? What was it? Murphy? That's a stupid name. What is it Polish? Is he a fucking Pollock? Did you say Murphy or Murphski? No, I don't know him. Sorry." I went on and on about a bunch of nonsensicle bullshit trying to confuse the redskin. I don't remember all of what I was saying. All the time I was trying to nudge my way past this drunken idiot, but he was staying with me face-to-face, step-to-step, move-to-move. Finally, I remember him telling me to SHUT UP! and to hold my breath or he was going to beat *my* ass. "SHUT UP AND HOLD YOUR BREATH, OR I'M GONNA BEAT *YOUR* ASS!!!!" he spit at me.

So I did hold my breath ……. for as long as I could because I'm a cowardly little man/boy. After degrading me for another ten minutes and making GOD DAMN SURE I was going to tell my FUCKING ASSHOLE BROTHER HarryassHarry that some drunk-fuck Indian was looking for him and he was going to BEAT HIS ASS, he let me go. What the fuck?

Chapter 33
Fights in High School

Naturally, in all high schools there are kids that just have to fight. I went to school out in the country and the rules read that if you came to our school in the middle of the school year and you are a big, muscular adolescent, you must seek out the toughest guy in the school and try to beat the crap out of them immediately. Remember that OCS was out there in South Onondaga. These kids were from South Onondaga, Navarino, Otisco, Nedrow, and the Onondaga Nation (formerly the Onondaga Indian Reservation). A lot of these guys were big ol' farm boys. Warm as mom's apple pie, but don't get 'm riled.

I don't recall this one kid's name but he was powerfully built. His hair was as white as white can be, his eyebrows were white and his eyes were a steel blue. He was like Ottar of Dublin; scratching 5' 11.", perfect lower body to upper body proportions, the "V" shape from the svelte waist to the rock-like shoulders with arms bigger than my thighs. You know the type. I don't know where he transferred from, but Earl Thompson and Raul O'Bierne, both Navarino boys, and this new guy did not see eye-to-eye. Earl was a little old and rugged to still be in high school. He was like 35. Raul was the right age and built very similar to Ottar. It was a toss up as to who would fight the Great Norseman, Earl or Raul. Raul won by the flip of a coin. The Stairway Brawl was arranged. They would meet in the east side stairwell on the second floor. Earl would guard the upper door to the stairway making sure the fight went on uninterrupted and Mark Roth, a pretty tough boy himself, would guard the bottom doorway. No one was allowed in but the two fighters. They battled it out for a good half hour slugging, punching, choking and throwing each other down the stairs until they came to terms with each other. They were the best of friends after that. I wish I could provide more details, but I can't. No one was allowed in.

When I was in the 11th grade I punched Mike Pascarella in the head for no reason. Mike was a skinny kid like me only a little taller. He was a senior. I was a junior. Everyone liked him. I liked him too. I never had any words with him about anything. It might have had something to do with Paula Babcock. But I just walked up to him and punched him in the side of the head. It was another one of the stupidest things I have ever done and it certainly didn't help my reputation any. Sorry Mike.

Fights were great in high school because they were always so well arranged. A time, a place, and the rules. Mark Roth and Jack Walsh cared little for each other. Mark, the guy that guarded the door for the Stairwell Brawl, was a mildly heavyset lad of average height, a wise guy and really a little too mouthy for his own good. He kicked my ass one time outside the Remedy a few years later. In my instance, I had just poured a pitcher of beer over my future ex-wife's head. He and everyone else had a thing for my ex. One of my best friends at the time ended up stealing her from me when all was said and done. I should've seen that coming. But she soon dumped him and went out with several other friends of mine. She was a good catch. I just wasn't ready. What I really mean is that I wasn't mature enough yet. I was an extremely jealous dude, but more on this later.

Back to the fight …..

At 3 p.m. the school bus dropped off Mark and Jack at the corner of Brookside and Dorwin. There was a nice grassy backyard there. It was a good place for a fight. Mark was dating Raul O'Bierne's absolutely beautiful, overly-developed, little farmer's daughter sister Autumn. Autumn was stunning. Mark? Not so stunning. Mark and I were similar in that we were immature, jealous, jerk-offs. Autumn was carrying Mark's child before we graduated from high school. They even married before school was out. Mark, if you think about it, had to be tough because his wife's brother was Raul O'Bierne. But really, Raul was a very gentle soul. I'm not kidding.

Jack Walsh was a tall, wiry guy. A punk really. Sneaky and dangerous. He had big fists, a big mouth and was very fast. He just wanted to prove the point that Mark's big mouth wasn't shit. The rule of this fight and all of the others was that no one was allowed to step in. Fights were always clean, one-on-one fights. I'll say that Jack threw a few fast head shots to set the tone for the late afternoon match. Mark was more of a wrestler than a boxer so Jack's strategy was to stay clear of Roth's bone-crushing, suffocating, bear hug. Roth got a few good shots in there along the way and there was some cat and mouse wrestling. But again, they came out as closer friends with a greater respect for each other. It wasn't that great of a fight. A punk and a loud mouth; both cowards when you come right down to it. The next two fights are much better.

Chapter 34

The Battle at James E. Heath Park

This was the best fight of all. I was in the 11th grade. Nedrow and South Onondaga had some tough boys, but there were a few viciously mean legendary families that lived in the Valley right around where the Nedrow and Valley border met. The McCartneys (crazy, dangerous Irish lads. Similar, but even more dangerous than the MacColloms), Warren Roberts, a real big guy who grew up next to the McCartneys, Oren Green, harmless, but still one of the Valley clowns, and Jimmy Parish. Jimmy was a drug addict and a drunk, as were most. The Valley boys loved Jimmy, but tortured him into oblivion. He was a full-fledged idiot by the time he was 25. These guys were close friends with the Elmwood Animals; serious shit.

A rumor began to spread that Chuckie Hayford, a Nedrow lad who liked to punch steel poles with his knuckles, had a verbal battle with Mike McCartney, the younger, redheaded McCartney, at McKinley Park Pool. McKinley was a public pool way down in the Valley on West Pleasant almost to downtown. It was quite a ways from Nedrow. Back in the day it was an all-white neighborhood, but eventually turned all black and was pretty much a killin' field. So Mike and Chuckie decided to meet ten days later at James E. Heath Park at 10 a.m. James Heath was a beautiful patch of undeveloped land just north of where Warren Roberts and the McCartneys lived and across from where the MacCollom family of spies lived. The fight would be held at the old water pump. The park was one of those pieces of land that was slightly out of place in the middle of a residential neighborhood. I drove or walked by it a million times on my way to Meachem Elementary when we lived on Salina or to the Valley Diner and church school when we lived in Nedrow, but never went inside the forest. The historic Iroquois Trail crossed here. This trail was later used by the Dutch in 1634 by Jesuit Missionaries. The property eventually became a part of Syracuse University's State College of Forestry until they turned it over to the City of Syracuse.

Chuckie never really knew why he was supposed to fight McCartney. All he knew was that he was being challenged and that he had to accept. You can't go around punching steel poles and then back down from a little fight with one of the most menacing families in the Valley. It just ain't proper behavior. At 10 a.m. everybody from Nedrow, even the Rags (the girls who hung around with us) and everyone from the Valley found their way inside the park. It was a thick woods with super tall pines and a blanket of pine needles a few inches deep covering the ground. There was a ditch down the center that at one time carried water to seedlings planted by the University. The now dry ditch was a good four feet deep and fifteen feet wide. The Valley spectators were on the north side of the ditch and the Nedronians were on the south, close to home in case we had to turn and run screaming like little girls. Mike McCartney, upon seeing Chuckie, comes to the realization that Chuckie was NOT the person he had words with at McKinley Pool. Chuckie agrees and states as he had several times that he had never met Mike McCartney before. The audience gasped in shuttered amazement and mumbled for a few moments while the situation was settled. Warren Roberts soon calls everyone's attention. "Ladies and gentlemen, distinguished guests. Since we have all taken precious time out of our work and family schedules to be here today and have all gathered together on this beautiful Saturday morning in James E. Heath Park (a very elegant language for such a brutal thug) our special guest representing Nedrow, Mr. Chuckie Hayford, and our own hometown lad Mr. Michael McCartney, not wanting to let their company of fans, brothers, sisters and erstwhile protectors down, being the men that they are, have decided to fight anyway." Holy Shit! The mumbling gets louder and louder like it may have during the renaissance before a torture session and hanging. Both sides start chanting, "Chuckie, Chuckie, Chuckie, Chuckie ..... Michael, Michael, Michael, Michael, Chuckie, Michael, Chuckie, Michael!!!!!!"

Really, Nedrow and the Valley could have broken into battle at this exact moment except, like I said, we Nedronians weren't known for our toughness. No one in Nedrow owned a gun. Everyone in the Valley owned a gun. We were smoking pot. They were robbing pharmacies. We had never been to jail. They had all been to jail. I was fighting girls ... well, they were too, only it was referred to as beating women. I was still being driven around by my parents. They were stealing and smashing cars. We were kids living at home. They were fucking real gangsters, gigantic men, many still living at home so there was that single commonality, but you get the picture.

It was decided that Warren Roberts would be the one and only judge and the only person who could stop the fight. If anyone from either side jumped in and tried to join the fight, Warren would personally beat them to a mutilated, unrecognizable pulp. Okay. I understand that. Off they went. Chuckie was a little taller than Mike, but they were both in their prime. Chuckie was left handed and had knuckles swollen by quarter-inch steel. He threw a strong left and nailed Mike in the head. Mike swiftly counterattacked with a right and a left.

Chuckie came back. This wasn't a wrestling match. This was a bare-knuckled fist fight in the woods. It was the real deal. Up and down both sides of the ditch. If someone slipped, the opponent would give them time to reestablish themselves and then they'd be back at it. Chuckie was bleeding. Mike was bleeding. Back and forth in the perfect bare-knuckle stance. It was like watching John L. Sullivan and Paddy Ryan in Mississippi City in 1882.

The fight lasted for a good half hour and then just like that it was over. Who won? Both were bloodied, but standing. Beaten, but willing to continue. Proud and willing to win at all odds for their people. Warren Roberts stepped in and stopped the fight. There were no contradictory statements from the audience. He carefully examined each man with Oren Green at his side. Everyone was quietly talking among themselves and then Warren turned and asked for our attention. "Ladies and gentlemen. Friends and perhaps even enemies. This has been the greatest fight I have ever witnessed, and I've witnessed many." There is dead silence. "These two soldiers," he continued, "came together today on neutral ground. One man from the north and one man from the south. Both similar in shape and size. Both of similar upbringings. Both not only representing their family's proud name and heritage, but representing entire communities. Communities separated by a single lane of pavement, Dorwin Ave. We, the northerners, live throughout this great Valley north to Elmwood. You, the southerners, live among the roads meandering through the great farms and townships of the beloved countryside.

We traveled here today to find an answer to much more than which of these strong men is more powerful. An answer to much more than who can knock the other down and bloody the other's face. This is about much more than who would win and who would lose. This union today drew blood from both sides. The blood of Charles Hayford lies on the fists of Michael McCartney. The blood of Michael McCartney lies on the fists of Charles Hayford. Bleeding flesh is not the answer. The bruised and battered bodies of these two men does not warrant a greater division of our peoples, but perhaps creates room for active, positive engagement. A solidarity among our people. A joining together of two unique forces that I see benefiting both communities. It was fate that drew us here to begin with if you recall. Some lying, sniveling weasel of a man, who shall be found and dealt with, spread a vicious rumor that one of these men threatened the other, thus leading to this challenge, to this very duel you witnessed today. It was an inner pride instilled in both these heroes that shone today like a beacon that can only be compared to the rising sun that provides our Earth with energy and light for daily growth. We, our two peoples, divided by a single lane of asphalt, represented by these men, are the true beacons of light. As two unique and shining peoples, let it be known that I am not suggesting we join forces under one rule, under one ruler and compromise the individual freedoms we each consider dear to our cultural heritage, but that we recognize our strengths and allow freedom of trade over the Dorwin Ave Compromise. That we may open our borders and not see our differences, but see our similarities." (Diane Johnston, a Nedrow girl half this giant's size, was swooning, weak at the knees, eyes batting like a starving monarch butterfly's wings, leaning into Robert's every word as if he was speaking to her and her alone. This was probably the first time Diane had ever been across Dorwin Ave. As tiny as Diane was, she would soon steal the heart of this great giant of a man). "Therefore, as the judge, referee, overseer, and chosen guard of the one-on-one battle of strength, maneuverability and cunning strategy, (he drew the two battlers together raising their arms to meet above their heads) I state before all of you that this match is a draw. That an equal amount of blood was drawn from both contenders and that this day be remembered in infamy for toughness, and above all else, for fairness. And that these two men, Michael McCartney and Charles Hayford both become part of our proud cultural histories." Everyone went wild. Both sides crossed the ditch and began mingling, joking and talking like we were one. Like we had always been one. It was an incredible moment. This boundary between the Nedronians and the Valley was never shaken again. In the history of the world, this is one of the few treaties that has lasted forever.

Later, it was found out that it was Johnny Moyle who had words with Mike McCartney at McKinley Pool. It was he who said he was Chuckie Hayford. Soon after this information was delivered to Chuckie, he found Moyle and beat the living crap out of him.

Chapter 35
White Man VS Indian

That same summer a big rumor began to spread that there was going to be an all out brawl between the alliance now forged between the white guys from Nedrow and the Valley, and the Onondaga Indians. The Valley turf was big. It stretched from the Valley where I used to live on Salina Street, over to Valley Drive stretching north to Elmwood. Elmwood was in a class all its own. They had the legendary Elmwood Animals who were real thieves who used real guns and real drugs – this was in the 60s and early 70s. Their fearless leader at the time that I was introduced to the Animals was Donnie Lugar. Donnie was this little guy about 5' 6" tall. He looked like a little version of Freddie (the Devil) Sowers. All the Devil guys I knew resembled Alfred E. Newman. They all had square heads, buck teeth, big ears and messy hair. But don't think for a moment they were stupid. You don't become the Devil or the leader of the Elmwood Animals by being stupid. You can look stupid, but somehow, by actions that others deem credible, you rise to the top and are not to be fucked with. The first time I met Lugar he was sauntering around, shooting the shit, laughing, smoking a cigarette, nothing really out of the ordinary. His voice and his mannerisms, not surprisingly, had a distinct tone and swagger that reminded me of Humphrey Bogart or Clark Gable, but Lugar was his own person, no doubt about that. He looked up to me, but only because he was shorter. I think it was Kipp Squirley who introduced us. Kipp is another Valley-boy story all together. Like I was saying, Donnie was smoking so he had a cigarette in his hand. As quick as lightning he cupped the cigarette so the burning end

was inside his palm rather than sticking out away from his fingers the way cigarettes usually are. He shook my hand firmly and burned the shit out of the inside palm of my hand with the lit end of the cigarette. It hurt like a bastard and naturally I pulled my hand away screaming, "WHAT THE FUCK! WHAT THE FUCK!
WHAT THE FUCK, MAN!
WHAT THE FUCK WAS THAT?"
Everyone got a huge laugh out of it. After a few moments I too gave into laughter. It was brilliantly executed. Masterful. A genius move. I'd never seen it before and have never seen it since. No wonder Lugar was the bossman. I was sold. "I will follow you anywhere. You is my new hero." Because really, he could have sliced my wrist off or something much more gruesome. Cut off my ear and shoved it down my throat, tied weights around my limbs and tossed me to the bottom of Onondaga Creek or just had me buried alive in Elmwood Cemetery. He could have done anything! So in a way I felt lucky. I also felt as though I was initiated into the Valley Brotherhood that day. Of course, that wasn't true and I knew that, but I felt a little bit initiated. These were the meanest fucking dudes on the entire planet and that was a brilliant handshake.

Musically, Donnie was a blues man. He and Kipp introduced the blues to the Valley and to everyone they came into contact with. I saw Donnie perform at a little club in Syracuse called the Foxy Lady down off Burnet Ave somewhere when I was maybe 18 years old. It was a 3-piece band. Don played guitar and sang. I don't remember who was backing him up. Bobby Neary could have been on bass I suppose. I had never seen anyone play guitar leads and sing before. To me it was like watching Hendrix. I was blown away.

A couple of years later I had the honor to play bass for Donnie. By this time he was either hooked on heroin or was trying to get off heroin. Maybe he would show up for the gigs and maybe he wouldn't. He was usually good for one or two sets and then he was gone, who knows where. He could take a perfectly tuned guitar and make it sound totally out of tune.

The drugs were just sucking him down into the Earth. When he placed his fingers on the strings his hands were so heavy that they bent the strings downward and out of tune. He could barely stand upright. He was a blurry human shape trapped in a shaking spoonful of junk sinking deeper and deeper in to the deep black tar pit of user hell. A black and blues globule. His face was drooping like it was made from hot wax. His beautiful, rich voice was slurred a few rpms below 33 1/3. His timing was one needle in the vein off. His eyes were somewhere back in his skull. Of course, Kipp, his feeder, who had one eye that looked over there and another eye that looked elsewhere, was usually hunched over, sniveling around somewhere just out of sight. Lugar was the original blues guy from Syracuse that I remember. I really thought the world of him. At least I got to play and record with him. He was a true hero of mine.

Somewhere along the way he ended up hating me for some blues-related reason. He stopped talking to me and considered me just another fuck-up. One lost night up in Elmwood he passed out drunk in a snow bank and the docs had to cut off one of his legs due to frostbite. He was also diagnosed with diabetes.

A couple of years later on one freezing cold winter's day I was walking through the icy slush and snow of downtown Syracuse and there on the corner sat this blanketed figure with his back to me stuck in the snow just sitting there helpless. I went over to see if he needed help. It was Donnie in a wheelchair waiting for someone, anyone, to help push him across the street. He was as surprised to see me as I was him. We laughed and talked for a bit. He was going to the County building to pick up his disability check or something. He apologized for treating me like shit for the past few years. I told him it was no big deal. I pushed him to the building, held the door for him, we shook hands and that was the last I ever saw of my hero Donnie Lugar. He died sometime later.

Looking back, in some ways, the real reason there may have been a co-mingling called for by Warren Roberts at James E. Heath was so the Valley gang could open up new avenues to sell their drugs. Nedrow and South Onondaga were like the Bobbsey Twins compared to those guys. While pot and hash were the big thing in the country, LSD, mescaline, mushrooms, speed, cocaine, morphine, reds and even heroin was available through the Valley. These delicacies suddenly became much more prevalent in God's special place on Earth we now refer to as Nedrow. The deluge was on. Drugs were everywhere. I'm not saying I didn't partake, but I am saying that serious drugs were never a real part of my life. I had enough mental problems without traveling into another dimension or hiding from the daylight or stumbling around unable to control my physical being. Where the hell is the fun in that? Pot was never even a favorite of mine for the simple reason that I was my own worst enemy. I hated myself. Pot always made me look farther inward than I was already looking. And besides, I've known the *Meaning of Life* since I was 15 and had no need to delve any deeper. I was the *Meaning of Life* - well, not really, but "I" meaning my bodily presence as a temple was the encompassed *Meaning of Life*. I *was* the Universe. I was filled with Life's Inner Galaxies. I was Who All Sought, the Deity, the Levitator, I could Walk Underwater, I was Scarred, I had been Stricken and Burned. I'd been Deviant, Credulous, in Love, Broken, Tied, Shamed, and All That Stuff. I was All God Ever Needed Within Myself.

Drugs, as we all know, are mind altering and I understood the fragile chemical makeup of Man. Believe me, I'm not alone when it comes to inner fragility. There were Justin Phillipses roaming all over the Valley. Justin was a long, wavy, blond haired drug servant (savant) who everyone worshipped because of his accessibility to drugs and his ability to correctly use drugs and still function. But to be honest, Justin wasn't really functioning. He could barely talk, at least by the time I knew him (I never really knew him very well. I wasn't a part of that deep inner circle). I don't think I ever heard him speak when I was around. He probably didn't trust me. I could give a shit really. I had other more pressing problems like remaining sane in my own little world of mass insecurity. Justin eventually overdosed on some "correct" mixture of one thing or another.

My new group of friends sure were a far cry from my old ones. These guys were dangerous, and like I said, I wasn't really into drugs all that much so they had reason to be suspicious. One thing for sure, I was not a narc. I just didn't want to lose my ability to think straight, but you had to do some type of drug if you were going to hang with these guys. I wasn't the only person accused of being a narc. Jake Byers was also. Jake was much more in tune with these guys than I was. He was more their age. Jake was a damn good artist and an all right musician. I don't remember Jake ever having a job, so he was doing something on the side to get by. There were a few Nedronians who never worked. As an artist, Byers was the type of artist who never sold his art. I wanted to buy a piece once and he wouldn't sell anything. What is the purpose of creating art if you can't let it go? Let's see, you don't work, you never have money, and you won't sell your art. Like I said, I'm not the only one with problems.

For about a week the rumor of the new Indian War was spreading. It would take place at 7 p.m. in the Rockwell Elementary School side yard next to the Nedrow Lumberyard up from the Holy Tabernacle Tiny House of Worship. The White kids and the Indian kids were going to settle the 200-year land dispute themselves. I was with these guys acting the role of a tough 120 lb guy, but I was pretty scared. There were probably, I'd say, 30 of us White guys. A fine mix of the Nedrow boys, South Onondaga boys and Valley boys. The tension was high and grew higher as the time passed. 6:30 came and went and the White folks were still arriving with their baseball bats, 2x4s, chains, branches and all kinds of hand-to-hand combat weaponry. No knives that I knew of and no guns, but I wasn't checking everyone so I really don't know what anyone was carrying. Ten minutes to seven came and slowly went. No Indians. No sign of them. We decided to be quiet and listen out the final ten minutes in silence. Cigarettes were being smoked. There wasn't any alcohol. No drugs (that was unusual). Seven o'clock came and went. No Indians.
COWARDS!

"No wonder we took their land from them!" "They deserve everything they get!" "Oh man, this would have been great!" "We would have kicked their asses!" There was nothing sweeter than this victory. This was the first time after the Hayford/McCartney Fight of the Century that we were all together. There was a true sense of camaraderie and fellowship. There were no grand speeches, although this would have been a good time for one. I don't know who would have spoken for Nedrow since we were on our turf. Not the Durochett's because they had a lot of close Indian friends. I'm surprised they were even there. Peter Farrington might have been the right person. He was already friends with Nedrow, the South Onondagans, and the Valley boys; loved by all, but he was dead. Who was our leader? Dean Krone? No. Tony? No. Curt or Carey Schneiderman, Neuman or Shorty Walker, Marc Sterns, Karl Craigue (too stoned or he might have been the Chosen One), Randy Ducane (Randy would have given a great speech. He had a gift with words, but his unique phrasing might have confused everyone even though his bent philosophy would have somehow been illogically correct), Manny or Chuckie Hayford, Mark Roth, Kerrie Rafter, Jake Byers, Fritz Kringle, Louis Paisley, Kelly Fitzpatrick, Scott West, Earl Thompson, the Boyds, Sean or Patrick MacCollom (who had moved to South Onondaga by this time). No one really fit the bill. We were leaderless and that was probably a good thing for everyone. We were just a bunch of kids from Nedrow and South Onondaga.

We were all in the middle of celebrating the White Man's second conquest of the Red Man and considering the best place to purchase and guzzle firewater when the next thing you know a cop drives east on Hudson Ave real slow. We were kind of hidden in a gully next to the school, but we were still makin' a ruckus. Silent warriors waiting in the tall pines and aspens we were no longer. He drove by slow again, slowing down to look right at us – shit! Somebody sold us out! Somebody turned us in! We ran like thieves in the night. No one got caught. We had won!

Fucking cowards. Stupid-ass Indians.

Chapter 36
Surprise Attack

The Onondaga Nation is a small reservation consisting of around 7,300 acres. 99.9% of their original land was taken illegally by the State of New York or some other government entity. The entire City of Syracuse and surrounding communities sit on Onondaga territory. As the treaty reads, or so I was told one day, the Indians still received blankets and some rice or something from the State every year. Something silly like that. Onondaga (the keepers of the Central Fire) is considered to be the capital of the Haudenosaunee, a name meaning "People of the Longhouse." The Haudenosaunee are sometimes referred to as the Iroquois Confederacy or the Six Nations. They are considered to be one of, if not the, oldest democracy on Earth and provided an important model for the White Man's Founding Fathers when developing the United States Constitution. They are known around the world as a peaceful, loving people and for having an oral history tradition that is passed down from generation to generation.

I was at the Remedy Tavern one night, a new bar that opened up sometime around 1972, right around the time I was getting out of high school. It was on the corner of Valley Drive and Seneca Turnpike. Everybody went there. We were all weaned in the Remedy and the Nedrow Tavern. I was standing at the bar minding my own business when these Indians came in. I had no idea who they were. Even though Nedrow shared a border with the Onondaga Nation and you knew everybody in Nedrow, not the same could be said for the Reservation. You only knew the Indians you went to school with. Inside the Reservation wasn't any place we hung around. Most of the Indians went to Lafayette High School anyway.

So I'm standing at the bar minding my own business and these Indians come in and stand pretty close to me and they're talking about this White guy they are going to beat the crap out of. Well, I'm only half listening because for one, I don't want to know who they're talking about, and two, it's none of my business, and three, I'm not going to mess with these gigantic, woolly primates. I have my couple of drinks and walk out of the Remedy. They follow me out and beat the living crap out of me. THEY WERE TALKING ABOUT ME! I don't even know who these guys were. Maybe I was singled out as 'a guy' who was at Rockwell claiming victory over the "stupid-ass Indians." Or maybe it was that drunken Indian from Dutton Ave getting revenge for me not telling HarryHarry that he was looking for him. Or maybe he found HarryHarry and HarryHarry beat the shit out of *him* instead of the other way around. I never did find out who they were or why I was targeted.

Chapter 37

High School Life

Skipping School

Life just keeps going on and on. There's no stopping it. Sometimes I win the toss, other times I get tossed. I get up in the morning, take a shower, brush my gnarly hair, brush my chipped teeth, put on some fairly clean clothes, grab a bite and head out the door. "Bye mom." I never intended to become a chronic school skipper like my neighbor down the street Tony was in the fifth grade, but who can really plan that far in the future. And as you might guess by now, I wasn't the smartest kid in school, but I'll have to agree with my mother, if I had only applied myself I might have been. Maybe if I was forced to apply myself I would have been. Maybe if we were educated and not brought up in a poor, work-for-a-living, you'll-never-get-anywhere-anyway environment, I might have been the smartest. We weren't poor poor, we were a regular working-stiff family. Bob the Father and the Virgin Betty did a good job with all of us. They truly did all they knew how to do. They taught us survival skills. They taught us to be polite. They taught us to respect others. They taught us to be patient. They taught us to enjoy life. Life is enjoyable no matter what level of financial security you are surrounded by. You are what you is. Our family credo was: work hard and you *might* get somewhere. It wasn't: study hard and you *will* get somewhere.

I skipped a lot of school between my sophomore and senior years. I wouldn't skip the entire day, that would be wrong. Here's how it worked. If you showed up at OCS by 10 a.m. your name appeared on the absent list so you could skip whatever class you wanted to from that point on and no one would know the difference. This didn't always work because the school was so small it was kind of hard to avoid people and avoid teachers. But also, by showing up prior to 10 a.m. you didn't need a written excuse as to why you were late.

More often than not, me and the boys, Fritz, Kerry Rafter and me, would drive out through South Onondaga or out to Otisco roaming the country roads. Sometimes we would ride with Chris Young in his new 289 Mustang over to Barker Hill Rd. There was this real steep uphill run on Barker and then the road immediately leveled out. If Chris got up enough speed, which was easy to do in the Mustang, we would fly with all four wheels off the ground. It was great fun. We would just drive down country roads not knowing where we were headed, take a right here, a left there, who cared? We had this one favorite stop along the way, an open-air barn where a farmer stacked his hay. We would climb on the stacks and make long tunnels and forts. It was amazing. Just good ol' country boy mischief. We never burned the place down or did any damage or anything.

Someone, and I think it was Chris, found this place he called the Blue Hole. It was way down this driveway, through the dark woods to this private summer home of a retired foreign agent somewhere off Case Hill Rd. An old couple seemingly from England or Australia lived there and they didn't mind us coming there as long as we stopped in, said cheerio or g'day, signed their visitor log and signed out when we were done goofing off. They never called the school. The Blue Hole was inspiring. It was a small waterfall or more like a water chute that the creek ran through and then dropped about twenty feet into this natural bowl hollowed out by the force of the water pounding on it for a million or so years. You could do one of three things at the Blue Hole, slide down the chute, I don't remember ever doing that, walk down a path to the creek, I did that plenty of times, or you could stand on this perch to the side of and above the falls and step off into the pool below. You didn't want to 'jump' off because you'd crash into the other side. The whole thing was probably only 10' wide from one side to the other. There was a fairly straight up shale wall on the opposite side. There was shale everywhere. When you did take that step off, it was frightening to say the least. The first time I stepped off I stood there for an hour before I got up the nerve. "Okay, I'm ready. No, I can't do it. Okay, I'm ready now. No, shit, I can't do it." "You Turkey," someone yelled. Meanwhile everybody else is stepping off. When you did step off you were falling into a small, deep pool of water. It was hairy, no doubt about it, but it was also great to be outdoors in the woods loving life in the cool, cool, rushing waters of South On and Otisco and not in school.

Chapter 38
The Chevy 409

At some point in the 10th grade my mom allowed me to be picked up in the mornings and ride with these juniors and seniors to school. Johnny Lightning, whose favorite saying was, "Life is one crazy thing after another," owned a candy apple red Chevy Impala convertible with a 4-barrel 409 in it. It was the talk of the town. I remember four instances with Johnny. He hung with Sammy Gaines, whose pet peeves were work and teachers and Luminous (Jimmy Waiters) who was also a close friend, and I can't remember who else, but I shouldn't have been allowed to be hanging with these guys. They were way to mature for me.

We were on our way to school, racing in Johnny's 409 down Rt. 11A through the reservation, up Indian Hill and south on Rt. 80 toward school. OCS, by the way, is the proud home of the Tigers. "O-N-O-N-D-A-G-A, Hu-rah, hu-rah, Onondaga Rah!" was our cheer. There was Rockwell Elementary in Nedrow, K-6 for the kids that lived in Nedrow. There was

Wheeler Elementary right next to the high school that was K-6 for the country folk. And the main building was for all junior and senior high school students together. There were 700 kids enrolled in K-12 and 111 kids in my senior class at the beginning of the year. I'm not sure how many finished.

On this day, instead of turning left onto Lords Hill which takes us to school, Johnny decides to go straight onto Tanner Rd. If you were to turn onto to Lords Hill toward school, the first part of it is a winding, snakelike road and then it straightens out to the school. Going down Tanner, the option we chose, is a long, straight run with a couple of nice, elongated dips along the way. On a normal day we would have taken Tanner to Makyes Road, taken a left on Makyes back down to Rt. 80, taken another left and gone to school. No big deal, it's just a couple more miles and a few more minutes of freedom before entering the halls of sub-par learning. So we jump onto Tanner and Johnny floors it. We are floating on the early fall pavement at an unexaggerated 90 mph. I'm developing one of those urges I have every once in a while where out of nowhere I have been able to take that soft, giant step .... and another step a bit further than the last .... and another one a bit further .... all the time in beautiful slow motion … and finally ..... I take my last step .... and I'm flying again. Oh my God, it's been a few years since I've tried this. The last time was when I shot out Gary Nielsen's windows. This is beautiful! This is so easy. Why don't I do this more often? I know I've talked about flying before, but one of the great things about flying like I fly is the total control you have over your flight pattern. It isn't necessarily about speed or dive-bombing although I've dreamt about flying at hyper-speeds and dive-bombing, it's really more about silence, freedom, no rules and nowhere to go. I swear to you, this time when I see my shadow on Earth it really is me flying and not the shadow of a bird. Maybe I just want it to be me so badly that I see my own image. Maybe I need it to be me. Maybe *I* need to be me. Maybe I need to *be*. Life is very confusing to me. Almost everyone seems so sure of themselves. They seem to know just what it is they're doing, where they're headed and how they are going to get there. I'm just going along for the ride. I *do* know what it is that I will and won't do so that's a good thing, but I'm still doing things that I shouldn't do. I've got to knock the pot smoking off. I'm just not into it. I think when I graduate from school I'm going to leave town and just get the hell out of here. Maybe Jennifer MacCollom was right. My fame and fortune just ain't happenin' here.

Enough of the daydreaming! Why am I daydreaming when I'm flying? What am I nuts? I haven't flown in years. Nobody I know can fly but me and I'm depressed? Come on Murf, snap out of it brother.

Oh, this is the life right here. I'm amazed at the simplicity of keeping aloft. No effort whatsoever. A quick head-nod to the right and I go right. A slight arch of the back and I gain in altitude. I do have to keep my arms out away from my sides. I have never questioned that, even when I flew as a bird, it's just natural. How can you fly if you don't have some sort of wings? I should show my flying skills off a bit more often, maybe I would get a few more girls. I've never even tested to see if when you hold a girl's hand if she automatically becomes a part of you, and as long as she holds your hand you both fly effortlessly like Peter Pan did. It should work that way (it worked a little when I supposedly kissed Cheryl Hartman). I've wasted a lot of time doing other stupid things, but from now on flying is part of my regular routine. But for now, I'd better pay attention to what's at hand and quit dreaming about the future. I find my way back to the 409. Nobody even missed me while I was gone. They were going too fast to worry about me.

At the very end of this section of Tanner Road, over this little knoll in the road, lies a stop sign at Tanner and Makyes. Unbeknownst to the rest of us I think Johnny was going to play chicken. I think his intent was to run the stop sign blind at 90 mph. Today there was only one problem. A fully loaded Samson Concrete truck with its first load of the day was glistening in the country sunshine and stopped at the stop sign. I'm surprised I didn't see this predicament while I was flying a few moments earlier, but I didn't. If I had seen it I wouldn't be strapped into the backseat of a candy apple red convertible with chrome trim Chevy Impala 4-barrel 409 with skinny whitewall tires going 90 miles an hour. I would have arched my back ever so slightly, easily risen above the cement truck and been on my way never giving it a second thought. But the fact remained that I was in the backseat of a candy apple red convertible with chrome trim Chevy Impala 4-barrel 409 with skinny whitewall tires that was cruising at 90 miles an hour!

I'm not sure how the miracle happened, especially since I don't believe in miracles or witchcraft or Jesus (well, I believe in Jesus, just not that He was the Son of God because I don't believe in God, and it's really not that I don't believe in God, it's just that I don't believe that God the creator of the entirety of everything for ever and ever including the wisdom He must possess and the vastness of His physicalness for holding all comprehension of all who are and all that is and ever has been and forever shall be, knows where Earth is). I also don't believe in Aphrodite, Venus, Bellona, Eos, Hades (well maybe, I mean you don't have to believe in heaven in order to believe in a hell), Chang Hsi, Fortuna, Geb, Magna Mater, Inanna, Lato, Nemesis, Ki, Pan, Quetzalcoatl, Rama, Ōyamatsumi, or Utu. What brought on this divine providence? What was it that saved our souls that day and allowed us to pursue our after-the-almost-certain-death-crash life? We were certainly flying eight feet in the air over the last knoll and with a little more advance notice we too probably could have cleared the top of the truck and continued down Tanner toward the Tanner Valley Golf Course. That was feasible; somewhat cartoonish, but possibly feasible. Fly over the truck and just keep going.

We all see the back-ass of the cement truck at the same time. Johnny does what comes naturally, he slams on his brakes. Chevy's are fucking great. The Chevy's brakes miraculously functioned in midair. We, still while in midair, somehow, in the slowest of slow motion, power-slide in silence to a hard right and came to a completely quiet, unjolting stop a mere inch from the back of the several-ton truck. We came to a complete halt eight feet in the air. It *was* a miracle! We could look around, but no one could speak a word, everything was perfectly still. Everything. There is no sound at this slow of a pace by the way. This must be where the Indians go when they are deep into their chanting. They go where only they can go. Others who chant; the Hindus, the monks and all the rest go elsewhere I'm sure. When the Indians reach this state, and as we can now see, they go back before recorded time; before the Intrusion. As I look around from my motionless state of consciousness, there are no houses, no roads, telephone poles, fences, stop signs or anything! Life is pure. Deer, buffalo, and all sorts of animals are everywhere and roam freely. The woods are densely thick because nothing has been cleared to make life easier for us Colonists. The world is in its natural state. This is the world the Indian came from and wishes to return to. We, the Intruders, unjustifiably took this from them, this beautiful, serene place. It's sad. The four of us are emotionally submersed in its natural beauty.

At a 90° angle to the back of the truck, in the superset of slow motion, we slid sideways and came to a stop, and then, ever so slowly were lowered to the ground by the grace of God or whomever or whatever. It *was* a miracle! We were all there. Holy Fucking Shit!

The Samson's driver, oblivious, put it in first gear and ground forward. Johnny slipped it into first gear and we pulled a cautious 180 and continued down Makyes and silently went on to school. It was an invisible miracle. That's what it was. A shocking miracle. A miracle beyond description. A miracle that we each knew had taken place, but were unable to rationalize. Like the giganticness of outer space, it was more than our mental faculties could piece together. It was a baby Jesus miracle. A lifting of the Jeep miracle. A Santa miracle. A little league miracle. A Nedrow African Tribal Women miracle. A hitchhiking miracle. A breast miracle. A Holy Roller miracle. A Vanessa Erekson miracle. A snowball miracle. A holding my breath miracle. We were healed, fed, clothed and sheltered. It temporarily changed all of our lives. We never spoke of it … ever, but when we would see each other in the hallways and after school we knew we were a part of something very special.

Chapter 39

The Rape

That weekend, right after this life-changing event where we learned our lesson in fragility, I was with Lightning and a couple of the guys and we did two things. Both events took place on the same evening. Again, I never should have been with these guys, they being 17 or 18 and me only 15.

No one ever had much money except for beer and drugs. What else would you need money for? Everyone was living at home. We were riding out through South Onondaga only this time we had a passenger. Johnny's beautiful, dirty-blond haired, countrified, honorably innocent, upright, law-abiding, squeaky-clean, inoffensively modest, undefiled, lily-white, gullibly virginal, easily persuaded, wet behind the ears, doe-eyed novice of a girlfriend. Just a regular old gal who was insatiably crazy about this strappingly tall, blond haired, blue eyed, very funny senior named Johnny Lightning. As we raced through the country roads we came to the realization that we were running low on gas. There were no gas stations in the country, but back in those days farmers all had their own giant tanks filled with gas. They never locked them because no one ever stole anything because they lived in the country. Doors were open, widows were open, cars were open, pretty much everything was unlocked. Peace reigned through the hills and valleys. Well, now the Nedrow boys were on the loose and nothing was safe, not even your lovely daughter. As we wandered through the country roads, we finally found a tank fairly close to the road. We quietly idled up next to it, partially filled up Johnny's tank and quietly drove off into the night. The mission was perfectly accomplished.

The next thing I know we've pulled over to the side of the road because Johnny wants to get laid by his countrified girlfriend. Okay, so she wasn't that innocent, she was still just a little girl to me. Johnny tells us all to get out of the vehicle and we oblige. He bangs her right there in the car while the three of us stand around smoking a joint, drinking a beer, shooting the shit, trying not to pay attention to the lucky fuckers sucking and fucking in the fucking 409. When he's finished he asks her to oblige the other two guys .... and me! He is telling her that if she really loves him, she will do this for him. It would mean so much to him. Of course he loves her he says. Why wouldn't he? "Come on, what's the big deal? A dick is a dick," he says. "No one is going to say anything." He would do it for her if the circumstances were reversed. If she wanted him to fuck her girlfriends while she stood by and watched, he would. All the while he is saying this he's still playing with her cum-filled, juicier than a mother fucker pussy, and occasionally leaning over sucking on her corn-fed tits. I couldn't believe it. I just couldn't believe it. I didn't like the sound of it. She's not saying much because when a woman's pussy is being played with especially after she just got fucked, she can't think straight. She'll do anything. She's in a pussy-rubbing trance. She's mentally blind. It's no different than playin' with a guy's pecker really. If you want your guy to do fucking anything for you, play with his dick. The pussy and the dick have more control over a person than anything else. We fall into a stupor. We become dumbfuckers. We do unreasonable requests. I will literally rob a bank if you play with my dick through the entire robbery. I will dress up like King Faruke and walk down the middle of Salina Street if you promise to play with my dick the entire time. Lightning's little country sweetie is no different that any other human. If she were stroking Lightning's cock and her girlfriends were standing in line, he would fuck all of them whether he wanted to or not. He would die trying to cum as many times as he could. If a woman really wants to kill her old man off, she doesn't need to waste her money on a hit-man. All she has to do is fuck the bastard all day, every day. He'll be dead in a week. One thing she *could* bet on is that she will get everything he owns because any man will gladly make a woman who sucks and fucks all day the only heir to his estate. That's the simple truth people. All men are simpletons. Stupid shits. Women fuck us up by not fucking us. Men have destroyed civilizations over the lack of nookie. We men want to get laid every fucking day. Please don't tell us no for any reason. Why do you do that? Humans have to fuck and be fucked. Especially out in the country. Especially in South Onondaga. While women may argue this point, men will not. Men don't fuck all day because somewhere along the way women persuaded us that we have other duties to perform. They threatened us with no pussy until the work was done, and even then they have to think about giving it up. Unfortunately, we men, we tortured poor souls became pussy-whipped and gave in. It's our own fault.

Oddly, women leave men because they don't get fucked enough, but they forget that they trained the poor fucker to only fuck them on command. Then some guy comes along and throws her on the bed or the floor or the backseat of a car and fucks her brains out. The defeated husband hates himself because he's wanted to do that every day for the last ten years, but he had been trained by the bitch not to touch her except when she wanted to be touched. It sucks, man. It sucks. It's unfortunate for everyone, but especially for us poor men.

In this particular case of the cunt in the country, our little waif does oblige, whimpering part of the time. It's really hard to tell the difference between whimpering and the low volume loving of probable enjoyment. She may have been whimpering just for Johnny's sake and truly enjoying the entire event. Think about it. She fucked three guys. She did what most or all women want to do. Fuck everybody in sight.

In any case, I did not partake. I just couldn't do it. I'm a trained humanitarian sympathetic to those of lesser means. Did I stand up and shout, "No, you can't touch this woman! She is a member of the weaker sex and deserves better than this type of barbarian treatment. You assholes! Leave her alone!" No, I didn't. However, this is about the end of me hangin' with the big guys. I'm not this type of person. Who the fuck am I though? Fuck!

There was one more incident. Johnny had this white '63 Dodge Polaris. He wanted to collect the insurance money on it because he didn't want the car anymore or it didn't run or something. So we either pushed it or towed it to Quarry Road on the Reservation. Sarah Nighthawk's stepdad owned a quarry up there. We put it in neutral and pushed it over a cliff. Johnny reported it stolen and got the insurance check in the mail.

Chapter 40
The Painting of OCS

As I have reiterated throughout this book, I've developed the accurate reputation for always being in some sort of trouble because to put it simply, I was always in some sort of trouble. Nothing major may I remind you. Maturing trouble. I was a good kid who was bored. In reality, all of my old friends were pretty much doing the same thing I was, but I did drift away from them and as we know, it's hard to go backward without asking for forgiveness of some sort. I didn't need forgiveness because I didn't do anything wrong. I had just moved onward and I would say upward, but that probably isn't right. It wasn't even a lateral move. I'm not sure what kind of move it was, but everyone gets into trouble at some point to some degree. The difference was that I kept getting into trouble most of the time. Nothing major. Did I already say that?

I was now in the summer between 11th and 12th grade. I had my driver's license. My dad bought me my first car for $400. It was a black Plymouth Belvedere with a blue interior. It had a 3-speed on the column and a 383 under the hood. It was awesome. Quite a few times I drove it over 100 miles an hour coming back from skiing at Song Mountain in Tully, NY. Going 100 miles an hour on a freezing cold winter's night with a carload of friends after drinking 32 ounce beers all night is just plain stupid to begin with, but we did it several times.

I was attending summer school for algebra at Corcoran High School that summer which was up past Elmwood. There were a few OCSers there so I wasn't alone. One day when we were all released from the morning session I see this cute little dirty-blond haired girl dancing up Corcoran's driveway with seemingly not a care in the world. She wasn't crazy, but she was looking for attention and she sure caught my eye. Somehow I got up the nerve to talk to her. Her name was

Melody Wadsworth. She said that I could remember her last name because if you chew your gum you get your wads worth. That was pretty clever. I'm sold. It doesn't take much to impress me. She was one of those hippie chicks I had been looking for all this time. The flowers-in-her-hair type. A free spirit. No attachments and no cares, just loving life. I really liked her and could have grown to love her had she grown to love me. We did start to innocently date for a while. She lived in this huge house on Roberts Ave across from Upper Onondaga Park. There was a lake there. More of a pond I would call it, but it was named Hiawatha Lake. It had a gazebo off-center in the lake not too far from shore, but just far enough where mischievous kids couldn't get to it. During the summers a small rowboat would take orchestra members out to the gazebo to perform. Ducks and ducklings were there, turtles and even schools of humongous goldfish. It was a beautiful place with huge oaks, elms and willows, winding park roads and cul-de-sacs for parking and making out. There was also an olympic size outdoor pool on the other side of the long clubhouse. My guess is that it was built in the 20s.

There are tons of parks in Syracuse. The great majority of them being quite large with a lot of trees and open space, basketball courts and in some cases golf courses, lakes and ponds. It is similar to Nedrow (the center of the universe) and therefore can be designated as bordering, but not being officially a part of God's country because God can only be from one country. He can make all of the other worldly and universal things, but He can only be from one place. Sorry, it's Nedrow.

Melody Chew Your Gum and I were doing pretty well. It was great having my own car. I could go over there whenever I wanted. Me and Melody never did do the do, but we came close. I think she had been around the block before and was taking her time before going around the block again. That was nice of her and all and I respected her wishes, but she had this bestest girlfriend named Saide Lee who was a direct descendant from the Civil War's Gen. Robert E. Lee. Saide was beginning to flirt with me pretty seriously. Melody was a lot of fun, but Saide was more fun. I really liked Melody, but then there was Saide. Melody was beautiful and Saide was beautiful. Two beautiful girls both interested in me ... at the same time? What the heck? This is because they didn't know me, or my past shall we say. And this was healthy for me. I could be myself with a few minor changes. I was growing up. I was beginning to sort things out. I was driving. Driving ain't easy.

One fine day I was at Saide's house and my good girl Melody happened by and saw my car parked out front. "What the hell is this?" she thought. "What the fucking hell is this? Mother fucker!" Saide and me were just, you know, getting to know each other when there was this loud, overly aggressive banging on the front door. It was the lovely hippie Melody totally enraged that I was there. Mel and Saide got into this hugely ugly verbal bashing. Not something you would hope two best friends would ever do, especially over some guy. But it wasn't just any guy. It was Little Jimmy Murphy. Master of the Universe, The Chosen One, He Who Shall Be, He Who Is, All That Is, All That Was, The Virtue Of Peace, The Floater, The Flier, The Transcended, The First Conception, The First Conceptor, The Reason For The Rhyme, The Toll For Whom The Bell Tolls, The Next Paradigm, The Reason For, Everything, Everyone, Consumed Darkness, Weight, Absence, Inclusion, Will, The Breath, The Light Within. I, Little Jimmy, was a good reason for their battle. I don't think they ever spoke to each other again. Stealing your best friend's lover is never a good thing. I don't think anyone has ever said, "Okay, you can have him," unless the guy had a little tiny dick or some other sexual abnormality that couldn't satisfy them. In which case the woman actually did love her man for who he was and not for what he was packing. I'm sure this is the case in many relationships. Some women would rather have a lover with a little dick (truly I doubt this, but thought I would be kind to those of you who quietly suffer with this). If the guy's a millionaire does it matter if he has pint-sized stub? Does a large bank account make up for a pinky-sized penis? Is a big damned diamond ring a good substitute for set of tiny family jewels? Is a fancy convertible a good substitute for a little hood ornament? Are your plated caviar the only eggs you need eaten? Is your bread in the oven the only thing you can get to rise? Does his key fit the lock? Is your fiddle in tune? Would you really rather be showered with gifts? Have you really had enough of someone fucking your brains out? Are you tired of the dick or tired of your current prick with the little dick?

These are only some of the reasons as to why someone might not be pissed that their man was stolen, so I felt pretty good about myself. Saide and I became a loving couple from that point on. I always felt bad about that because I originally fell in love with Melody and then I got stolen away. Some things you just can't do anything about. I'm just a guy. Whoever has the pussy leash, that's where I'm going.

One day that fall after we'd all returned to school I'm sitting in one of my classes daydreaming about pussy and I happened to look out the window. There's this chick standing out there by my Belvedere in a full length fur coat. Holy Shit. It was Saide! She'd hitchhiked all the way from Corcoran to OCS to visit me. She'd never even been to OCS before. This was pretty impressive I must say. Thankfully, this was my last class of the day. It was great to see her. I think I was really falling in love this time. Up to this point I had made out with quite a few gals, the Krone sisters (who once baked me a small birthday cake and after I ate it they told me it was filled with dead flies), Samantha Walsh (I wanted that. Other people were digging in, but she wouldn't give it to me.), Vanessa Erekson (my next door, built like a brick shit house ballerina neighbor who dated the idiot Dennis the Menace all through school), Linda Kompf (I liked Linda, not sure why we didn't hook up), Candy Burtone who was handing out her sweetness to everyone but me, Michele Black (I did some serious making out with her), Mary Glason (maybe I got a peck. I did see the U.S. astronauts land on the moon at her house), Nancy Clark (she was tall and all woman even as a young woman. Steve Young from the Valley snagged that thing up), Janet Silver (she and I made out for an entire party once, like for four hours. We hid under the stairs. It was great. My lips were killing me for days afterward.) There was the Lynnette Kelley debacle (coming up) and maybe a couple more, but it was all innocent stuff. Oh yeah, Cheryl Hartman. How could I forget her. I'm not saying that we did kiss in the first grade or anything. I'm just sayin' that since we were in love I should probably add her to the list. But here's this girl Saide who hitchhiked all the way to OCS to see me. That was something no one had ever done before. She went out of her way to find me. She was for me. She was my true love for ever and ever and ever.

One snowy day Saide and I were driving up Glenwood Ave in the Elmwood area just past South Ave. About half way up Glenwood there is this guy yelling and screaming at his poor little girlfriend on someone's front porch. Hers more than likely. So I stop my Belvedere with a 383 in it and yell over to him, "Hey, knock it off!" At first he ignored me so I shouted it again, "HEY, knock it off!" This time he looked over at me, turned back to his victim and continued bitching her out. And then I shouted, "Leave her alone, Dickhead! Who the fuck do you think you are, GOD?" This caught his attention. He comes walking down to my car all hunched over. He was a lot bigger than I thought. He arrives at my rolled down window, looks in, leans back, slugs me in the side of the face, turns and walks back toward the bitch-out session. That didn't work out too well for me, but maybe it gave the poor girlfriend enough time to go back inside and lock the door. Swollen, I drove off.

One of the best times I remember with Saide was on a Christmas Eve. I picked her up and we found a back road to the roundhouse up next to the Woodland Reservoir so we decided to go parking. We took off our clothes, steamed up the windows and did the do. We were doin' the do a lot. It was really a good relationship; meaningful. Our original intent this evening was to go to midnight mass so we put our clothes back on and drove down to St. James Church where I regularly attended Sunday mass, went to church school, made my communion and made my confirmation. We smoked a joint right before we went into church. I would never suggest that anyone ever do this. The words of God Almighty while under the influence of the God Cannabis Sativa take on an entirely different meaning. The two of us could not stop laughing. It was c - a - r - a - z - y!

This was my church. It was even named after me. The real St. James Minor was an actual cousin to Jesus. James' mom, Jesus' auntie, asked Jesus one day if James could sit at his right hand. Jesus thought for a moment and said, "No, I don't think so." This is a true story. Look it up in your bible. For me it has never been easy to carry this weight of Superior rejection around, but I've managed the best I can.

Anyway, I knew a lot of people attending this mass. The two of us just could not stop laughing. I'm sure those people who knew me weren't the least bit surprised and more than likely disappointed once again. I was probably beyond disappointing by this time. I'm sure we smelled like freshly smoked pot. We ended up leaving. It was the best thing to do. We finished our joint, drove back to the reservoir and fucked some more. This was the best relationship ever. All said and done, I never saw Melody again and slowly but surely Saide and I drifted apart. I can't recall why. I remember her moving into this apartment right around the corner from her parents and meeting some other guy or something. Something happened. She wanted more out of a relationship than a dick. It was very confusing to me. "Do you love me," she would ask. "Of course I do," I would say. She would say, "Why don't you show me then?" I would say, "What are you talking about?" She would say, "I just don't think you really love me." I would say, "What do you want me to do?" "I don't know. I just don't think you love me." "What are you talking about? We do everything together. I'm here all of the time. We have fun. We talk. We laugh. We fuck. What else is there?" "You never tell me you love me." "Well, I was never told that I was ever loved so I have a hard time saying those words. Maybe that's why I don't tell you." This went on for hours, even days ..... fucking weeks. After a while, no matter what you do or say there's no turning back, you're done. The relationship is over. I never saw Saide again. Whatever it was, I got the boot. Saide was gone and Melody wouldn't speak to me. I got screwed and fucked. Melody married some Pollock who she had a couple of beautiful girls with, but he was an abusive, drunken idiot with tons of issues. She had a secret P. O. Box that I mailed letters to for a few years and then that faded away. Being a Superhero isn't easy. I always felt that maybe Melody and I might have another chance at love some day, but that never happened.

Soon I was back hanging out with the OCSers and found a fancy for the stunning Sarah Nighthawk. She was in the next grade above me and had never been in trouble her entire life. I really did like her a lot. Sarah is your perfect mental image of an Indian Princess. My Pocahontas or Sacajawea. I called her Squatch. She called me James R. She was just the right height at 5' 6". Long, straight, glistening black Indian hair, earth-brown eyes, a perfect nose and lips, she was more than beautiful. Her favorite saying was, "With me, it's really very simple," which for me made things that much more difficult. Sarah was voted "Best Looking" in her senior class. When she signed my yearbook she filled an entire page with loving text. She claimed to have given me a very difficult time. "One of these days we'll get it together." After stating that, she probably shouldn't have told me how she really felt, but she did. She said, "I really love you a whole lot. Did you get that? I love you. I hope you don't rip the page out okay? But as you know I got certain problems and when that someday comes, I hope you will still be there." She goes on to say, "The answer to your question on page 52 is you." (Page 52 was the *Life at Central* page where the seniors listed their Favorite Song, their Hangup, their Favorite Hangout, their Favorite Kick, and what they'll be remembered for). Under Sarah's Favorite Kick column she writes: "Cheering (she was a cheerleader), being happy, and liking a certain someone" [me]. Wow! I'm such a dumbfuck. A senior girl in high school states in her class yearbook for the world to read that she likes a certain someone and that someone was James R? I'm just way too naïve to get these things. I don't know how to react or what to do next. I'm just a stupid kid. I should have swept her off her feet. I could have. It could have been like that scene in *It's A Wonderful Life* when George Bailey and Mary Hatch are at the bottom of the stairs in Mary's foyer talking on the phone to George's best friend in New York City, the guy who's supposedly courting Mary. They're both sharing the phone with their faces and bodies as close together as two people can get. George is smelling her hair and he is just dying to kiss her, but he's pissed-off at her (actually at himself). Mary is leaning against George and the guy on the other end of the phone is yakking away with some nonsensical bullshit and Mary and George are totally lost in each other. It is an unbelievable scene. One of the most powerful love scenes ever filmed. I could have done that same thing. I just don't know how to do that shit. Besides, you can't plan that stuff. Love happens because of innocent, unplanned incidents like George and Mary's. I know there are arranged marriages where people eventually, because of their shared life-circumstances, learn to love each other, but this is America and we don't cotton to that sort of crap.

Sarah was a purebred Onondagan. She lived in the nicest house on the Reservation. Her stepdad owned the trucking/excavating company where we dumped Johnny Lightning's car. She was the most beautiful girl on the Res. She liked me? How lucky was I?

We dated for a while. I use the word "dated" very loosely. She was a braincell, super smart and beautiful. I had 'a' braincell, weighed in at 120 and had a broken face. We used to talk on the phone for hours and hours. The only date I really remember going on with her was going parking down at the end of West Roswell in her dad's Buick Electra 225 and making out. I was trying to get at her nice little Indian boobies but she wasn't about to let me. I love boobs. Unfortunately, for me and all the other guys standing in line, she decided that she was going to save herself for an Indian man. She felt it was her obligation as a purebred to marry another purebred in order to carry on the Native American bloodline. Much to the chagrin of every White guy in Onondaga County, a collective "What the fuck!" was heard throughout the entire county at 8 p.m. when this announcement was made to me from the end of West Roswell in the backseat of the Electra. Everyone was listening in. Sarah did eventually marry an Indian ironworker and had bunch of little Indians.

One summer night, I think it was Sarah, myself, maybe Mindy Ordino, Shelley Bussinger, and Cindy Jones; a skinny little piano-playin' senior with hefty boobs that kind of or almost kind of, but not really, fell into my grubby little paws. I'm not sure why Cindy Jones and I never tried anything. I know *I* was considering it. My lips around her nipples may not have been considered by her because she was a best friend of Sarah's. These chicks were tight. Friendship was everything. Relationships in high school are very territorial, proprietary, and for the most part "ownership" was respected, by the girls at least. Guys are guys. We fuck anything we can. Can you imagine a guy apologizing to another guy? It might go something like this: "I'm sorry for your loss. I mean you guys breaking up and all. I'm sorry I fucked her before you did. I didn't know you guys were serious. All you ever do is fight. It just happened. We didn't plan it. She came on to me. She offered her honor, I honored her offer and all night long I was on her and off her. Anyway, you can have her back. I really don't like her anyway. But she's a great fuck if that makes you feel any better." Guys seek, destroy and move on. There isn't any time or any need for an apology.

This particular beautiful country evening, me and the gang decided to paint one of the brick walls at OCS. We got a five gallon bucket of white paint from somewhere, probably Sarah's house, and climbed up on the roof over the cafeteria on the back side of the school and painted in huge ten foot letters, CLASS OF 1972. How stupid was that? Within a day we were all caught. We had paint all over ourselves. I'm sure I was ultimately blamed for it. I don't believe this adventure was my plan, but if you're the one who is usually in trouble, the trouble-pointing finger can easily waver toward you like the finger of a compass, no matter what direction you face, the finger always points in the same direction. In this case, and many other cases, toward Murphy. Our punishment? We had to scrub the paint off the wall with hot soapy water and stiff brushes and then we had to work with the maintenance crew for the remainder of the summer helping to prepare the school for the coming school year. I learned how to paint properly from the oldest maintenance man, Mr. Clark – "go with the grain son, go with the grain. Take your time. Nice even strokes. That's right. It's like fucking (no, he didn't say this, I made this line up)." On a sad note: Sarah's and my dating days were over from this point forward.

Chapter 41
Parking With Lynette

As my quest for the breast continued down the dirt road of teenage love, one evening at my schoolmate Lynnette's request, she and I went for a ride in her daddy's blue station wagon. Leaving from the Nedrow Tavern we drove up into the woods across from where my sister was caught parking a few years earlier. Lynnette knew exactly where she was going so I am assuming she had been there at least a hundred times before. There were some notches carved on a gun handle in the back seat that I saw out of the corner of my good eye, but I couldn't really make out how many notches there were. I was very attracted to Lynnette and apparently she was attracted to me. I was in line to be the next notch. What more could one hope for? She was a damn good looking brunette with a finely toned body. Everyone was pounding her, but I was way too stupid to take advantage of the free-fuck situation. Damn Catholics and all their guilt. There was a time when I was pretty good at fucking or at least trying to fuck every tiny thing, but in reality I was still a very shy, introverted person. Being shy and introverted is a horrible condition and something that you can do absolutely nothing about. People mistake it for being stuck-up or for being full of your own shit. Some introverts react violently and eventually explode and cause irreversible harm to others. On the other hand, some introverted people are very strong people who have faith that their shyness will fade and someday be gone forever. It usually takes someone to fall in love with them to make them blossom into the true artistic person that most of them are.

It was getting harder for me to simply act (or fuck) without solid reasoning behind the action (fucking). Fucking had its religious mental consequences. How could I be so smart and so stupid at the same time? Instead of a good angel on one of my shoulders and the bad angel on the other (not that there are angels), I have a smart angel and a stupid angel (not that there are angels). Why do I let emotions get in the way of screwing chicks? Why do I feel guilty all of a sudden all of the time? Why can't I just fuck and run like everyone else (including girls)? Why can't I just love the physical joy of the moment and walk away like everyone else does? Why do *I* have to suffer for my brothers and sisters? Why do *I* carry the weight of their sins on *my* shoulders? Why do *I* have to say penance for *all* Man?

After my breakups with the Corcoran girls I'm wondering how it is that you can fuck someone if you aren't in love with them? And when guys think like this there's no way their pecker is going to stand at attention and drive its way into the back walls of the impatiently awaiting pussy. You can have the most gigantic hard-on you've ever had while your clothes are on and even while you are taking your clothes off, but as soon as your prick head touches that pussy juice your stupid-ass conscience says, "Do you love this woman, Jimmy?" "Why aren't you answering me? Do you love her or don't you?" You drive your dick in there while you're answering, "Yes, of course I love her." By this time it's too late.

Your date has graciously provided you with everything she has, everything you've dreamt of, the nothin' could be finer than to be in her vaginer piece of ass, and really? You can't fuck the pussy? You're a fucked up dude. You couldn't fuck Lynnette Kelley? Jesus Christ, where's that fucking gun? After my embarrassing little-boy failure to perform my manly dick duties, she never paid much mind to me ever again.

That following summer, Lynnette was being gang-banged upstairs in one of my neighbor's homes. At least that was the story being told. And a couple of bed legs crashed through the oak floor and down through the living room ceiling. Yes, through the ¾" oak flooring and down through the first floor ceiling. You really have to be raising a ruckus to break through oak flooring and then continue down and break through the ceiling below. My dad and I were hired to repair the floor and the ceiling. He was befuddled. "How could this have happened?" "I don't know," I said. "I just don't know." Lynnette was eager to please the entire male community. After our incident she started hanging around with older, more experienced guys.

Chapter 42
The Thief

One nice feature to our Nedrow house was one of the pine trees. It was right next to my brother HarryHarry's bedroom window that eventually became my window after my sister moved out (HarryHarry got her room). Pine trees are God's natural ladders. Lynn Kelleher's father owned Ned's Drugs. Ned's was way ahead of its time. It wasn't your local, trashy, cramped, jammed-packed, drug store. It was clean and organized. Mr. Kelleher was a very nice man. I knew all of the girls that worked there because they all went to OCS. I would go in and look through the new albums; Jimi Hendrix, Janis Joplin, the Doors, Cream, Black Sabbath, Crosby, Stills, Nash and Young, and any new album release representing several genres. I would buy one and then I would steal whichever ones I wanted and simply walk out of the store. No one ever stopped me. What a jerk. I would walk home, climb up the pine tree, sneak into my room, put on my headphones and listen to my new albums. All in all I probably stole 25 or 30 albums. Not cool, I know. I was probably talked about as a thief by the prettiest girls in school. I wasn't the only thief in the neighborhood, not including my sister, but I was one of them.

Chapter 43

High School Sports

When it finally came time for graduation, things were kind of shaky in the grade department. I was a B, B- or maybe even a C student at best. "With a little effort," I could have easily been an 'A' student. It wasn't really a goal of my family to raise 'A' students. My father and mother both dropped out of high school. My sister did all right when she wasn't doin' the Hoodie-Do with some guy in the backseat, but she never went on to college. Instead, as I mentioned earlier, after she and Jonn Tarrow broke it off, she went to church everyday praying that she would marry our cousin, and she did. She and my cousin have pretty much worked their entire life in the middle to lower middle-class arena. There isn't anything wrong with that. That's where most of us end up, struggling to get by.

HarryHarry, whose favorite saying was "What a braincell," dated some beautiful girls like Bennie Bussinger, who believed, "Love will triumph over all." Bennie was a pretty little farm girl (I think they had a rather argumentative, rough relationship). She was a cattle rustler, a tough farm gal, and HarryHarry was a regular guy. He would have made a great farmer. She missed out on a good catch. Then HarryHarry went out with and married the sportily delicious cheerleader Eileen Mary Martin who once suggested that I, "Try to be good at least once in a while." I'm not sure what happened to that relationship, but I did see Eileen downtown a few years later after a couple more of her failed marriages. She was as beautiful as ever. She told me she was headed to the courthouse to "get her name back." HarryHarry and Eileen had a son together, but my family never shared in that joy. His name was Robert. My parents always wished Robert would come to visit them, but he never did.

HarryHarry was a worker bee. He never went on to college. He had a tough time in school and never wanted to go back. He was pigeonholed as a student who needed extra help. Part of the reason my brother's marriages failed is that HarryHarry would do anything for anybody at any time of the day or night, except for our sister Eileen that is. They hated each other, but how ironic that HarryHarry married someone named *Eileen*.

My younger brother Michael eventually married Contessa de Luca, one of the Italian waitresses from the Valley Diner. Michael was pulled out of OCS after a witch hunt that booted my brother, me and Spike Cardigan off the Varsity basketball team. Someone saw the three of us drinking at a party way out in the boondocks one weekend. Are you kidding me? Was it just the three of us who were drinking? What about the cheerleaders? You mean to tell me they weren't drinking? What about the rest of the Junior Varsity and Varsity team? You mean out of the hundred and fifty people at the party only the three of us were drinking???? Bullshit! Believe it or not it was Spike Cardigan's sister-in-law Gabby McPherson, now a dairy farmer's wife and Spike's sister-in-law, who fought before the school board to have us booted off the team. What the hell was that all about? You're ratting on your own brother-in-law? I hated that utter-sucking bitch from that day forward. Her birthday was the same day as mine too. What a fucking curse! Every year I celebrate my birthday I can see that bitch standing up before the school board demanding that we get removed from the team. If my brother Michael was going out with his cute little Italian mafia babe at this time I'm sure our families would have pitched in to have some sort of "accident" mysteriously happen on one of those dark country roads. BAM! "Fuck you, you horse fucking bitch!" BAM! BAM! "Cunt!" BAM!

I was a starting Varsity basketball player when I was in the 10th grade. Let me rephrase that. I was the ONLY 10th grader on the team and I was a *starter* on the "Varsity" basketball team. This didn't go over well with some of the junior and senior players. One of them sabotaged the basketball team's picture in the yearbook that year. They swiped something across the photo blocking half my face. It was like that in all of the yearbooks. I know who it was.

My parents were crushed by the allegations made by the utter-sucker and they fought right back. As uneducated as my parents were they loudly spoke their minds. My dad was the youngest drum major of the Auburn Drum & Bugle Corp when he was a lad. He was in the Navy. He was president of the Valley Little League and he was a lieutenant in the Nedrow Fire Department. Bob and Betty were huge supporters of the OCS sports teams. My parents went to nearly every basketball game the entire time we went to that school. My brother HarryHarry was a real scrapper on the basketball court. He didn't mind blatantly crushing the opponent five times a game and fouling out for the advancement of the OCS Tigers. Spike Cardigan was a tall, lanky farmer boy, also a scrappy player and a good shooter. These two boys never got to play their senior year because of that bitch. It would have been my junior year. We were finished! No basketball ever again! Unfucking real. I guess I should apologize for carrying this anger with me for so many years and still expressing it so vehemently, but I'm not going to. Fucking horse-fucking Bitch!

Coach Fletcher had retired by now or this never would have happened. I, for one, was a proven idiot, but I was obviously an above average b-ball player. I WAS A VARSITY STARTER IN THE TENTH GRADE!!!!! This bullshit mishap was all under the eye of the new basketball coach Mike Cod, a former OCS basketball player, OCS graduate and resident farmer. You prick! You think he would have stood up for us. We were the fricking stars! Jerkoff! Asswipe! Dickhead! After all this hoopla and fighting, and after ruining our lives forever, the school board finds out that Cod never even had a college degree. Imagine that! They hired him on his word that he had a degree. WELL HE DIDN'T you fucking Jerkoff, Asswipe, Dickhead Mother Fuckers!

Because of this, my hard working dad pulled Michael out of OCS and sent him to Christian Brothers' Academy (CBA). An all-boy, private, Catholic school. Out of Farmerville and into the life of luxury. Michael himself wasn't a terrible basketball player. He was one of those guys you would throw the ball to and he would just stand there because he lacked so much self-confidence he was afraid to shoot. He might miss, God forbid. "What would people think of me if I were to miss?" You could read the audience's mind, "Please get OFF the fucking court."

Michael was raised at the bottom of the Murphy family totem pole and knew he had to get out. We were workers. CBA taught him that he could be and should be more. He received scholarships for all of his years of college. He went on to receive his graduate degree and earn his Ph.D. He works for the University of Auburn in Alabama. Smart kid, sucky basketball player. So from this fucked up year on, the only sport I played was ping pong in Chris Young's basement.

Chapter 44
The Principal Wants to See Me

My hair was pretty long in my junior and senior years. It was as thick as all get out too. My senior picture is really something to admire. I wore a suit and tie, but I had this huge pile of hair on my already huge head. I had a favorite pair of really wide bellbottoms that I wore all of the time until they were paper thin, and even then I sewed patches on them so I could wear them a while longer. My chosen nickname was Roger Willnot. A willnot is one of those little chunks of shit that gets stuck in your ass hairs and 'will not' come off. Back in these days several of the guys had long sideburns or somewhat long hair, whatever their parents would allow. One time the school stated that we couldn't play basketball for OCS unless we got our hair cut and shaved our sideburns. A bunch of us went over to my house and completely shaved our heads. The school wasn't too happy about this either. We even held sit-ins over the right for girls to wear pants and for everyone's right to wear sandals and no socks to school. The principal, Mr Hilbert, came out and talked to us giving us time to think about the consequences of our revolution. He said he had called the county Sheriff and that they were on the way. We didn't believe him and refused to move. Within a few minutes the Sheriffs pulled up in front of OCS with their lights flashing and we quickly disbanded. Eventually, we did get our way though. Other schools like Central Tech, down in the city, were having full blown violent race riots. We were having peaceful little sit-ins. We didn't know how to have a race riot.

The 60s and 70s were times of tremendous change in American culture. Technology was making major breakthroughs which allowed for the media to spread the word of the latest trends in peace and anarchy quickly across the nation, and to some extent, globally. FM radio came crashing in. The bands were a bit sloppier and more vulgar than the doo-wop and Elvis Presley sound alikes that preceded them. The beat was a lot more aggressive and tons louder thanks to advances in technology. The early Beatles music was recorded on a measly 2-tracks and then advanced to 4-tracks. 4-track recording changed everything because you could record on three of the tracks and mix (or dump) them down to the fourth track and then record on two more tracks and mix those two new tracks and the already mixed 4th track down to the new 4th track, and so on. It wasn't until 1968 that 8-track recording began.

Fashion was becoming much more daring and pleasing to the eyes of Man as well. Mr. Blakely, our social studies teacher, used to put all the girls with miniskirts in the first two rows and just stare at their panties all class. Linda Bell, Susie Manar, Happy Reynolds, Mary Glason; all in the front row. He would pretend to be sleeping, squinting his eyes, shading his brow with his hand, tilting his head to tweak the peek, and just stare at their white undies for 45 minutes. I think they all gave him the pantie show he needed and they all passed with flying colors. In the mean time, while Blakely, the perverted panty peeper peered precociously into the open slot and played pocket pool with his pulsating penis, everyone else in the class was cheating. I know I was.

In general, besides being at all of the great fights, coming in late hundreds of times and several other offenses I haven't mentioned, I was a good kid. I could have been a veterinarian. Right before the end of my senior year I was called down to Mr Hilbert's office. When I got there he told me to go ahead and take a seat. He was carefully going over my grades and finally let me know that it appears as though I failed geometry a while back and that I never made it up, and now I don't have the credits to graduate. This is not good news. Geometry was one of those pre-10 a.m. classes. "But," he says as he stares squarely at me, "we are going to give you a passing grade to get you out of here Murphy!"

I'm not sure what just happened. What did he say? As usual I wasn't paying attention. "What did you say Mr. H?" "I said that you don't have the credits to graduate, but we have decided it would be best for the school to give you the grade you need simply to get you out of here Murphy. If you ever mention this to anyone, it will be impossible to prove, now get out of my office!"

"Oh my GOD! You're kidding me right? Are you really? Oh my GOD! Thank you so much! Wow! Aw man I can't believe it! You're the best principal ever! This is the best school in the entire world!" I stand up and shout, "GO TIGERS! GO TIGERS! O-N-O-N-D-A-G-A Hu-rah, hu-rah, Onondaga Rah!" The ladies in the office and students walking down the hall were all wondering what the hell was going on inside Mr. Hilbert's office. "Oh my GOD! Oh man, I can't believe it! Yes, yes, yes!!!!" I stand at attention, salute, and begin to sing our school Alma Mater with lyrics written in 1950 by Dorthy Gann and music byWilliam Peters, "In this wide and spacious valley, she stands beautiful to see (you can hear the office staff and students in the hallway and outside joining in). Tis our own dear alma mater, school of youth and gaiety. We will strive to ever serve her, carry onward through the years (the chorus gets louder and louder. There are a hundred students or more singing in the hallway). Goals once reached by those before us, reached with smiles as well as tears. Proudly now come join the chorus, join with us and gladly sing, (everybody!) of our dear Old Onondaga, may the JOYFUL ECHOES RING."

I graduated with the class of 1972, sideburns, ponytail and all.

Years later, when asking for my transcript because I was thinking of going to college, my transcript said I graduated 7th. It doesn't say 7th from the top or 7th from the bottom. I'm assuming it's 7th from the top. Otherwise, I would have graduated like 97th don't you think?

At a class reunion a few years later, one of my classmates sat across from me during dinner. She was a real hard worker in school and a smart girl. She was never late and never in trouble. We were just talking, no big deal. She told a story of how she failed her fourth year of German by one point. A 74 instead of a 75. She was called down to the Mr. H's office too, but was NOT allowed to graduate with the class. She had to go to summer school and make it up. That's not cool.

Chapter 45

Life's Final Chapters

The '53 Chevy

In my senior year and right out of high school I worked at the Van Dyne Laundry up on Seneca Turnpike by Community General Hospital. One of my classmates, Bob Bugnaski, got me the job. His mom worked there and a couple of other young guys, Don Peck and Steve Young worked there also. We sorted and washed all the laundry from Community General, Van Dyne Nursing Home and the city or county jail, one of them. There was a special needs young man who worked there that we frequently tortured. He wasn't pigeonholed, we were all tortured in one way or another, wrestled down and stuffed into a laundry bag, sent down the line and dumped into the industrial washers or driers. Everyone was game for fowl play.

While sifting through the hospital laundry we would find cut off fingers, guts, blood-soaked jelly type stuff and even umbilical cords. We would set the umbilical cords out on the windowsill to dry. We would also sort contaminated laundry that came in special red bags without wearing the gloves we were supposed to wear. We would drink beer on the job, smoke pot and all kinds of crazy shit. There was an old black guy named Bill who would boil steak at lunch in water and make us laugh all through the day. He was tellin' tales of gamblin' weekends, flashin' wads of money in my eyes while we were doin' LSD and goin' down inside. Eventually, I think I got fired. After that I mainly worked for my dad in the construction trade and for a few other local contractors along the way, but mostly with my dad. Low expectations are easily met to keep the uneducated life pleasing.

Long-haired and still ragged, as I like to say, I sold my Belvedere to neighbors across the street and purchased a 1953 Chevy pickup truck with a split, two-piece front windshield, wing vent windows and three windows in the back. I think they were called port windows. It was beautiful. Not beautiful in the restored sense, but beautiful to me. My friend Keith MacCallom, no relation to the MacColloms, and me had painted the body primer red and the roof battleship, primer grey. The truck came without your standard pickup truck bed on the back so we built a flatbed out of 1x6s and 2x4s. Keith was a good friend to everyone and a handy guy with cars and just about everything else. He was musical, sharp-witted and very clever. When we were kids his dad came out into the garage with a shot glass full of something. He set it on fire and drank it down. That was fricking amazing! With his eyes closed his dad could also tell you how many coins he had in his hand by their weight. Keith, his little brother and awesomely built-like-my-truck little sister Valerie, lived straight down the street across Rockwell Road. Right by where I blew up Ian-the-Pion's Madras hat. My '53 Chevy had chrome front and rear bumpers (no relation to Keith's little sister), vacuum wipers, a straight-6, and a four-speed tranny with a real low 1st gear. I usually started out in 2nd because 1st was so low it just didn't make any sense to use it most of the time. This truck was a workhorse for somebody in its day. It also had a starter button on the floor. If you put the key in the ignition and turned it on, nothing would happen. You had to turn the key to the on position and then step on the gas pedal and this starter button to the right all at the same time all with your right foot. It was the only way the truck would start. I'm sure it was a genius piece of modern technology when it first came out. I really loved this truck.

In the wintertime on nights when it was snowing as hard as it could, my friend John Eaglefeather from the Onondaga Nation and I would buy some beer and ride through the Valley streets, through Nedrow and out through South Onondaga in 1st or 2nd gear just purring along. The vacuum wipers worked perfectly if you kept the engine idling steadily. If you stepped on the gas a little too much, air would be sucked away from the wipers to feed the carburetor. The wipers might not stop, but they would barely move anymore. It was a delicate balance, but much better than no wipers at all and who cared about wipers anyway?

During these heavy snowfalls nobody would be on the streets and it was snowing so hard that the plows hadn't yet made a dent in any of the streets. John and I were making the first tracks in the 6" to foot-deep snow .... windows down .... no radio .... elbows resting on the doors .... going about five miles an hour .... dead silence .... no people .... just quietly talking, smoking cigarettes and drinking beer .... this is the life my friends. This is the life.

The following summer me and my truck were down at the end of Ruhamah on Brookside hanging around with Curt, Carey, Shorty Walker, Neuman and a couple of the Rags. We were tossing the football and frisbee around and just being regular kids on a regular summer day. Nowhere to go and nothin' to do. Niagara Mohawk, the Upstate New York power company, had left one of those big wooden spools down there. The spools they used to roll power lines off of when they were stringing new lines in a community. They're a good five or six feet across and maybe 30" high. A lot of people had them in their backyard and used them for picnic tables. We got the bright idea to roll it out into the street and push it up the street with someone's car and see how fast we could get it going. I forget whose car we were pushing it with, maybe Shorty's, but it was a blast. We pushed it north on Brookside and got it up to about 30 mph and let it go. It eventually went off the road and flipped over. No harm done. We got it back out and placed it in

the middle of the road, lined up Shorty's car and pushed it south from Dorwin, slightly downhill back toward Ruhamah. Again, we got it going about 30 mph, slowed our vehicle down and let it go. It was going exactly down the middle of the street. It was perfect! "Look at that sucker." And then it started to veer slightly right. And a little more right. And a little more.
"Holy Shit! No, no, no, no, no, no, no, no, no!!!!!"
A hugh frickin'

<u>S ... M ... A ... S ... H</u>

like you have never heard a smash before in your entire life. Everyone stopped dead in their tracks. The spool rolled directly into the front of my beautiful 1953 Chevy truck. It was totaled. I never drove it again.

Chapter 46

Love in the Funeral Home

After my favorite truck was demolished I bought some nondescript, forgettable piece of shit to drive. Life as a teenager is tough enough while you're in school and even tougher when you get out. There are no clear cut answers to anything except for the fact that you have to work in order to survive. All through high school and after high school I was trying desperately to figure out love and life. What do I say that's meaningful to a girl? How do I say it, and all that happy crap.

One evening I went to an in-law's father's wake at Ballweg & Lundsford Funeral Home after I ate dinner at the Valley Diner and had a drink at Mondo's. I'd always had a thing for one of the just-married sisters in the immediate family who was in mourning, but I wasn't going to try anything at the funeral of her father for Christ's sake. Not to say that I wasn't thinking about it. She and I had innocently flirted through the years and we had some real good, meaningful conversations as well. I always wondered why we didn't hook up and do something. Like fuck for instance. Maybe because her sister was going out with my brother, but most likely it was because I really didn't have a good job. I worked for my father in the residential remodeling business and there wasn't a secure financial future in that.

This girl was high maintenance, spoiled, fine and dandy tasty candy - slim, bendable and dependable - just my size if she would realize I was the prize. I could bring rise to her aspirations, relieve her from her complications, make her beg please as I made her drop to her knees. She could be mine for all time temporarily, in the form of won't you marry me. How could I, how can you, move in the groove, in the groove, in the groove. She had been looking for me for ever, forever and a day, what do you say, leave your husband for a minute, it won't take long and I'll be in it. He'll be wondering where you are. You'll be on a floating star. You won't know where you are, twinkle twinkle on my dinkle dinkle. You won't have to worry. I'll cream on your curry. I'll be the shoulder you can cry on while I dip between what you rely upon, up on, my horse, it's healthy, your wealthy, and I'm wise. I'm the bottom line between you and a good time. I'm the thread for your needle. You can be the skin wrapped tight around my potato. The jel for my j-e-l-l-o. I'll be the message in your bottle. I'll be the love in your tunnel, if you want to funnel, just a moment of your time, I'll help you unwind, forget about your daddy's death, if only for a second, I'll be your second, I won't mind. Up upon the alter, I'll alter your sorrow, I'll turn your down into a pick-up as I pick you up and set you down on my golden Jesus rod. By the power vested in me I now pronounce you my wife to be, in this funeral home, I want to take you home and let you play with my bird *and* my bees. I can see your golden locks all out of place and your naked, slim body in a race to succeed. To suck, to seed. I'll be your farmer. I'll plow your field and make your garden grow. I'll be your tractor, your milk cow, you can stroke me for my milk to feed your hungry throat while I stand above you straightening your crown. No one has to know that you went down, in this side room full of dead bodies, full of gloom. I'll take you to your groom, place your hand in his, talk to you together, like you're the birds of one feather, and then I'll turn and go, because I know, he's got the money, but I got the honey ..... on my lips.

Shhhh, I'm next in line ... she is beautiful. Look at her. More beautiful than I remember. Maybe one Irishman is all that's allowed in an Italian family. It's an unwritten, but fully understood Mafioso law. And this is good for all Irishmen because it creates fervor for Italian chicks to find and dig into the Irish guys. It's like a race. It's a sister to sister race to find the Irishman. I can say this, that Italian women in Irish families usually is not a good thing. They're powerful females. They're demanding. They know everything and always run back to daddy with tears in their eyes. It can be very dangerous for the little Irishman who thought he found a good partner. Daddy's the partner, not you. Fortunately, this family of girls were already mixed with Irish blood from their mother's side. The old man was connected to his gambinos and so it should be. The Italians really help each other. The Irish help each other help themselves.

My lovely lady's father passed away somewhat suddenly from cancer. He was a great guy. Gentle, funny, humble, and self-employed. He did well for himself and treated his family well. My father hired him occasionally to work for us. He knew what he was doing and always treated my father fairly.

So I'm standing in line to offer my condolences and I come face to face with this incredible woman of special interest. Our eyes meet and we can both tell that there is still this thing going on between us. Damn, how did I miss the boat on this one? I lean forward to give her a, "Hello, I'm truly sorry for your loss" hug and then I figure I'll back off, look deeply into her swollen, baby blue eyes and move on. I proceed to hug her and she holds on to me for a moment longer; a nice tight hug. She rubs her little nippled breasts against my shirt and tie covered chest. She has one arm wrapped over my shoulder outside my jacket and her other arm is inside my sport coat. She slowly slides her hand down my back and gives my ass a nice, firm, comfortable squeeze.

Was I wrong to think what I had thought?

Chapter 47

The New York State Trooper (unbelievably stupid)

Life is funny. You can never guess anything about the future, and many times we end up pleasantly surprised by the here and now. People always say, "I knew that was going to happen. I told you." But that's bullshit. The things we are most fearful of are usually the things we gain the most from. The things we take for granted usually end up fucking us over or we fuck them over. Somebody's always plotting something, myself included.

Before I get to the heart of this particular adventure, I need to tell you of another mishap that took place not too soon before my interaction with the afore mentioned NYS Trooper.

We used to party once in a while at this little bar on Rock Cut Road off Brighton Ave. It was called Cindy's or Linda's or something like that. It was a little tiny dive bar slash biker bar that used to be a strip joint. Me and a few buddies were out on the town one evening and decided to stop by for one more drink before we called it a night. We strolled in, ordered our beers and before you know it a fight breaks out in the parking lot. We were parked across the street. The cops were called and all this shit started happening just as we got our beers. Being from Nedrow, we decided to leave because we had nothing to do with, or wanted anything to do with the dispute. It wasn't my car that we came in. I was just a passenger sitting in the backseat. I think Shorty Walker was driving his Lincoln again. But before I got into the car I put my hands up over my head and waved them back and forth like a signal, "Hey, look over here! Look over here! Help! Save me! Save me!" Unfortunately, the cops did look over and within seconds a dozen of them surrounded our car. Being the youthful protesters that we were, we locked the doors and refused to let the cops in. They were shining their lights in the car, tapping on the windows with their nightsticks and demanding that we unlock the fucking doors before they smash the windows all to hell, beat the living shit out of us and drag us all to jail for resisting arrest. After a very brief discussion among ourselves, like for maybe a second, and being the kind, courteous, law-abiding young men that we were, we decide to open the doors. They immediately grabbed *my* ass, handcuffed me and threw me in the back of a police car. I had never been arrested before and I was pretty drunk. And I was pissed because they arrested me instead of arresting the people who were still fighting in the parking lot. I was shouting, "Look! The fight is over there. Those guys are killing themselves and you're arresting me? I was just waving my arms over my head joking around. There's the fight! Right over there!" They could care less about the real fight. They made an arrest so they could close the books. Everyone I was with was told to go home. The one phone call I was allowed to make went to my parents. My father phoned Dave Campbell from Campbell's Valley Diner in the middle of the night and had to borrow the $100 it cost to bail me out. It was very embarrassing for everyone. The court fined me and let me off. I had to pay a lawyer his fee and pay Dave Campbell back too. Shit!

There were plenty of times I wasn't looking for, nor did I want anything to do with trouble, but I ended up in trouble anyway. One Saturday afternoon I drove out to Cliffside Trailer Park off Rock Cut Road (again). I wanted to test drive a van somebody was selling. The van wasn't on the road so it had no insurance, an expired inspection sticker, it wasn't registered, it didn't have any plates, and so on. How was I supposed to buy it if I couldn't test drive it? I took the plates off whatever car I was driving at the time, threw them on the van and took it for a spin. What could possibly happen?

On my way back to the trailer park, as Murphy's Law would dictate, a New York State Trooper pulls up behind me and turns his lights on. I pull into the park and find my way back to the trailer where I got the van. The trooper says he pulled me over because he noticed regular plates on a commercial vehicle and this is illegal. He wanted to see my license, registration and proof of insurance. I had my license, registration and proof of insurance for my real vehicle, but nothing else. I politely explained my situation to him, that I was simply test driving the vehicle and meant no harm, but he felt he still had to write me up for something. State Troopers, if you don't already know, are very similar to the Mounties in Canada. They are impeccably dressed with dark grey stripes down a light grey pant, black shoes, a grey, neatly pressed shirt with a purple tie and a beautiful, wide brimmed tan hat. These men are perfect. They're like German Shepherds.

We were standing about two feet from each other. His head is tilted down as he writes out my ticket. Uncontrollably, I take my hand out of my pocket and with my first finger sort of knuckled in, I reach under the front brim of his just-right-hat and tip the hat up backward on his head. This is not a good idea. I sense this immediately. He calmly looked up from writing the ticket and looked at me like he wanted to kill me on the spot. Not with his gun, but with his bare hands like my father wanted to so many years before when he caught me smoking in the barn, and quickly snap my neck. I wouldn't even see his hands move. I wouldn't even feel it. My expression would never change. My head would just tilt slightly to the right. CRACK! No pain whatsoever. He would release my throat and then I would drop to the ground in the same rumpled heap with the same old jeans, flannel shirt and worn out shoes from an era gone by.

Troopers, fortunately for me, are a special breed. They are trained to think, assess, evaluate, and then react properly ensuring the safety of those around them. If the table had been turned, trained or not, I think I would have killed *him*. But instead of rapidly snapping his neck, I would slowly snap his neck, gleefully watching every twitch. I'd keep my left hand on his throat, place my right hand on the left side of his head, quickly cracking his neck to his right, and then pull out my gun and shoot him with several rounds, reload and unload again. Done!

Instead, this gentle giant writes me out about eight tickets. My insurance skyrocketed for years and I had to hire another lawyer. Brilliant!

Chapter 48
The Lighter Trick

That evening I was at a party over the Nedrow Hardware Store between Leonard and Lindberg in Section 2 drowning my sorrows. I can't remember who was renting the place. I think it may have been Jack Clawson. We were performing the lighter fluid trick. You squeeze a drop of lighter fluid on the table or on your hand and light it and then you put the fire out really quickly. No harm comes to the furniture or to your flesh. It was the extreme opposite version of Russian roulette. Maybe a little burn, but no bullet to the head.

One of the new kids in town was Willie Peevs. His family moved to Nedrow from somewhere inside the city of Syracuse. Willy decided to be cool and show off his ability to master the new trick. He could do something no one else could do. Here goes …. watch carefully …. Willie pours lighter fluid all over his arm and begins to shoot the shit for a minute or so because Willie is Willie and he can't just do something, he has to bullshit for ten minutes and then complete his task. Willie was a real funny guy. One of those guys that always knew a new joke, a *good* new joke. The Peevs fit right into Nedrow. There were like eight kids in the family and they were regular white trash as were the rest of us. They bought this place down at the end of Meredith by the creek in Section 3. I knew Willie, the twins Ronnie and Dell and their sister Dawn. Willie was a trouble maker. He was in with the deviant crowd immediately. He was big time trouble compared to little ol' me, and that was fine. He had new connections to drugs from the inner city so all was good in that world.

Willie was a wheeler and dealer. One deal led to another and another and another. That's what he was always bullshitting about. "If I make this shot (at the pool table) what will you give me?" And he was the type of opponent that would never shut up while you were trying to concentrate on making your shot. What's the first rule in sportsmanship? Shut up while your opponent is concentrating. Not Willie. He would talk about rumors that were going around about you or your interests. He was an asshole when you came right down to it, but we tolerated him.

Willie had this stringy, mid-length, blond hair that was always greasy. He was almost always sweaty and greasy. It was probably the drugs and alcohol trying to escape from his seedy personality. “I know I’m a drug, but I gotta get the fuck out of this guy!” DRIP ... DRIP ... DRIP. His brother Ronnie was cool. He was left handed so what would you expect? Dell was cool. He was a little light in the loafers, but still a really nice guy. I liked Dawn and I’m pretty sure she liked me, but I had my sights on a bigger prize. Finally, after about ten fucking minutes of Willie-shit, he gingerly lights his arm on fire. It was orgasmically breathtaking. Of course, for you reading this, this is a gentle bit of wisdom. You should probably never attempt this trick before a stoned, slightly inebriated audience.

“Now that’s a fucking fire!”

“Look at the colors!”

“Whoohoo!”

“N ... i ... c ... e!”

“Aw man, that’s fucking great!”

“You da man Willie! You da man!”

Willie starts sweating, which is nothing new, and acting a little stressed out. And then he tries to put the fire out by waving his arm. And then he waves his arm a little harder. And then REAL fucking hard! Well two things happened. He took too long to light his arm. The fluid had soaked into his skin. And while he was frantically waving his arm he was adding fuel to the fire. It was like the Santa Ana offshore winds sweeping through California. The fire only got bigger and bigger immediately! Needless to say, Willie ended up in the hospital for the next few days with a severely burned arm. Welcome to the neighborhood! "You cool, you cool. Love ya, man."

Chapter 49

One Timothy Leary Experiment

It was common for friends to move from one apartment to another. Nobody stayed anywhere too long. We were teenagers. We could do anything we wanted to do. We didn't have much in the way of material possessions so moving wasn't very time consuming and there were always people around to help you move. Not too long after Willie's fiery escape, me, Jack Clawson, Shorty Walker and some girl, I can't remember who, were at another apartment Clawson was renting. This time we were almost to downtown up over the Dolphin Bar & Grill, an all black nightclub in the middle of Boonieville. What was he thinking? We decided to get together and do some acid. I've told you this before, that me and drugs really didn't see eye to eye, but here I was and because of peer pressure, personal insecurity and wanting to fit in, I did the do. We stayed in Jack's apartment all night long. Whoever's girlfriend was with us flipped out on the acid almost immediately. She was a friggin' whack-job all night. Somebody, and I think it was Jack, catered to her well-being periodically. After a while we just left her in a heap on the couch. She was better off alone. There was nothing we could do. We certainly weren't going to take her to the hospital or for that matter we were never going to leave the apartment even if she convulsed and died a horrible, drooling death. We were all too fucked up.

We sat there for hours listening to side one of Pink Floyd's *Dark Side of the Moon* over and over. We never even knew it until someone finally asked what time it was. We had been sitting in the same spot listening to the same music for four hours! No one said a word that whole time except for Jack early on trying to comfort his wigged-out girlfriend. The album just kept repeating itself. And then somebody mumbled something. Somebody else turned another light on and said something about "the room is changing color" and all of us at the same time saw vibrant Peter Max, Yellow Submarine, Robert Crumb, Mr. Natural's Keep on Truckin', and Zap Comix drawings leisurely wash over the entire room. It wasn't that it all happened in a split second, the colors started where the light was turned on in the corner and washed out along the ceiling, the walls and the floor. Colors crept over the tables and chairs, the light sockets lit off a spectronically fantastic fft, fft, fft, fft, fft!, the colors seeped into the light switches (zing, zing, zing!), the doors were awash with bright pastels, the brass door hinges shot off a sparklie, sparklie, sparklie!, door knobs threw globular flashes ... fffssseeewww!, the shag carpeting ends spit golden ping, ping, ping, ping, pings a trillion beautiful times!, windows, window sills, curtains, oak trim, and the oak baseboard all rolled waves of Nestle's pure milk chocolate, the bible opened to the Sacrament of Penance on page two hundred seventy-three and Joseph and Mary rose with their right hands raised toward us penitents and together like delicate baby's breath from within they monotoned, "May the Almighty and merciful Lord grant you pardon, absolution and remission of all your sins. May our Lord Jesus Christ absolve you; and I, by His authority, absolve you from every bond of excommunication, suspension and interdict, insofar as I am able and as you require." A golden chariot wheeled up with Charlton Heston at the reins. The old book slammed shut. Joseph and Mary jumped on with Charlton and off they rode into the kitchen. Our sneakers changed to platform shoes, our jeans to stay-press polyester pants, t-shirts to paisley and tie-dye prints, old belts to white belts, rusted belt buckles to silver, white socks suddenly had colored rings around the tops; jewelry, ashtrays, ashes and drug paraphernalia all changed into delicious colors. And the music, especially the music … it was LIFTING OFF THE FUCKING RECORD twisting and turning and tumbling. If you blew on the notes they scattered like bubbles in the wind. "This is the finest exposé I have ever experienced," I whispered. "This is cool, man."

After a few days the 8-hour trip was almost over. "Fuck. That shit's exhausting!" One of the problems with drugs is that it takes days if not years to recover from evenings like these. Human biology isn't meant to be altered to that great of a degree. "I'm going home." "Me too." "See ya." "Later man. That was fucking great dude." "I'm still all fucked up." "What about her?" "I don't know. We'll see." "Later man." "Yeah, later." "Watch out for the Neebros." "It's okay, man. They don't come out in the daylight." "Watch out for the dolphins." "Watch out for *your* dolphins." "See you on the dark side of the moon."

Several Timothy Leary experiments later, me, my compadres and the Rags decided to drive to the far end of Skaneateles Lake, another one of the Finger Lakes. There were a good six or eight of us. I have no idea why we were where we were. Normally we didn't stray very far from the Holy Land. But here we were on the south end of this beautiful Upstate New York lake in this tiny bar in a one-horse hick of a town. It was another one of those towns where everyone trusts everyone because no one ever steals or gets into trouble because everyone knows everyone and is related in some form or fashion to one another. Well, here come the Nedrow boys and girls. We all order a beer. There is no one in the place but us. It's fairly late, around 11 p.m. or so. Ronnie Peevs and I decide that we will stage a fight. While we're fighting, Jack Clawson will go behind the bar and steal a bottle of whiskey. How simple is this? So Ronnie and I start to argue, stand up and start swinging a few phony punches. The poor old man bartender does exactly what he is supposed to do. He comes out from behind the bar, breaks up the fight and throws us out. Clawson in the mean time had gone behind the bar and stolen a bottle of Jack Daniels. Off we go. Another mission perfectly accomplished.

Chapter 50

Revenge

As time went by, little pittie-pooh Ian-the-Pion Edwards (from the third stone from the Madras hat experience) and I became close friends. He had a great connection to hash, and who doesn't love people who have great connections to hash? Pencil-necked geek or not, Ian was a smart kid so I secretly envied him and learned from him. He had been stationed in Germany as a translator for the American Army. If I remember correctly he brought his hash back *from* Germany. He had the ivory meerschaum pipes and everything. He taught me to mix tobacco in with the hash. It would last longer, be less harsh and stay lit longer.

We would sit in my parents' backyard when nobody was home, put on some music and smoke up a storm. We always had a great old time reminiscing. One day we were walking back toward the house after smoking some hash and shooting Ian's pellet gun out under one of the trees. It was me first and Ian behind me. There was a short staircase to walk up in order to get to the back porch and then to the kitchen for some munchies. I take the first step, the second step, and all of a sudden I hear this abrupt "pop!" and my ass starts killing me and burning like hell. "What the hell was that?" I'm thinking. The stupid-ass, fuck-face, pencil-necked geek shot me with his 'most powerful pellet gun ever made' at point blank range! "Ow! Man! What the hell are you doing? What the fuck is wrong with you? Jesus H. Christ! What's wrong with you? Holy shit you idiot! Are you crazy? I'm not a fucking German, you asshole! Translate this (as I flip him the bird). Talk about a downer. You are a downer. You are a life-size depressant. You are diarrhea. You make me want to shit."

Ian on the other hand was elated. He had the smoking meerschaum hanging out of his mouth with his Scottish golf hat tipped down over his eyes, blowing smoke away from the gun barrel at the same time he was blowing smoke out of his mouth from the hash, looking over his gun like he'd just killed Hitler or something. Very nonchalantly he proudly says, "That's for blowing up my Madras hat."

Chapter 51

Drugged For Love

After years of searching for love all over Onondaga County, I finally meet this sleazy little gal named Patty from North Syracuse. She was a well-trained, cute little underage hussy. A bit loud and mannerless for me, but crazy, rabbit fun. Someone who had the same relationship mentality that I did. Fuck, fuck and fuck some more. She was brainless compared to everyone else I'd dated. Her brain was in her pussy. She loved being sedated and having her brain stimulated with my dick of knowledge. Not to belittle her too much, she was *very* religious. A few minutes into our brain-stimulation sessions and she would start screaming, "Oh God. Oh God. Jesus! Jesus! Oh fucking God," and so on. It was hilarious and yet I always felt like the administrator of the sacrament when she cried out. I felt like she was talking to Me. Like I was looking down at her naked, writhing teenage body from heaven and my dick was a mile long. I felt like I had deeply cleansed her. Like I had just performed a royal anointing. This was the only reason I got such a chapter and verse stiffy. My brain thought it was okay to fuck her because she was swearing to God, and my dick thought that the more I fucked the bitch in her pussy-brain the Holier I became. It was normal for me to spend eight straight hours screwing her in the back of my van at parties we went to in South Onondaga. We never came up for air, never even attended the party, we just screwed each other all damned day and night. It was another very healthy relationship.

One night we were at the Nedrow Tavern shooting pool with Willie and Jack Walsh (aka: Fucking Idiot), the Fucking Idiot put some kind of drug in the beer I was drinking so that this other guy, Leslie Johansen (Fucking Idiot #2), a Valley guy no less, could make a pass at the Patty with the Pussy. It was probably her idea. Leslie had all the prescription pharmaceuticals Patty would ever need. The next thing I know I'm waking up from a drug induced coma in my truck the following morning and my religious affiliation is gone forever.

She ended up marrying Fucking Idiot #2, having his kid and soon leaving him.

Drugs were everywhere in these times. Once I went for a ride with David Urias in his jeep. We were going out to smoke a joint. We got along okay, but he fucked me over big time a year or so later. But on this night we were riding in his jeep up through Nedrow coming back down Macon when all of a sudden he cuts onto Clooney's lawn doing like 30 miles an hour heading toward their driveway that cuts across the lawn. The Clooney's had chopped down the five gigantic elms that bordered their driveway a little while ago. David, the experienced, cross country jeep excursionist, nails the trunk of a tree on his side of the jeep. I'm sitting on the passenger side with half-filled rolling papers in my right hand while sprinkling pot onto them with my left hand. Miraculously, and I can't explain this one either, the jeep rolls 360 degrees in midair. I'm tossed up in the air still in the sitting position and land right back in my seat still holding the partially filled papers in my right hand, pot in my left hand and baggie in my lap. I didn't spill a seed. Nothing happened to David either (probably because I was with him). The jeep tranny had slipped into neutral and the engine was still running. There we sat, a bit bewildered and shaken up, but all was good. I finished rolling the joint, lit it, and on we went back to the Tavern.

Chapter 52
Suicide #1

Arthur Paisley, like the Peevs, came from somewhere down in the inner city to OCS. He was one of the tough guys that had to battle it out because he arrived mid-year. The Paisley's lived on Seneca Turnpike half way between the Valley and Marcellus. I'm surprised they didn't attend Westhill instead of OCS, but they didn't. Arthur and I got along for the most part. He ratted on me once for some unknown reason. I didn't think that was too cool. Like Willie Peevs, Arthur was close with the

Navarino boys, the Nedrow boys and the Valley boys. Wherever there was illicit activity, Arthur liked to be there. One night a few of us got drunk at his house. His mom was coming on to me and I went for it in a sloppy, disrespectful manner right in front of Arthur. I never had sex with her but the foreplay was heavy. Arthur never said anything about it to me, but it was totally not cool on my part.

Arthur was into guns too. He had a German Shepherd watchdog that would let you in the house, but wouldn't let you out without Arthur telling the dog it was alright for you to go. This way if you broke into his house and were robbing it and you gathered all that you needed to and thought the dog was just being a cool, dumb dog, and you then decided that you were ready to leave, the dog would not let you leave. You were trapped *in* the house. How cool is that? His mom eventually moved out and went back to Syracuse. Somehow Arthur got ownership of the house. His younger brother Jimmy was the nicest guy ever, straight laced and honorably intelligent. His sister was as nice as pie, pretty cute with some big bazonkers. She was a braincell too. I kind of had a hankerin' for her but she was a little too intimidating for me. She could break me in two in a heartbeat if I ever wanted to break up with her, and besides that, her brother was Arthur Fucking Paisley for God's sake! Break up with her and they both would have killed, maimed, branded and broken you or something along those painful lines.

Forever, OCS had the same phys ed teacher, Coach Fletcher (that is until they hired the fuckhead liar Tommy Cod). I've mentioned Fletcher before. He was the gym coach, the soccer coach and the basketball coach. He was the greatest basketball coach OCS ever had. He always wore a dark suit, white shirt, black shoes, a red bow-tie and red socks to the games for good luck. He was tough. He loved winning and he had some unbelievable teams in the late 60s with Larry Behm, Jerry Cardigan (Spike Cardigan's older brother who married the bitch that got us kicked off the team), Mark Clark, the Dixon brothers, Mike Boland, the asshole mother fucker Tommy Cod, Mackie Bertrand, Frank Fey, John Ders, Bob Group, and John

Barmonde. These guys were real showmen and kicked everybody's ass. Entire families would go to these games. They would all be sold out.

Coach Fletcher ended up being the Health teacher as well. This was in the middle of the free love era in American history when they started to teach us about sex and abstaining from sex. I don't think he was too comfortable teaching it. He retired soon thereafter. The replacement coach, after Cod, was this newly retired commandant from the U.S. Marines. This guy was a real bastard. The Paisley family joined our school around this same time. A few gym classes came and went and everyone clearly hated this coach. Gym class was no longer an exercise class mixed with fun, it was now a regimented, no laughing allowed, bullshit class. And then one day, Coach Suck the Fun Out of Your Life, is picking on some poor schmuck military style, sergeant style, face-to-face screaming style. We were all taken a little back by this new type of public humiliation. We were just old time country folk used to organizing sit-ins in the hallway so we didn't have to wear socks with our sandals. The new kid, Arthur Paisley, steps out of line and asks the coach to cool his jets. Coach Dracula loves this. Instead of teaching us a lesson through his militaristic, tyrannical public humiliation method, he is going to challenge Arthur. In a split second, faster than the blink of an eye, Arthur pounds the life-sucking commandant rapid-fire in the head a few times. It was unfrigginbelievable, well deserved, and over in five seconds. The coach, with his own blood dripping off his face, left the gym without a word. The gym erupted with applause. Arthur became the school hero and we soon had another new coach.

A few years after graduation, the cops and the Feds and everyone were onto Arthur and the various dealings going down at his house. It eventually all caught up with him. Arthur was found dead with a toxic amount of something in his blood and a rifle and his dog by his side. At least that was the rumor. Arthur killing himself wasn't a rumor. True to form, the dog let the cops in, but he wouldn't let them out. He was killed too.

Chapter 53
Suicide #2

One of the Navarino boys, Sean Eastman, was a fun-loving, good ol' boy. His sister married Manny Hayford while still in high school. Sean was madly in love with my soon-to-be wife, Nicki. He was heartbroken when she and I started dating and I'm quite sure he wanted to beat the hell out of me, but out of respect for Nicki, he never did. He was great fun. He owned an orange Dodge Super Bee for a while. I think this thing had a 440 six-pack in it (three 2-barrel carburetors). He'd just bought the car from Dean Krone. Being from Navarino, it was the ultimate car for Sean to have. Nobody could beat this sucker. It was a sleek looking, extremely fast car. The speedometer went up to 160.

I was with him right after he bought it. It was going through gas like there was no tomorrow. The six-pack wasn't known for getting great gas mileage, but this was ridiculous. I mean, all of a sudden it was leaking gas all over the place. I think we were at Arthur's house. We jump in the car and head down through South Onondaga at an easy 80 or 90 mph; gliding, floating, barely touching the pavement – he's focused on finding Krone. It's a great ride, but as usual, I'm a little scared. He's driving this way because his gas gauge is emptying out before his very eyes. He thinks Krone sold him a lemon and he ain't happy about it. Sean Eastman and Arthur Paisley – both of these guys looking for you – not good.

We race down through South Onondaga and down Rt. 80. He's doing an honest 130 mph and decides to turn right onto Indian Hill. Holy SHIIIIIIIIIIT!!!! The car leans way left up on two wheels. The tires smoke and scream as we burn through the loose gravel into a 180. Without stopping, Sean floors it and down Indian Hill we go. We made it to Nedrow. He was going to beat the hell out of Dean. We wheel into Dean's driveway and we're out of gas. The problem? A bad fuel pump. Fixed it that afternoon. No fights, just one hell of a wild ride.

Sean was a great guy and eventually moved to Dallas with Patrick MacCollom and married a redheaded gal from Austin.

They had a couple of kids. He was an avid hunter. I had a picture of him in camouflage gear from head to foot in the middle of the woods holding up a dead wild turkey. He returned to Navarino from Texas annually for a family reunion in July. He would always stop by my house for one or two hours. We would have the best time drinking beer, reminiscing about high school days and making silly fun of everyone we knew. It was the same old thing every year, but how I looked forward to it. I really treasured those times. One day I got word that he'd killed himself. Shot himself. I just couldn't believe it. That guy was one of the nicest people ever. I loved that guy and was so honored that I was one of the people he stopped by to see every year because I knew he had a lot of friends to visit. Damn fool.

It wasn't long after high school ended that we started to lose a couple of people to various forms of death. The ones who die first are never the ones you expect to die first or the ones who should die first or the ones you'd hoped would die first. As the saying goes, it's always the good who die young. Buddy Neumyer went first. He died of a heart attack. He was 300+ pounds when I met him in the 4th grade. He used to break boards in two with his hands and feet when he was like eight years old. He was a karate expert. He used to let us punch him as hard as we could in the stomach. He would never even flinch. Peter Farrington died while driving with the Devil. The beautiful Nancy Clark died (from what I don't know), Gary Nielsen and Arthur Weiton died; they were both gay. The bare-knuckled fighters Chuckie Hayford and Michael McCartney died too. Oren Green, Donnie Lugar and a few more of the Valley guys passed as well. We weren't dropping like flies, but we were dropping.

Chapter 54

My Suicide

I was crazy in love with my wife, Nicki Catalano. What insanely jealous man isn't crazy in love? Nicki was one of the original Rags. She had that same carefree, love-for-life swagger that Melody Wadsworth had. I was automatically drawn to her. Sometimes there really aren't words to describe the most beautiful person. She was just that regular ol' gal who everyone loved. She was a natural. Nature's choice morsel. An actual sunbeam. The one lightning strike that gave life to planet Earth. The cell that first wiggled and divided while fighting for individuality. The single seed that first broke ground, and with its little leaves wide open, followed the sun's heated path across the sky. She was the first perfect diamond formed from the rough, the amphibian who dared to leave the water. She was Eve, the Virgin.

I had always been smitten by the beauty of the female. All of the girls and young women I had been attracted to up to this point were beautiful: Cheryl my little bubble, Shelly and Sandy my little circus neighbors, Samantha, Michelle Barnes (my fifth grade love). The Beatles released their song *Michelle* during this affair; she was Michelle, Ma Belle. Her family moved to Camillus leaving me heartbroken. The Traylor sisters, Melody Wadsworth, Saide Lee, Vanessa Erekson, Cindy Jones, Patty from North Syracuse, Linda Bell, Mary Landly, Michelle Black, Dawn Peevs, Little Lisa, Rene Debro, Sandra Lynch, Eileen Mary Martin, Harmony and Serenity Riley, Candy Burtone, Mindy Ordino, Janet Silver, Valerie MacCallom, Lynette Kelley, the MacCollom sisters, Melinda Richenbacher, Susie Manar, Happy Reynolds, Sarah Nighthawk, Mary Glason, and the 127 other young women attending OCS at the time, I was attracted to all of God's finest children.

Nicki and I started hanging out between the summer of my senior year and her junior year, after the Melody, Saide, and Squatch tribulations. There were a group of Nedrow girls that us Nedrow guys called the Rags. You've heard me mention them a few times. Yes, the name does refer to the well aged tale that a woman is bitchier when she is on the rag, and since they always seemed to be bitching about something we appropriately nicknamed them the Rags – something disgusting, something used, and something you would discard after you were finished with it. But in reality, it was great to have them around and they were all good girls who liked hanging around with us guys. Plain and simple; they were a lot of fun. As I've also mentioned, my girl, Nicki Catalano (an Italian), was a Rag. So was Marie Hyland, Bonnie Haines, Kathy Kotarski, Sharon Reinhardt, Karin Kilmer, Patti Phelps and Debbie Alumbaugh. They considered it an honor to be a Rag.

My nickname for Nicki was Elizabeth, after Elizabeth Taylor, and I called her Kidd, after a famous line in the movie *Casablanca*, "Here's lookin' at you, kid." I added an extra 'd' because Nicki was special and deserved an extra 'd'. She and Kathy Kotarski lived across the street from one another. Another one of the Rags, Sharon Reinhardt, lived a couple of doors up. There was a time after we started dating, when Nicki moved out of her parents' house and into Kathy's Rag-house where the parental rules were a little less stringent. There was some heavy petting going on that summer on the living room couch. I was knocking on that zipped up pussy-door for months. "Holy shit! You're killin' me! Come on man, give it up! Jesus Christ! I'm killing myself over here! What the hell do you want? Look, I've told you that I love you. What else do you want me to say?" My balls were as blue as blue-balls can get. Fuck! I walked around with a hard-on all fucking day and night long. It was embarrassing. "Jesus Christ! Give me a fucking break!"

Nicki had a great personality, a beautiful body and was just a natural human being. She was who she was and that was good enough for everyone. I lived across Salina St. in Section 6, she lived a couple blocks away in Section 2. It was perfect. Her father, Ricky, worked behind the scenes for a local TV station, and her mother, the Wicked Bitch of the East, worked for the phone company. Ricky lived in a little stone house behind the main house. Wifezilla and the four kids lived in the big stone house. Her mother was a hell-cat on wheels and treated the old man like shit. The old man was a nice little Italian guy who loved his kids and put up with his ignorant wife who was a big-nosed, bouffant-haired, self-imposed goddess. My future wife had a younger brother and two younger sisters. Nicki raised these kids from infancy while the parents worked. Because of this she didn't want any kids of her own. She felt she had already experienced all that having children might offer. That made sense I guess. In my own mind I was good with the decision, and as a guy who wanted kids, you always hope you can spring the unwanted pregnancy on your lovely bride. Of course, holding and wiping the tears and baby-bottom of your sister or brother is nothing like holding your own child. When you can look into your child's eyes and see your spouse's eyes, or best scenario, your own eyes, or your parents' eyes (unless it's your rag-ass mother), nothing can compare to that. And because of who Nicki was - God of Goddesses - she would be the best mom ever.

Up to this point in time, secretly (well, maybe not), I had always been a shy, introverted individual with plenty of troubles of my own. Peer pressure was a killer and trying to fit in with who I wanted to fit in with was never a given. I never did fit in, but I tried to make it seem as though I fit in. My real problem was that I liked everybody. I didn't want to be friends with the bad guys and not be friends with the good guys. I wanted to be a nerd and be a non-nerd. I wanted to smash things and be completely negligent of my daily duties, but also complete my daily duties and never smash anything. I wanted to be stoned, but I wanted to be straight. I wanted to be the life of the party, but I also wanted to be left alone. I wanted to be in drama club, but was way too shy for that. I wanted to be in several clubs, but what would the thugs I was hanging around with think of me? "You're in fucking drama club? Faggot!" "You're in German Club? Sprechen ze dick?" "You're in track? What the fuck is wrong with you? Run to the refrigerator and get me a beer." Instead of joining these clubs I settled for rolling joints and drinking. I even sold a pound or two of pot just to fit in.

One time I bought a pound of pot for $165 from some guy up at Syracuse University. I was living in an apartment on Hobart Ave. Shorty Walker and his wife Rhonda lived upstairs. They fought like cats and dogs, holy shit! But they were in love. That's more than I could say for myself at the time. On this fine day I think Mary Landly and Little Lisa were with me. We were in my downstairs apartment and had the entire pound broken up on newspapers in the middle of the living room floor getting ready to weigh it up into ounces. It smelled great. There is little in this world that compares to the smell of raw pot. All of a sudden there was a polite knock on the door. I stood up and looked out the window. It was a Syracuse policeman. HOLY FUCKING SHIT!!!! WHAT THE FUCK!!!!! ARE YOU FUCKING KIDDING ME!!!!! Innocent Little Lisa and Mary Landly! HOLY *SHIT*! I'LL GET *KILLED* FOR THIS! OH MY FUCKING GOD!!!!! ARE YOU FUCKING KIDDING ME!!!!! WHAT THE FUCK!!!!! HOLY *FUCK*!!!!! OH MY GOD!!!!! FUCK *ME*!!!!! OH FUCK!!!!! I'm just twisting and turning with my hands up to my face, looking back and forth and rocking like a retard. FUCK FUCK FUCK FUCK FUCK FUCK FUCK FUCK FUCK!!!!!

All of a sudden it dawns on me. No problem Einstein. All my life I've heard that if you are about to get busted, take the reefer that you have and flush it down the toilet. Bingo! Away it goes. Down into the city sewer lines. No proof of anything. You lose your pot and your money, but it's better than going to jail. The doorbell rings again; ding-fucking-dong. FUCK!!!!! "Just a minute," I politely said. So we pick up the freshly broken apart pound of pot and all of the newspapers and run to the bathroom. And there we stand. Looking down at the tiniest little flush hole you've have ever seen. Are you kidding me or what? And then I look at the massive collection of sticks, stems, buds, leaf and today's newspaper in my arms. NO FUCKING WAY JOSE!!!!! HOLY FUCKING *SHIT*! HOW THE *FUCK* ARE YOU SUPPOSED TO FLUSH A POUND OF POT DOWN A FUCKING TOILET HOLE? TELL ME THAT WILL YOU? WHO THE *FUCK* THOUGHT OF THIS BRAINY MOTHER FUCKING IDEA? WHO THE FUCK THOUGHT OF THIS? CAN YOU TELL ME? WHO THE FUCK THOUGHT OF THIS FUCKING INGENIOUS IDEA? FLUSH IT DOWN THE FUCKING TOILET? COME ON, MAN!

Holy shit! Let me think. Some stupid asshole in California, that's who fucking thought of it. Some stoned mother fucker that's for sure. Some stoned idiot with a fucking nickel fucking bag. "Oh, simply flush your pot down the toilet," said the fairy. Ding - - - - - - dong.   Fuck!

I run to the back porch and shove the pound on a shelf. I go back to the front door and open it. I expect to see a gun in my face and expect that we are all going to be carted off to jail. It would be about time I suppose. All of the predictions would have come true. The church bells would ring at St. James like they had just confirmed a new pope. There would be a special mass held for those whose lives I'd fucked over. "Today my friends," Father Cardigan would say (no relation to the South Onondaga Cardigans), "Today is a day of great sorrow and a day of great joy. A day of sorrow because a young man who was raised in our congregation, a young man of good upbringing by caring, loving parents, Bob the Father and the Virgin Betty, will forever be encased behind the stone walls of the Jamesville Penitentiary (another institution named after Me). A young man, a young sinner who has disrupted this church on holy occasions one time too many. I am sad because not every human being can be saved by the grace of God our Heavenly Father. Not every young person has the strength to win over the evil deeds asked of by the Devil. Not every young person can see the light of Jesus and feel the warmth of His calling. I am saddened that the stench and filthy sexual deviancy that exists behind the walls of Jamesville Penitentiary will now become the daily ritual for our sinner James Robert Francis Murphy, instead of what his daily ritual *should* be, his praising of the Lord Our Father. Do I hear an Amen?" "AMEN!" they all rejoiced.

"I am saddened my friends, but I am also joyful. Joyful that the stench of Mr. Murphy is encased inside the those thick stone walls. That his meals will taste like the slop fed to filthy pigs. That he will be beaten and penetrated by a greater sin than he shall ever have known outside those walls. I am joyful that his antics have cost him. I am joyful that his sins have shown *us* the Way. I am joyful that his ignorance has provided a guideline for those of us who stand on the razor thin blade wavering between sinning and praising the Lord Our Savior. Do I hear an Amen?" "AMEN!"

Father Cardigan went on and on for almost an hour. Sometimes it was unclear as to who he was praising, Jesus or Me. Sometimes his capital H's got mixed up. "We may never see Him again." Is he talking about Me or Jesus? "May He have the power to withstand and destroy those who prey upon Him and his message." Who is he really talking about here? I even think the congregation was getting confused. It was as if he actually remembered that I *was* Jesus and I *was* God Our Savior. You could see his confusion when he looked up at Jesus bleeding on the crucifix over the altar. He would tilt his head slightly to the right, stop preaching for a moment, squint, take off his glasses, clean them, take a drink of wine before it was time to drink the wine, and then reexamine the face of Jesus because it really did look like Me. He *was* confused. When you see *My* face instead of *God's* face peering down through the heavens, this might be disturbing. There are moments in time when the truth reveals itself, especially when those abusing their power create untrue scenarios. Father Cardigan was leaning against the Devil's shoulder during this tirade. *He* was beginning to tremble. *He* was sinning! It's his job to run the parish, not to pass judgment. He isn't allowed to sway the thoughts of those who have come to worship. This isn't a political race. This is about Me! Father Cardigan should be the voice of Me, not the voice of his weakened, greedy, graying self.

He died soon thereafter from unknown causes. Rumor was, he tripped on a fallen oak branch and it pierced his chest going clear through the center of his heart and it burst into flames as it bluntly forced its way out through his back. Others said his electric shaver fell into his bath and fried his holy ass to an unrecognizable black crisp. Still others said that he didn't die at all, he simply vanished during the first light of a cresting St. Patrick's Day sun. Many thought he was murdered, cut up into little pieces and distributed throughout the Valley, Nedrow, the Reservation and South Onondaga. I don't know where they got that from. My parents stopped going to St. James after his death and started going to St. Michael's up on the Turnpike. That's all I know.

As gentle and kind as my parents were, they would, by all rights, finally have the right to disown me if they cared to. I am a fuck-up. My pot smoking friends who always considered me to be a narc would now be extremely paranoid because they would be sure that I would rat on every one of them while I was in prison. I was stuck in Purgatory; nowhere to go. I'm sure I'm going to get busted so I may as well face the music.

I open the door and the policeman says, "Did one of you park your car over the sidewalk? You can't block the sidewalk. Is this your car?" He should have known I was up to no good because I'm sure my ragged hair was all fucked up and my eyes were probably bulging out of my head. "Yes. It's my friend's car. I'll have her move it." "Okay, and your name?" "Jim Murphy." "Okay Mr. Murphy. We have to leave the sidewalks clear for pedestrians. We aren't allowed to park vehicles over the sidewalk." "Okay. I'll have her move it right now. Thank you."

UNFUCKINGBELIEVABLE. This was an earth shattering, mind blowing experience. What the fuck am I doing? What the FUCK am I doing? WHAT the FUCK am I doing? WHAT the FUCK am I DOING?

Nicki, my wife-to-be, in her senior year at her graduation ceremony was recognized as the "Most Improved Student of the Year." What a proud moment for us all. It was all her doing, believe me.

We dated for a couple of years prior to getting married. Her dad Ricky liked me because his daughter liked me, but I'm sure he'd wished for better. I had no clear future. Nicki was young and inexperienced, but oddly enough, as inexperienced as she was, she never wore a bra. She didn't like them. Me and every guy that ever met her loved her for that. She wasn't well endowed, she was perfectly endowed. Her breasts were the perfect breasts. I loved each of them equally. And they were always there. No bra to fuck with, just beautiful, soft, mildly olive skin-wrapped breasts. She was the virgin of all virgins. She was more pure than Eve. She was like the Virgin Mary. She radiated the light of life that no one could resist. And again, I have the opportunity to love the most beautiful young woman on the planet. As for me, on a manly level, I'd been in and out of a few things, but Nicki was different. She was, like I said, a natural human being. Unlike her mother, she really was goddess-like. It was the best of times. Lot's of good, innocent fun. We would ride to school together, go to Otisco Lake and hang out at parties in the country on weekends. Nicki was funny. She had my ticket punched the minute she met me. She wasn't afraid to wisecrack right back to me. She didn't suck any of my powers from me (what little I had left). She didn't need them. I could tell just by holding her hand that she was much more powerful than I would ever be. I'm not exactly sure how we officially hooked up. I don't remember the "exact" moment. I don't have a list of our best 100 moments together, but I do know that she was an extremely nice, down to Earth person and that nice, down to Earth people are hard to find. She just wanted to be herself and she just wanted me to be me. How comforting is that?

One summer night we were parking in a gravel bed on Hitchings Road in South Onondaga steaming up the windows, gettin' down to the nakedness of it all in the backseat of my parents' Chevy, when out of nowhere a County Sheriff pulls up and shines his damn 9,000 watt floodlight toward the car and caught us fighting to get our clothes back on before he, the idiot cop, ran up to the car with his megawatt flashlight to see what he might see. Our shirts were on inside out, Nicki hurriedly put her head through her tank-top sleeve, our pants were half on. Hair was everywhere. It was bad, man, it was bad. It scared the hell out of the both of us. What the hell was he doing there? Nothing else to frickin' do? Turn the God damned light off Officer Dickhead!

After our brief, to-the-point interrogation: "What are you doing here?" I'm thinking, what the hell do you think we're doing here? I'm trying to fuck my sweetie! "What's your name?" "What's her name?" "Do you know this is private property?" (So what! I'm trying to fuck my girlfriend!) "OK, you'll have to move along. Have a good evening." (How fuckhead? Asshole!). We drive back to Nedrow to Bailey's Ice Cream, get a Spanish Sundae and a cone and drive down to the Rockwell Elementary playground and sat on the swings to cool down. It was funny, man. We were still shaking, but we were laughing too. Asshole cop.

One day I pulled up to pick up Nicki in an old Dodge van that I had remodeled. I'd hung curtains in it, carpeted the floor, made a bed in the back and put barn siding on the walls with shelves, deer antlers, photos, an antique mirror and whatever else. It was really a nice job, but her dad wasn't too happy about the bed. It was clearly a fuck-your-daughter over and over machine.

We were married on Oneida Lake shores in northern NY at Wysocki's Lake Park Manor. We were both 21 at the time. It was a big to-do. Everyone was there. We were friends with everyone so we didn't exclude anyone. The weather was as good as New York weather can get. A crisp morning followed by a mid-70s temperature in the afternoon. Everything was just right. The bride was angelical in her white gown. The bridesmaids were dressed in light blue to match the sky. The celebration lasted all day and into the night. We postponed the honeymoon because we didn't have the money to go anywhere. But we were together and that's all that mattered. We moved into this cute little four room home on Macon Street, still in Section 6, close to both sets of parents. We repainted the four rooms and cleaned the place up real nice. There was a tiny bedroom, tiny living room, tiny kitchen, tiny bathroom and tiny, low-ceiling basement – that was it. It did have a beautiful, long backyard with some nice trees and shaded areas. There were always people over, mostly my guy friends and her Rag friends. We would have cook-outs and just sit in the back yard and have fun. Not too long after we were married Nicki would begin to criticize these fun times and complain that we never spent time alone. Looking back on it, the reason there were always people over is because we always hung around with everyone. We were never alone to begin with. It was fun being with everyone, roaming around, going to everyone's apartments, drinking, laughing, and pulling pranks. That's what life was all about. That's how we grew together as a couple. Were we supposed to isolate ourselves now that we were married? I thought we were alone plenty. In these days you just stopped over to people's houses, you never called in advance. I really thought things were fine. Party with your friends, fuck your wife, party with your friends and fuck your wife some more. What is it about a relationship that I'm missing? Everyone was doing the same thing. That's why people get married, so they can legally fuck each other with their parents' blessing. "Now that you've married my daughter, I don't mind if you fuck her brains out in the back of your beat-to-shit Dodge van." "Why thank you, Ricky."

Where and why did things start to go wrong? More and more that's what I was wondering. It's not like I was running around town with the guys. That really wasn't my thing. I liked being with Nicki. I went to work every day with my dad so it's not like I was hanging around the house like some slouch being supported by my wife. I was working. I'm sure there was more to it than that, but I remember 'not having time to ourselves' as being one of the main reasons for the rapid termination of what should have been a life-long marriage. What the fuck was I doing wrong? Is anyone going to tell me or am I supposed to figure this out on my own? There were also some heavy outside influential sources tugging at her to get rid of me. Kathy the Cunt Kotarski, who was going out with this nonworking, illegitimate scumbag, decided I wasn't good enough for my wife and since her relationship sucked, she relentlessly pulled my wife away from me. Hiding Nicki and lying to her and lying to me for her. It was fucked, fucked, fucked, fucked, fucked! Some older guy, Tim Janes, who owned a house right near the Remedy, was taking my wife over to his place up to his white, shag carpeted, love shack attic with the awesome stereo system, comforting her, listening to her, paying attention to her, giving her everything she complained about that she wasn't getting from me, and then slamming the hell out of her little tiny pussy all the while. But he was so nice to me when I saw him; calm, justified, understanding. I should have beaten the fuck out of that asshole; he was fucking my wife! What the fuck was wrong with me? I should have beaten the fuck out of that dude twice in a row.

The negative outside forces were a greater influence over the relationship that I could ever hope to have been. The people that she wanted to move away from, the one's that we were always hanging around with, were the same people that she ended up being persuaded by. How did that fucking happen? Eventually, I threw her across the kitchen a couple of times trying to prove how much I loved her. I smashed a bunch of our stuff and pretty much became a nonstop, raging torrent of misunderstood emotions. Within six months after we were married she had left with one of my best friends, the Dickhead David Urias. He was living in a fucking tree fort that he'd built in South Onondaga. She left me for a guy living in a tree fort. That's how fucking bad it was. I hated the fact that Nicki and I were breaking up. I hated the fact that she was hanging around with one of the guys that I always had at the house. While we were married, Dickhead David got her a job where he worked so they rode to and from work together, ate lunch together and everything else. This too sucked. Toward the very end, before she moved out, she wrote this in one of my songbooks:

"They all told me it was bound to happen. It was just a matter of time. Now I've come to my decision – it's one of the hurtin' kind. It seems you wanted a martyr, just a regular girl wouldn't do. Oh baby, I can't hang around a lover's cross for you."
This is from the Allman Brothers' song, *Lover's Cross*.

Holy shit! What the fuck are you talking about? You feel like a martyr? I've never forced you or stopped you from doing anything. So are you saying you married me against your will? Everyone told you it was just a matter of time? You're going to back out after six months of marriage?

I hated everything. Everyone at the fucking Remedy would protect her. I was definitely the odd man out. Everyone kept telling me, "It's over man. Forget about it and move on. You'll find somebody else." There were plenty of girls to go around and I did try out a few here and there much later, but I just couldn't get over Nicki. I would break down and cry in public if I saw her somewhere. It was beyond the clearest definition of devastating. There was no one to turn to. I was completely alone. No one wanted to talk about it with me. They were sick of it. They were sick of me. They liked my wife and they liked me. They weren't about to get in the middle of it. "Get over it!" "Move on!" they would say. "Fuck you! You get over it!" I would shoot back.

Almost three years went by. I had left town and hitchhiked all over the country. To Florida, Colorado a couple of times, California and Wyoming. I ran into lonely women everywhere, but I just couldn't let go. And then one day I was back in Syracuse working for my father somewhere in Eastwood building a dormer on the back of a house. I was the only one there, upstairs, alone, standing on a ladder, holding onto a crossbeam crying my eyes out, screaming, mentally disturbed, mentally fractured and mentally exhausted. Still, I was asking the question, why is no one willing to help me? Why had I failed so badly as a person, as a husband, as a friend? Why wouldn't she take me back? I have admitted to all of my wrong-doing. I have begged her and pleaded with her several times for forgiveness for Christ's sake. I WAS NOW A CHANGED PERSON! I promised her that I wouldn't crush her against the kitchen wall anymore! How could she not know that? Everyone in town is still *against* me and *for* her. Everyone! Everyone still wants me to, "Get over it!" "You want me to get over it? Here, I'll get over it!" "Fuck You!" "Fuckers!" "Fuck you!" "Fucking Friends!" "Fucking Bitch!" "Fucking Rag!" "Fucking Rag-ass!" "Fucking Cunt!" "Fucking Pussy Shit!" "You Fucker!" "Fucking Stupid-ass Bitch!" "Fucking Friends!" "Fucking Best Friends!" "You Fucking Assholes!" "You Fuckers!" "Fuck you!"

"Fuckers!"

Sometimes
this life
can be
so sad

Sometimes
this life
can be
so sad

My friends Lord
they're gone
the cup had done run dry

My friends Lord
they're gone
the cup had done run dry

this is
this is
this is the south side of blue

I was found dead late that afternoon by my father. I was hanging from a ceiling rafter with 12-gauge electrical cable wrapped around my bruised neck. Bob was pissed and immediately shouted, "Jesus, Mary and Joseph! For Christ's sake! God dammit! Holy Shit! For the Love of Christ! Give Me Strength Dear Lord! Stupid Fucker!" I'd never heard my father say the 'F' word before. He rummaged through my toolbox tossing shit everywhere, finding my wire cutters, calling me a 'stupid fucker' again and a 'real idiot' under his breath as he forced his way through the kicked over debris scrambling to set the ladder in place. "Why aren't you using your Superpowers?" I thought. He climbed up a couple of steps and cut through the wire. I dropped.

There I was ..... again, crumpled up on the floor in the same fetal position I had been in so many times before. Wearing the same old rags I had always worn.

My dad was my superhero. My one and only. The carpenter who gave me life. The man of steel. The drier of my tears. The one who gave me the shirt off his back and cleansed blood from my face. He bragged about me. He was my teacher of measurement and reason. He was the dog chaser, the ice rink maker, the catcher to my pitches, the fighter, the architect, the self survivor, the president, the worker for his family, the one who stood tall against all odds, the man who kept me clothed, fed and sheltered, the man who taught me everything. He once again held my lifeless, quivering body and rocked me in his arms.

"Come back to me."

"Come back to me," he whispered.

"Shhhhhh."

Come back to me Jimmy."

"Shhhhhh."

"Shhhhhh."

"Shhhhhh."

Dead. Numb. Ashamed. Shut out from the world around me. Worn down and broken. A complete failure in life. Unable to communicate. Unable to trust. Lying in the safety of my dad's arms. Dammit! A couple of more minutes and my troubles would have been over! Why do people have to save other people? Why did he have to show up with coffee and plain donuts at that exact moment? Why did he have to ask for assistance from Jesus, Mary *and* Joseph? Why did he have to save me for *Christ's* sake? Why did he have to ask God to *damn it*? Why did he have to use the same cursing phrase that Adam first used that in-turn made God first curse? Why did he have to ask for the *Love of Christ*? Why in the name of our Lord did he have to ask for God to *give him strength*? Why didn't he just use his Superpowers? Why did I do something stupid enough to make him use the 'F' word? Son of a bitch.

End Note

Life is a most fantastic journey. Most of which we choose to conveniently ignore, try to forget, and then store in the "bruised file" in a fold of our mind. I hate that shit don't you? It may seem like I hate a lot of things after reading this book, but I didn't then and I don't now. I was honestly searching for love and understanding. I was searching for someone to share this crazy life with. I just didn't know how to go about it. I had many, many good friends. I was messed up, insecure, and intimidated by everyone and everything. I crashed and burned big time. I was a mental wreck for eight years after Nicki and I broke up. Life was a struggle, make no mistake about it.

The simple act of staying alive is the greatest challenge of all. Over the years since my breakdown I have grown so much stronger as an individual. Most importantly, I have succeeded in making a difference in other people's lives who exist in and around my little world. Making a difference, no matter how big or small, is what life is really all about.

Nicki Catalano died on August 25, 2009. No one from my hometown contacted me.

Epilogue

My Life Before I Decided To Commit Suicide - A Love Story is a true story. This is the way I once dealt with and felt about all things. I want everyone mentioned in my book to know that I love you and truly appreciate that you were, and are, a part of my life. Thank you all for being there. You have made my life so interesting. I hope each of you who read my book found some joy within my verse and that you have remembered a few fond memories of your own while reading my Nedrownian tragedy.

Life is so worth living.

References

The Marian Bible, To Jesus through Mary.
This is the Murphy Family Bible. It was issued to celebrate the Marian Year. On September 26, 1953, His Holiness, Pope Pius XII, announced that the year 1954, [coincidently the same year I was born] the hundredth anniversary of the proclamation of the Immaculate Conception, as a dogma of the Church, would be a Marian Year. The Marian Bible was printed in the U.S.A. Copyright 1954, 1953, 1952, 1950. The Catholic Press, Inc.

To find out more about Auburn, NY's newspaper, *The Citizen Advisor*, and what happened on Saturday, September 11, 1954, visit www.fultonhistory.com

To find out about Auburn, NY visit www.tourauburnny.com

To find out about Nedrow, NY visit http://en.wikipedia.org/wiki/Nedrow,_New_York

To find out about the Onondaga Nation visit: www.onondaganation.org

To find out about the Finger Lakes visit: www.fingerlakes.org

To find out more about James E. Heath Park visit http://www.baltimorewoods.org/Data/Documents/CityParksHEATH.pdf

To find out about what happened on a particular day in history visit: www.historyorb.com

Songs referenced:

P17 and 107, *Eyesight to the Blind*, Sonny Boy Williamson

P39, *The Thrill is Gone* (I'm free, free, free), B.B. King

P42, *Snakebite* (Legs crossed and all), Austin Jimmy Murphy

P43, *Smoke, Smoke, Smoke (that cigarette)*, Merle Travis and Tex Williams

P56, *Tutti Frutti*, Little Richard

P100, Earth, Wind and Fire

P106, *She's Alright, She's Alright*, Austin Jimmy Murphy

P109, *It Should've Been Me,* Ray Charles

P127, *This Girl is Mine* (I'm a lover not a fighter), Michael Jackson

P172, *Black Bill Blues*, Austin Jimmy Murphy

P198, *South Side of Blue*, Austin Jimmy Murphy

About the Author

Jim Murphy holds a B.S. from SUNY with a concentration in Arts Management, and an M.A. from the University of Oklahoma in Administrative Leadership. He is the principle founding member of the New York State Blues Festival, serving as festival director from 1992-2003, and co-founded the Guinness Irish Festival, serving as its festival director from 1999-2003 and 2013-2014. Both of these community events continue in Syracuse, NY. He and his family moved to El Paso, TX in 2004. Mr Murphy has been serving the City of El Paso, TX as their director of development for the El Paso Museum of History since 2006.

ACCOMPLISHMENTS / AWARDS

- 2015, Released the following four books: *My Favorite El Pasoans: Past and Present Vol.1*, *The Right to Kill*, *My Life Before I Decided To Commit Suicide-A Love Story,* 2nd Edition, and I'm So Pissed Off!. All through BLBM Publishing
- 2015, Founder and President of El Paso Music Society, Inc.
- 2013, Worthy of being called Excellent, *My Life Before I Decided To Commit Suicide*, Book Publishers of El Paso
- 2013, SAMMY (Syracuse Area Music Award), Best Blues CD, *A History of Blues*
- 2010, Co-edited for the El Paso Museum of History, *El Hilo de la Memoria*, Fresco Fine Arts Publications, LLC
- 2009, *El Paso: 1850 -1950*, Arcadia Publishing - Images of America
- 2004, *Selfless Service to Music and the Arts*, for service as the NYS Blues Festival founder/director
- 2003, *Keeping the Blues Alive – Best Promoter/Festiva*l, Blues Foundation, Memphis, TN (NYS Blues Festival)
- 2001, 1999, 1997, *People's Choice Award* (Best Festival) Syracuse New Times (NYS Blues Festival)
- 1999-2003, Festival Director Guinness Irish Festival, Syracuse, NY
- 1996, SAMMY for Best Concert Event or Series (NYS Blues Festival)
- 1995, *Service to the Arts*, Cultural Resources Council of Syracuse and Onondaga County
- 1992-2004, 2013-2014, Festival Director, New York State Blues Festival, Syracuse, NY

<u>Additional books by James Robert Murphy</u>

The Right to Kill
I'm So Pissed Off!
My Favorite El Pasoans: Past and Present, Vol. 1
El Paso: 1850-1950
Available at: wwwjamesrobertmurphy.com